MICROSOFT

Visual Basic 6

Introductory Concepts and Techniques

Gary B. Shelly
Thomas J. Cashman
John F. Repede
Michael L. Mick

Contributing Author
Deborah L. Fansler

COURSE TECHNOLOGY
ONE MAIN STREET
CAMBRIDGE MA 02142

an International Thomson Publishing company   I(T)P*

SHELLY
CASHMAN
SERIES.

CAMBRIDGE • ALBANY • BONN • CINCINNATI • LONDON • MADRID • MELBOURNE

MEXICO CITY • NEW YORK • PARIS • SAN FRANCISCO • TOKYO • TORONTO • WASHINGTON

COURSE
TECHNOLOGY

Course Technology
One Main Street
Cambridge, Massachusetts 02142, USA

International Thomson Editores
Saneca, 53
Colonia Polanco
11560 Mexico D.F. Mexico

ITP Europe
Berkshire House
168-173 High Holborn
London, WC1V 7AA, United Kingdom

ITP GmbH
Konigswinterer Strasse 418
53227 Bonn, Germany

ITP Australia
102 Dodds Street
South Melbourne
Victoria 3205 Australia

ITP Asia
60 Albert Street, #15-01
Albert Complex
Singapore 189969

ITP Nelson Canada
1120 Birchmount Road
Scarborough, Ontario
Canada M1K 5G4

ITP Japan
Hirakawa-cho Kyowa Building, 3F
2-2-1 Hirakawa-cho, Chiyoda-ku
Tokyo 102, Japan

ISBN 0-7895-4653-1

PHOTO CREDITS: *Project 1, pages VB 1.2-3* Wedding photo, wedding rings, Courtesy of PhotoDisc, Inc.; baby Courtesy of Digital Stock; doll on tricycle, robot toy, Courtesy of KPT Metatools; *Project 2, pages VB 2.2-3* Painted mountains, Courtesy of Digital Stock; computer, slides, Courtesy of KPT Metatools; male model, girl with hat, Courtesy of Fargo; happy couple, Courtesy of PhotoDisc, Inc.; *Project 3, pages VB 3.2-3* Chalkboard, circuit board, microscope, rat, Courtesy of PhotoDisc, Inc.

2 3 4 5 6 7 8 9 10   BC   03 02 01 00 99

MICROSOFT

Visual Basic 6
Introductory Concepts and Techniques

C O N T E N T S

⬤ PROJECT THREE

MULTIPLE FORMS, DIALOGS, DEBUGGING, AND EXEs

Preface

The Shelly Cashman Series® offers the finest textbooks in computer education. In our Microsoft Visual Basic 6 textbooks, you will find an educationally sound and easy-to-follow pedagogy that combines a step-by-step approach with corresponding screens. An Introduction to Visual Basic Programming section at the beginning of the book emphasizes good programming practices and gives students the foundation to produce well-written Windows applications. The Other Ways and More About features offer in-depth knowledge of Visual Basic 6. The project openers provide a fascinating perspective on the subject covered in the project. The Shelly Cashman Series Microsoft Visual Basic 6 books will make your programming class exciting and dynamic and one that your students will remember as one of their better educational experiences.

Objectives of This Textbook

Microsoft Visual Basic 6: Introductory Concepts and Techniques is intended for a one-credit course that includes a survey of Visual Basic programming. No experience with a computer is assumed, and no mathematics beyond the high school freshman level is required. The objectives of this book are:

- To teach the basic concepts and methods of object-oriented programming
- To teach the fundamentals of the Microsoft Visual Basic 6 programming system
- To acquaint students with the three-step process of building Windows applications using Visual Basic 6
- To use practical problems to illustrate application-building techniques
- To take advantage of the many new capabilities of building applications in a graphical environment
- To encourage independent study and help those who are working alone in a distance education environment

When students complete the course using this textbook, they will have a basic knowledge and understanding of Visual Basic 6.

Obtaining a Copy of Microsoft Visual Basic 6 Working Model

Microsoft Visual Basic 6 Working Model can be bundled with this textbook for a minimal charge, so your students will have their own copy of Microsoft Visual Basic 6. Bundling the textbook and software is ideal if your school does not have Microsoft Visual Basic 6 or if you have students working at home on their own personal computers.

All the projects and exercises in this book can be completed using the Working Model. The only significant limitation of the Working Model is that it does not provide the MAKE.OLE DLLs command and the MAKE.EXE command.

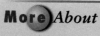

Other Ways

1. On Project menu click Components
2. Press CTRL+T

More About

Writing Code

Code in a Visual Basic application is divided into blocks called procedures. You write code for the Visual Basic application in a separate window, called the Code window. Using the Code window, you can view and edit any of the code quickly. You can choose to display all code procedures in the same Code window, or display a single procedure at a time.

The Shelly Cashman Approach

Features of the Shelly Cashman Series Microsoft Visual Basic 6 books include:

- **Project Orientation:** Each project in the book builds a complete application using the three-step process: creating the interface, setting properties, and writing code.

- **Screen-by-Screen, Step-by-Step Instructions:** Each of the tasks required to complete a project is identified throughout the development of the project. Steps to accomplish the task are specified, accompanied by screens.

- **Thoroughly Tested Projects:** Every screen in the book is correct because it is produced by the author only after performing a step, resulting in unprecedented quality.

- **Other Ways Boxes for Reference:** Visual Basic 6 provides a variety of ways to carry out a given task. The Other Ways boxes displayed at the end of many of the step-by-step sequences specify the other ways to do that task. Thus, the steps and Other Ways box make a comprehensive reference unit.

- **More About Feature:** These marginal annotations provide background information that complement the topics covered, adding interest and depth.

Organization of This Textbook

Microsoft Visual Basic 6: Introductory Concepts and Techniques provides detailed instruction on how to use Visual Basic 6. The material is divided into an introductory section and three projects as follows:

Introduction to Visual Basic Programming   This section provides an overview of application development, user interface design, program development methodology, structured programming, object-oriented programming, and the Visual Basic development system.

Project 1 - Building an Application   Project 1 introduces students to the major elements of Visual Basic. Students develop Calculating Sales Commission, a sales commission conversion application. The process of building the application consists of three steps: creating the interface, setting properties, and writing code. Topics include starting Visual Basic; designing a form and adding labels, text boxes, and command buttons; changing the properties of controls; specifying an event procedure; using a function and a method in code; running and saving applications; documenting applications; starting a new project and opening an existing project; and accessing information about Visual Basic using Help.

Project 2 - Working with Intrinsic Controls and ActiveX Controls   Project 2 presents additional properties of the controls used in Project 1, as well as several new intrinsic controls. ActiveX controls also are explained and used in the project to build the Theater Box Office application. Topics include copying controls; copying code between event procedures; using variables and constants in code statements; and using code statements to concatenate string data.

Project 3 - Multiple Forms, Dialogs, Debugging, and EXEs   Project 3 extends the basics of building applications. The SavU Loan Analyzer application in this project consists of multiple forms and dialog boxes. Topics include additional properties of the controls presented in Projects 1 and 2; WindowState and modality; adding an icon to a form; using Image, Line, and ScrollBar controls; debugging applications using the features of Visual Basic's Debug window, and creating EXE files.

End-of-Project Student Activities

A notable strength of the Shelly Cashman Series Visual Basic 6 books is the extensive student activities at the end of each project. Well-structured student activities can make the difference between students merely participating in a class and students retaining the information they learn. The activities in the Shelly Cashman Series Visual Basic 6 books include:

- **What You Should Know** A listing of the tasks completed within a project together with the pages where the step-by-step, screen-by-screen explanations appear. This section provides a perfect study review for students.

- **Test Your Knowledge** Four pencil-and-paper activities designed to determine the students' understanding of the material in the project. Included are true/false questions, multiple-choice questions, and two short-answer activities.

- **Use Help** Any user of Visual Basic 6 must know how to use Help. Therefore, this book contains two Help exercises per project. These exercises alone distinguish the Shelly Cashman Series from any other set of Visual Basic 6 instructional materials.

- **Apply Your Knowledge** This exercise requires students to open and manipulate a file on the Data Disk that accompanies the Visual Basic 6 books.

- **In the Lab** Three in-depth assignments per project require students to apply the knowledge gained in the project to solve problems on a computer.

- **Cases and Places** Seven unique case studies require students to apply their knowledge to real-world situations.

Shelly Cashman Series Teaching Tools

A comprehensive set of Teaching Tools accompanies this book in the form of a CD-ROM. The CD-ROM includes an electronic Instructor's Manual and teaching and testing aids. The CD-ROM (ISBN 0-7895-4655-8) is available through your Course Technology representative or by calling one of the following telephone numbers: Colleges and Universities, 1-800-648-7450; High Schools, 1-800-824-5179; and Career Colleges, 1-800-477-3692. The contents of the CD-ROM follow.

- **Instructor's Manual** The Instructor's Manual is made up of Microsoft Word files. The files include lecture notes, solutions to laboratory assignments, and a large test bank. The files allow you to modify the lecture notes or generate quizzes and exams from the test bank using your own word processor. Where appropriate, solutions to laboratory assignments are embedded as icons in the files.

- **Figures in the Book** Illustrations for every figure in the textbook are available. Use this ancillary to create a slide show from the illustrations for lecture or to print transparencies for use in lecture with an overhead projector.

- **Course Test Manager** Course Test Manager is a powerful testing and assessment package that enables instructors to create and print tests from the large test bank. Instructors with access to a networked computer lab (LAN) can administer, grade, and track tests online. Students also can take online practice tests, which generate customized study guides that indicate where in the textbook students can find more information for each question.

- Lecture Success System Lecture Success System files are for use with the application software, a personal computer, and projection device to explain and illustrate the step-by-step, screen-by-screen development of a project in the textbook without entering large amounts of data.

- Instructor's Lab Solutions Solutions and required files for all the In the Lab assignments at the end of each project are available.

- Student Files All the files that are required by the student to complete the Apply Your Knowledge exercises are included.

- Interactive Labs Eighteen hands-on interactive labs that take students from ten to fifteen minutes each to step through help solidify and reinforce mouse and keyboard usage and computer concepts. Student assessment is available.

Student Data Disk

A few of the exercises in this textbook, especially the Apply Your Knowledge exercises, require that students begin by opening a file on the Student Data Disk. Students can obtain a copy of the Data Disk by following the instructions on the inside back cover of this textbook.

Acknowledgments

The Shelly Cashman Series would not be the leading computer education series without the contributions of outstanding publishing professionals. First, and foremost, among them is Becky Herrington, director of production and designer. She is the heart and soul of the Shelly Cashman Series, and it is only through her leadership, dedication, and tireless efforts that superior products are made possible. Becky created and produced the award-winning Windows 95 series of books.

Under Becky's direction, the following individuals made significant contributions to these books: Doug Cowley, production manager; Ginny Harvey, series specialist and developmental editor; Ken Russo, graphic designer and Web developer; Mike Bodnar, Stephanie Nance, Mark Norton, and Dave Bonnewitz, graphic artists; Jeanne Black, Quark expert; Marlo Mitchem, production/administrative assistant; Nancy Lamm, copyeditor/proofreader; Cristina Haley, indexer; Sarah Evertson of Image Quest, photo researcher; and Susan Sebok, contributing writer.

Special thanks go to Jim Quasney, our dedicated series editor; Lisa Strite, senior editor; Lora Wade, associate product manager; Tonia Grafakos and Meagan Walsh editorial assistants; and Kathryn Cronin, product marketing manager. Special mention must go to Becky Herrington for the outstanding book design; Mike Bodnar for the logo designs; and Stephanie Nance for the cover design and illustrations.

Gary B. Shelly
Thomas J. Cashman
John F. Repede
Michael L. Mick

Microsoft
Visual Basic 6

```
txtAmount.SetFocus
Else monthlypmt = Pmt
hsbRate.Value / 12
* 12,-1 * txtAmount       txtAmount.SetFocus
1b1Payment.Caption                    = Pmt (0.0
(monthlypmt, "c    mC
1b1Sumpmts.Cap
(monthlypmt * hsb
"currency")
End If
```

Microsoft **Visual Basic 6**

INTRODUCTION

I

Introduction to Visual Basic Programming

OBJECTIVES

You will have mastered the material in this project when you can:

- Describe programs, programming, applications, and application development
- List six principles of user interface design
- Describe each of the steps in the program development life cycle
- Define structured programming
- Read and understand a flowchart
- Read and understand a HIPO chart
- Explain sequence, selection, and repetition control structures
- Describe object-oriented programming
- Define the terms objects, properties, methods, and events
- Read and understand a generalization hierarchy
- Read and understand an object structure diagram
- Read and understand an event diagram
- Define and explain encapsulation, inheritance, and polymorphism
- Describe rapid application development (RAD) and prototyping
- Describe VBA, VBScript, and the Visual Basic language

Microsoft Visual Basic 6

Microsoft Visual Basic 6

Introduction to Visual Basic Programming

INTRODUCTION

I

Introduction

The **Visual Basic Programming System** encompasses a set of tools and technologies that are being used by more than three million developers worldwide to create computer software components and applications. At the release of an earlier version of Visual Basic, Bill Gates, chairman and CEO of Microsoft Corporation, said, "It has been a long time in coming, but the industrial revolution of software is finally upon us." Although not all people would agree with Mr. Gates's characterization of Visual Basic, most would agree that it is an extremely versatile, powerful, and yes — complex development system (the Professional Edition of version 6 contains more than 5,000 pages of user documentation). The popularity and complexity of Visual Basic is evidenced by the several Internet discussion groups dedicated to Visual Basic as well as the many World Wide Web sites and the wealth of books written about Visual Basic.

Schools across the country are teaching Visual Basic in a variety of different settings. These range from using Visual Basic as a general introduction to computer programming to two- and three-semester course sequences with prerequisite courses in subjects such as logic, software design, and structured programming. The editions of this book are designed to provide an introductory to intermediate working knowledge of Visual Basic and the software development concepts and technologies upon which it is built.

You may come to this course already having studied subjects such as systems analysis and design and structured programming, or this may be your first exposure to how a computer is programmed. The purpose of this introductory section is to provide the *big picture* of software design and development. You easily can find entire books and courses on each of the topics covered in this introduction, and your instructor may decide to spend more or less time on these topics depending on your background and the nature of the course you are taking.

Programming a Computer

Before a computer can start to produce a desired result, it must have a step-by-step description of the task to be accomplished. The step-by-step description is a series of precise instructions called a **program**. When these instructions are placed into the computer's memory, they are called a **stored program**. **Memory** stores the data and instructions that tell the computer what to do with the data.

Once the program is stored, the first instruction is located and sent to the control unit (**fetched**) where it is translated into a form the computer can understand (**decoded**), and then the instruction is carried out (**executed**). The result of the instruction is placed in memory (**stored**). Then, the next instruction is fetched, decoded, and executed. This process, called a **machine cycle**, continues under the direction of the operating system, instruction by instruction, until the program is completed or until the computer is instructed to halt.

In the Windows operating system, you can have multiple windows (programs) open on the desktop at the same time. Unless the computer has more than one CPU (each with its own memory), called **parallel processing**, it still executes only one instruction at a time. It carries these instructions out so fast, however, that it can move back and forth among programs carrying out some instructions from one program, and then some instructions from another program. To the user, it appears as though these programs are running simultaneously. This moving back and forth between programs by the processor is called **multitasking**. Even in a multitasking system, a processor can execute only one instruction at a time.

For the computer to perform another job, a new program is read into memory. By reading stored programs into memory, the computer can be used easily to process a large number of different jobs. The instructions within these jobs can be written, or **coded**, by a computer programmer in a variety of programming languages. Today, more than 2,000 programming languages exist. The process of writing the sets of instructions that make up these jobs is called **computer programming**.

Most computer users do not write their own programs. Programs required for common business and personal applications such as word processing or spreadsheets can be purchased from software vendors or stores that sell computer products. These purchased programs often are referred to as **application software packages**, or simply applications. **Applications** are programs that tell a computer how to accept instructions from the end user and how to produce information in response to those instructions. The process of using a programming language or development environment to build software applications is called **application development**.

User Interface Design

The way that a program accepts instructions from the user and presents results is called the **user interface**. Today, most applications have a graphical user interface (GUI). A **graphical user interface** (**GUI**) provides visual clues such as small pictures, or **icons**, to help the end user give instructions to the computer. Microsoft Windows is the most widely used graphical user interface for personal computers.

After working only a short time with different applications within the Windows operating system, you will begin to notice similarities in the user interfaces — even among applications created by companies other than Microsoft. This is not a coincidence and this similarity greatly reduces the time required to learn a new application.

Examine the packaging for software applications the next time you are in a store that sells software. Many applications have a Windows logo with the words, Designed for Microsoft Windows. These applications must follow an extensive set of requirements in order to display the Windows logo on the package. These include requirements ranging from supporting the use of long file names to adherence to very detailed Windows interface guidelines. Whether you want to display the Windows logo on your software or not, some basic principles need to be followed in designing a graphical user interface.

The application always should be under the user's control. The application should present choices that allow the user to initiate and control the application's events. One example would be a user's capability not only to initiate a print function, but if necessary, to cancel the print function before it is completed.

User capabilities and preferences vary greatly and change over time. The user should be able to customize the application to meet his or her preferences. For example, the **ToolTips** (pop-up help bubbles) that are valuable to a new user of an application may be annoying to a proficient user. A color scheme that one person finds attractive may be distracting to another. The application should allow, but not require, customizing. An initial default interface should be provided for those who do not want to specify customizing options.

Form should follow function. The interface should be designed to provide direct ways to accomplish tasks and not to be glamorous or trendy. Avoid the temptation to try to find some use within the application for your favorite visual elements. For example, a Drop-down ComboBox control should be used when the control you want to give the user is best accomplished with a combo box and not because you feel that combo boxes make your application more professional looking or fun to use. Some of the best interface elements are ones the user does not notice because their use is so intuitive, they do not have to consciously think, Now how do I do this? or What does this thing do?

Use concepts and metaphors that users are familiar with to make the interface parallel real-world experience. A familiar GUI metaphor for lifting and moving a real-world object from one location to another is to use a mouse to complete a drag-and-drop operation. Dragging and dropping an image of a file folder onto an image of a recycle bin is closer to real-world experiences than typing the characters del filename.doc next to the c:\windows> characters.

Applications should follow basic graphic design principles and should be consistent visually and functionally. For example, each time a dialog box is used to provide a message to the user, it should have a similar shape, location, color, font size, and style. Functional consistency means the user initiates the same set of events in the same way throughout the use of the application. If the same set of print options is offered to the user when printing report A or report B, then report A's options should not be presented as a menu and report B's options presented as a set of check boxes.

The user always should receive immediate feedback after initiating an event. You probably at one time or another have experienced the frustration of clicking a button or icon and then wondering whether anything was happening. When you click an icon and the mouse pointer changes to an hourglass or animated image, you understand that processing has been initiated in response to your click. If you have ever heard the Windows Chimes, Chord, Exclamation, or other sounds, you have experienced **auditory feedback**.

The application should attempt to prevent users from making mistakes as much as possible, rather than allowing mistakes and then pointing them out to the user. Nevertheless, users will make mistakes, and the application should be capable of responding to their mistakes. The user never should be told that he or she made a mistake. Instead, he or she should be told politely why a function cannot be carried out or prompted to reenter data. These messages often are conveyed in dialog boxes, called **error dialogs**, but they should never use language that implies the user is at fault. Many individuals learn how to use an application by trial and error and so the error dialog is a way to provide positive rather than negative feedback to the user.

The Program Development Life Cycle

When programmers build software applications, they just do not sit down and start writing code. Instead, they follow an organized plan, or **methodology**, that breaks the process into a series of tasks. There are many application development methodologies just as there are many programming languages. These different methodologies, however, tend to be variations of what is called the program development life cycle (PDLC).

The **program development life cycle (PDLC)** is an outline of each of the steps used to build software applications. Similarly to the way the system development life cycle (SDLC) guides the systems analyst through development of an information system, the program development life cycle is a tool used to guide computer programmers through the development of an application. The program development life cycle consists of six steps, summarized in Table 1.

Table 1		
STEP	PROCEDURE	DESCRIPTION
1	Analyze the problem	Precisely define the problem to be solved, and write *program specifications* — descriptions of the program's inputs, processing, outputs, and user interface.
2	Design the program	Develop a detailed logic plan using a tool such as *pseudocode, flowcharts, object structure diagrams*, or *event diagrams* to group the program's activities into modules; devise a method of solution or algorithm for each module; and test the solution algorithms.
3	Code the program	Translate the design into an application using a programming language or application development tool by creating the user interface and writing code; include *internal documentation* — comments and remarks within the code that explain the purpose of code statements.
4	Test and debug the program	Test the program, finding and correcting errors (debugging) until it is error free and contains enough safeguards to ensure the desired results.
5	Formalize the solution	Review and, if necessary, revise internal documentation; formalize and complete end-user (external) documentation.
6	Maintain the program	Provide education and support to end users; correct any unanticipated errors that emerge and identify user-requested modifications (enhancements). Once errors or enhancements are identified, the program development life cycle begins again at Step 1.

Structured Programming

Structured programming, or **structured design,** is a methodology used to facilitate translating the problem analyzed in Step 1 of the PDLC into the specific program instructions in Step 3 (coding). Each module identified in the design step of the PDLC may be broken into a number of smaller and more precise instruction sets. This process can continue for several levels of even smaller, more precise instruction sets. The lowest-level instructions often are called **procedures.** A **hierarchy chart,** also called a **top-down chart** or **hierarchical input process output (HIPO) chart,** is a common way to represent this subdivision of activities visually. A hierarchy chart is shown in Figure 1.

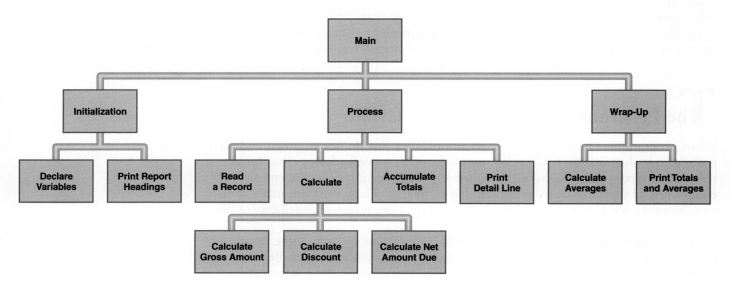

FIGURE 1

A **flowchart** is a design tool used to represent the logic in a solution algorithm graphically. Table 2 shows a standard set of symbols used to represent various operations in a program's logic.

Table 2

SYMBOL	NAME	MEANING
	Process Symbol	Represents the process of executing a defined operation or group of operations that results in a change in value, form, or location of information. Also functions as the default symbol when no other symbol is available.
	Input/Output (I/O) Symbol	Represents an I/O function, which makes data available for processing (input) or displaying (output) of processed information.
Left to Right Right to Left Top to Bottom Bottom to Top	Flowline Symbol	Represents the sequence of available information and executable operations. The lines connect other symbols, and the arrowheads are mandatory only for right-to-left and bottom-to-top flow.
	Annotation Symbol	Represents the addition of descriptive information, comments, or explanatory notes as clarification. The vertical line and the broken line may be placed on the left, as shown, or on the right.
	Decision Symbol	Represents a decision that determines which of a number of alternative paths is to be followed.
	Terminal Symbol	Represents the beginning, the end, or a point of interruption or delay in a program.
	Connector Symbol	Represents any entry from, or exit to, another part of the flowchart. Also serves as an off-page connector.
	Predefined Process Symbol	Represents a named process consisting of one or more operations or program steps that are specified elsewhere.

In structured programming, all program logic is constructed from a combination of three control structures, or constructs. A **control stucture** is a series of instructions that control the logical order in which the program instructions are executed. The three basic control structures are sequence, selection, and repetition.

Sequence Control Structure

The **sequence control structure** is used to show a single action or one action followed in order (sequentially) by another, as shown in Figure 2. Actions can be inputs, processes, or outputs.

Selection Control Structure

The **selection control structure** is used to tell the program which action to take, based on a certain condition. When the condition is evaluated, its result either is true or false. If the result of the condition is true, one action is performed; if the result is false, a different action is performed. This is called an **If...Then...Else structure** (Figure 3 on the next page).

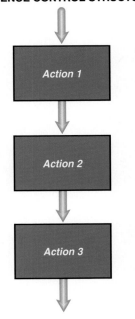

SEQUENCE CONTROL STRUCTURE

Action 1

Action 2

Action 3

FIGURE 2

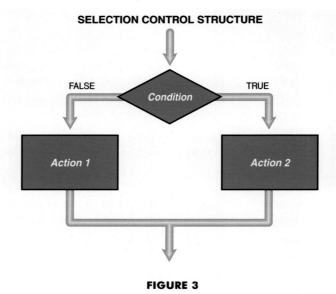

FIGURE 3

The action performed could be a single instruction or the action itself could be another procedure. The **case control structure** is a form of the selection control structure that allows for more than two alternatives when the condition is evaluated (Figure 4).

Repetition Control Structure

The **repetition control structure**, also called **looping** or **iteration**, is used when a set of actions is to be performed repeatedly. The Do...While and the Do...Until loops are forms of repetition control structures. The **Do...While loop** repeats as long as a condition is true (Figure 5). The **Do...Until loop** is similar, but it evaluates the condition at the end of the loop (Figure 6). This means the action(s) in the Do...Until loop always will execute at least once, where the actions in a Do...While loop may never execute.

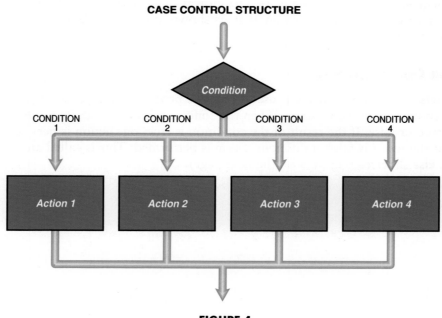

FIGURE 4

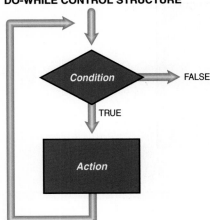

DO-WHILE CONTROL STRUCTURE

FIGURE 5

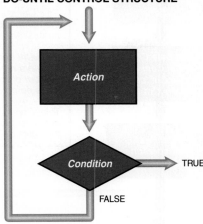

DO-UNTIL CONTROL STRUCTURE

FIGURE 6

Procedures commonly contain more than one control structure. The action specified within a control structure may be a single instruction or may activate other procedures. **Nested control structures** are control structures contained within other control structures. Figure 7 on the next page shows a flowchart that illustrates the processing required to compute the average commission paid to a company's sales personnel and determine the number of male and female salespeople. The flowchart illustrated in Figure 7 contains sequence, selection, and repetition control structures. The selection control structure is nested within the repetition control structure.

Object-Oriented Programming and Design

Object-oriented programming (OOP) and object-oriented design (OOD) represent a more recent methodology of application development than structured programming. This is a methodology that is not as well-defined as structured programming. Today, a number of Internet newsgroups exist in which the definitions, constructs, and implementations of OOP are debated hotly. **Object-oriented programming** has evolved as a way to better isolate logically related portions of an application than is possible in structured design. The benefit is that it is easier to develop, debug, and maintain applications that are becoming tremendously more complex than those created even a few years ago.

Object-oriented design represents the logical plan of a program as a set of interactions among objects and operations. An **object** is anything real or abstract, about which you store both data and operations that manipulate the data. Examples of objects are an invoice, an organization, a computer screen used to interact with a computer program, an airplane, and so on. An object may be composed of other objects, which in turn may contain other objects. A **class** is an implementation that can be used to create multiple objects with the same attributes and behavior. An object is an **instance** of a class. For example, Engine 15 located at 5th Street and Main is an object. It is a member of the class, Fire Truck.

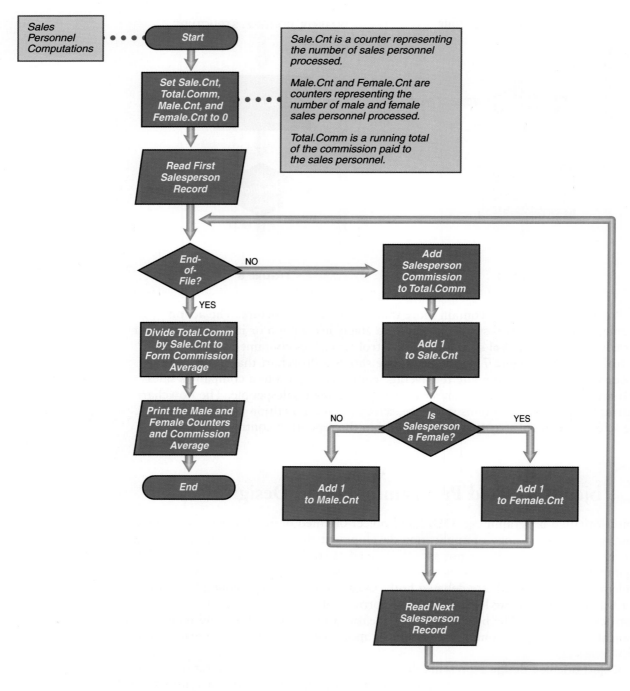

FIGURE 7

Each class can have one or more lower levels called **subclasses** or one or more higher levels called **superclasses**. For example, Fire Truck is a subclass of Truck. Motor Vehicle is a superclass of Truck. The relationship among the classes, subclasses, and superclasses is called the **hierarchy**. A **generalization hierarchy** (Figure 8) is an object-oriented design tool used to show the relationships among classes of objects.

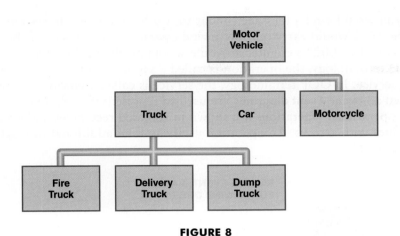

FIGURE 8

In object-oriented terminology, the data stored about an object is called an attribute, or property. **Attributes** are identifying characteristics of individual objects, such as a name, weight, or color. An **operation** is an activity that reads or manipulates the data of an object. In OOD, an operation is called a **service**. In OOP, the code that may be executed to perform a service is called a **method**.

An **object structure diagram** is used to provide a visual representation of an object, its attributes, and its methods (Figure 9 and Figure 10).

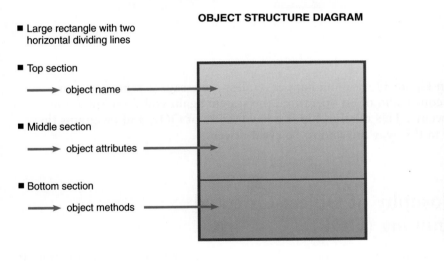

OBJECT STRUCTURE DIAGRAM

- Large rectangle with two horizontal dividing lines

- Top section
  → object name

- Middle section
  → object attributes

- Bottom section
  → object methods

SAMPLE OBJECT STRUCTURE DIAGRAM

TRAFFIC LIGHT

Color

Turn Red
Turn Yellow
Turn Green

The operations are described in terms of what they do — not how they do it.

FIGURE 9   **FIGURE 10**

For an object to do something, it must be sent a message. The **message** must have two parts — the name of the object to which the message is being sent and the name of the operation that will be performed. An **operation** is an activity that reads or manipulates the data of an object. An operation also can send additional messages. As an example, consider a VCR as a class having a rewind operation, a serial number attribute, and a counter attribute. Your VCR serial number 0023 is an instance of the class, VCR. The tape inside the VCR is not at its beginning and so the value of the counter attribute is something other than 000. To rewind a tape in the VCR, you would send a message similar to, vcr0023_rewind. In response to this message, the VCR would carry out the rewind operation. As a result of the operation, the value of vcr0023's counter attribute would be changed to 0000.

In OOD terminology, the operation is called a **service** and the message is called a **request for service**. In OOP terminology, the service is called a **method** and the message is called an **event**. **Event diagrams** are used to represent the relationships among events and operations. Operations are shown in rounded rectangles and events are shown on lines with arrows. An operation itself can send additional messages (events) (Figure 11).

**SAMPLE EVENT DIAGRAM
FOR REWIND OPERATION**

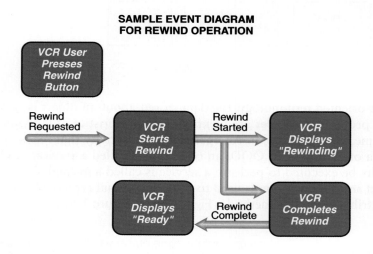

FIGURE 11

As shown in Figure 11, nothing happens unless a message is sent (an event occurs). At the conclusion of an operation, the system again will do nothing until another event occurs. This relationship is a key feature of OOP, and programs that are constructed in this way are said to be **event-driven**.

The Philosophy of Object-Oriented Programming (OOP)

OOP is not just a different set of tools and methods from structured programming. It represents a different philosophy about the nature of computer programs and how they are assembled. The following case scenario is designed to help illustrate these differences and provide an analogy for discussing the OOP constructs of encapsulation, inheritance, and polymorphism.

Paul Randall is a student of structured programming. He wants to create a work and study area in his room where he can write and draw and be able to cover his work. He wants to sit at the work area, and he wants to store his papers. Paul views the system as a set of functions — sitting, writing, and storing.

After a great deal of effort in drawing up blueprints, Paul has designed a one-piece, integrated study unit consisting of a writing surface with rolltop cover, a bench, and two drawers. By designing an integrated unit, the functions of sitting, writing, and storing will be compatible with each other and he will save on material costs and construction time. Paul travels to several lumber and hardware stores and purchases all the materials.

After considerable construction time, Paul is finished and satisfied with the result. He can work comfortably and does not reach too far to lift up the desktop or pull open the file drawers. Several weeks pass and Paul begins to think about making enhancements to his system. His bench is not as comfortable as he would like, his writing area feels cramped, and his two drawers are full. Paul decides to live with his system's shortcomings, however, because any change would require a substantial effort to dismantle and rebuild the entire system.

Mary Carter is a student of object-oriented programming. She would like to have a study area with the same functionality as Paul's. Mary, however, views the system as a set of objects — a sitting object, a writing surface object, and a storage object. Even though they are separate objects, Mary is confident she can make them interoperate with each other for an effective study area. Mary travels to a furniture factory warehouse and begins evaluating the hundreds of different chairs, desks, and file cabinets for their suitability to her needs and their compatibility with each other.

Mary returns to her room with a chair, a two-drawer file cabinet, and a rolltop desk from the Contemporary Oak line of the Devco Company. The desk has a handle similar to those on the drawers of the file cabinet. When the desk handle is pulled, it activates a hardware mechanism that raises the rolltop. Without too much effort arranging the furniture, Mary's study area is complete.

Although Mary's furniture cost more than Paul's materials, her savings on her labor costs have more than made up for the difference. After several weeks, Mary's file cabinet is full. She returns to the furniture store, buys a three-drawer cabinet from the Contemporary Oak line, and replaces the file cabinet in her study area.

Encapsulation, Inheritance, and Polymorphism

Just as sequence, selection, and repetition are the major constructs of structured programming, encapsulation, inheritance, and polymorphism are the major constructs of object-oriented programming.

Encapsulation

Encapsulation is the capability of an object to have data (properties) and functionality (methods) available to the user without the user having to understand the implementation within the object. Structured programming separates data from procedures. In the object-oriented world, an object contains functions as well as their associated data. Encapsulation is the process of hiding the implementation details of an object from its user. This process also is called **information hiding**. Users know what operations may be requested of an object but do not know the specifics of how the operations are performed. Encapsulation allows objects to be modified without requiring the applications that use them also to be modified.

In the case scenario, both Paul and Mary want drawers that cannot be pulled all the way out accidentally. In constructing his system, Paul had to attend to the details of how drawer stops work, which ones to use, and how to build them into the system. Mary, on the other hand, did not concern herself with *how* the safety stops on her drawers work; only that they *do* work. For Mary, the safety stop functionality and behavior is encapsulated within the file cabinet object.

Inheritance

Inheritance means that a descendent class (subclass) that differs from its superclass in only one way contains just the code or data necessary to explain the difference. Its status as a subclass is enough to give it access to all the superclass's functions and data. This is a very efficient way of reusing code. Also known as **subclassing**, this provides a way for programmers to define a class as an extension of another class, without copying the definition. If you let a class inherit from another class it automatically will have all the data and methods of the inherited class.

Mary's desk, chair, and cabinet all have similar wood grain, color, and style. If you think of the Devco Company's Contemporary Oak line of furniture as a superclass, then Mary's furniture objects are instances of subclasses of that furniture line. Because they are subclasses of the same superclass, they *inherited* the same wood grain, color, and style attributes from the superclass.

Polymorphism

Polymorphism allows an instruction to be given to an object in a generalized rather than specific detailed command. The same command will get different, but predictable, results depending on the object that receives the command. While the specific actions (internal to the object) are different, the results would be the same. In this way, one OOP function can replace several traditional procedures.

Paul must lift up his desktop when he wants to open it. You could say he must perform a *lifting* operation. To open his drawers, he must perform a *pulling* operation. Recall that Mary's rolltop desk has a pull handle with hardware *encapsulated* within the desk that translates the pull of the handle into the raising of the desktop. Mary's desk and file cabinet objects are *polymorphic* with respect to opening. Mary applies the same method, *pulling*, to open either object. She knows that the pull method will result in the object opening. How the object opens, or even that the object does open differently, is not a concern to Mary.

Rapid Application Development (RAD) and the Benefits of Object-Oriented Programming

Rapid application development (RAD) refers to the use of prebuilt objects to make program development much faster. Using prebuilt objects is faster because you use existing objects rather than writing everything yourself. The result is shorter development life cycles, easier maintenance, and the capability to reuse components for other projects. One of the major premises on which industry implementation of OOP is built is greater reusability of code.

The adoption of an object-orientation means that not all members of a development team need to be proficient in an object-oriented programming language such as Visual Basic, Delphi, PowerBuilder, Smalltalk, or C++. A more practical and economical approach is to separate the task of creating objects from the task of assembling objects into applications. Some programmers can focus on creating objects while other developers leverage their knowledge of business processes to assemble applications using OOP methods and tools. The benefits of OOP are summarized in Table 3.

Table 3	
BENEFIT	EXPLANATION
Reusability	The classes are designed so they can be reused in many systems or create modified classes using inheritance.
Stability	The classes are designed for repeated reuse and become stable over time.
Easier design	The designer looks at objects as a black box and is not concerned with the detail inside.
Faster design	The applications can be created from existing components.

What Is Microsoft Visual Basic 6?

The **Visual Basic Programming System version 6**, is a tool that allows you to create software applications for the Windows operating system. With **Microsoft Visual Basic 6 (VB6)**, you can create Windows desktop applications, reusable software components for building other applications, and applications targeted for the Internet and intranets.

Visual Basic 6 incorporates a set of software technologies called ActiveX. **ActiveX technology** allows the creation, integration, and reuse of software components called controls. **ActiveX controls** are reusable software components that can be integrated into a large number of different software products. More than 2,000 ActiveX controls currently are available. VB6's ActiveX technology also allows you to create ActiveX documents. **ActiveX documents** are applications that can be delivered dynamically over the Internet or intranets with browsers such as Internet Explorer or Netscape Navigator.

Version 6 of Visual Basic is available in four editions — Control Creation, Learning, Professional, and Enterprise. The Visual Basic 6 **Control Creation Edition (VB6CCE)** allows developers to build ActiveX controls from scratch, customize existing ActiveX controls, or assemble multiple existing controls into new controls. It does not include some of the functionality found in the Learning, Professional, and Enterprise editions and it cannot be used to develop stand-alone applications. The Control Creation Edition is available free to download from the Microsoft Web site. In addition to including control creation capability, the Learning, Professional, and Enterprise editions each offer progressively more application development and project management features.

Visual Basic 6 is based on the **Visual Basic programming language**, which evolved from the Beginner's All-Purpose Symbolic Instruction Code (BASIC). In addition to four editions of Visual Basic 6, two additional editions of the Visual Basic programming language itself are available. The **Applications Edition (VBA)** of the Visual Basic programming language is included within Excel, Access, and many other Windows applications. You can use VBA to customize and extend the capabilities of those applications. The **Scripting Edition (VBScript)** of the Visual Basic programming language is a subset of Visual Basic you can use for Internet programming.

Is Visual Basic Object Oriented?

Visual programming languages are languages where you create the entire program by *visual* means. With Visual Basic, only the interface is created visually. The program still mostly is coded. Visual Basic, therefore, is not a visual programming language in the strict sense.

One of the strengths of Visual Basic is that it is very easy to put the basics of the interface in place, and then go on to develop the functionality of the application a little at a time. Visual Basic is well-suited to prototyping. **Prototyping** is a process where developers iterate between refining the specifications and building working models of the system.

Since its first release in the early 1990s, Visual Basic always has been event-driven and object-based. It does not, however, meet all the requirements to be called an object-oriented programming language. One of the principal distinctions is that Visual Basic implements subclassing through something called *aggregation* and *containment* rather than through inheritance.

In Visual Basic, you create applications by assembling components. Visual Basic has a set of predefined objects and also allows for user-defined objects. Objects have attributes called **properties**. The visual elements common to Windows applications such as check boxes, option buttons, and list boxes, are called **controls** in Visual Basic. The windows that contain an application's controls are called **forms**. Controls and forms are objects that have properties, methods, and events. Messages or requests for service are called **events**. Operations or services are called **procedures**. Procedures include **methods, functions,** and **subroutines.**

Applications are created with Visual Basic in a **three-step process** —creating the interface, setting properties, and writing code. Although Visual Basic has a number of built-in methods and functions that can be applied to objects and controls, you still must write many of the procedures that *glue together* the components. These procedures are written instruction by instruction. The constructs and syntax used to write the procedures are based on the BASIC language. In fact, the approach to coding procedures in Visual Basic uses the constructs and control structures of traditional structured programming.

Visual Basic is well established in the industry as a commercial-grade RAD tool. Thousands of large-scale, complex applications have been built with Visual Basic. Visual Basic also is a powerful tool for learning programming and application development, because it requires an understanding of the concepts and techniques of both structured programming and object-oriented programming.

Summary

This introduction provided an overview of application development, user interface design, program development methodology, structured programming, object-oriented programming, and the Visual Basic software development system. This overview has provided a context within which you can better understand the concepts and technologies involved in the projects that follow. Visual Basic is a powerful and complex event-driven, object-based software development system. Creating applications with Visual Basic is a challenging and exciting undertaking.

Test Your Knowledge

1 True/False

Instructions: Circle T if the statement is true or F is the statement is false.

T   F   1. The program development life cycle is an outline of steps used to build software applications.

T   F   2. The selection control structure also is called looping.

T   F   3. A flowchart is used to show the relationships among classes of objects.

T   F   4. In OOP terminology, a message sent to an object is called an event.

T   F   5. Inheritance also is called information hiding.

T   F   6. Visual Basic is an object-oriented programming language.

T   F   7. Event diagrams show the relationship among events and operations.

T   F   8. Applications always should direct the user what to do next.

T   F   9. In a multitasking system, a processor executes multiple instructions at the same time.

T   F   10. The function of an interface should follow from its form.

2 Multiple Choice

Instructions: Circle the correct response.

1. A method is another word for a(n) _____.
   a. service
   b. request for service
   c. event
   d. property

2. Of the following, which is not a structured design tool?
   a. HIPO chart
   b. flowchart
   c. generalization hierarchy
   d. top-down chart

3. The correct order of operations in a machine cycle is _____.
   a. store, decode, fetch, execute
   b. fetch, store, decode, execute
   c. decode, execute, fetch, store
   d. fetch, decode, execute, store

4. An If...Then structure is an example of _____.
   a. sequence
   b. pseudocode
   c. selection
   d. iteration

(continued)

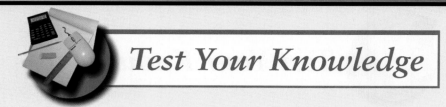

Test Your Knowledge

Multiple Choice *(continued)*

5. An object is a(n) _____ of a class.
   a. instance
   b. attribute
   c. encapsulation
   d. inheritance

6. _____ allows objects to be modified without requiring the applications that use them to be modified.
   a. Inheritence
   b. Polymorphism
   c. Encapsulation
   d. Instantiation

7. Of the following, which is not a benefit of OOP?
   a. reusability
   b. disposability
   c. stability
   d. faster development

8. In Visual Basic terminology, check boxes, option buttons, and command buttons are called _____.
   a. elements
   b. objects
   c. controls
   d. events

9. _____ refers to the use of prebuilt objects to make application development faster.
   a. SDLC
   b. PDLC
   c. RAID
   d. RAD

10. In the PDLC, internal documentation is written during the _____ procedure.
    a. documenting
    b. maintaining
    c. designing
    d. coding

Test Your Knowledge

3 Understanding Flowcharts

Instructions: A flowchart representation of part of a cariovascular disease risk assessment is shown in Figure 12. The higher the point total, the greater the risk. In the spaces provided, write the point total for the following persons.

1. A 33-year-old non-smoker with normal blood pressure who eats a high fat diet

_____

2. A 19-year-old non-smoker with high blood pressure who eats a high fat diet

_____

3. A 50-year-old non-smoker with high blood pressure who eats a high fat diet

_____

4. A 27-year-old smoker with high blood pressure who eats a low fat diet

_____

5. A 43-year-old smoker with high blood pressure who eats a high fat diet

_____

6. A 17-year-old non-smoker with normal blood pressure who eats a high fat diet

_____

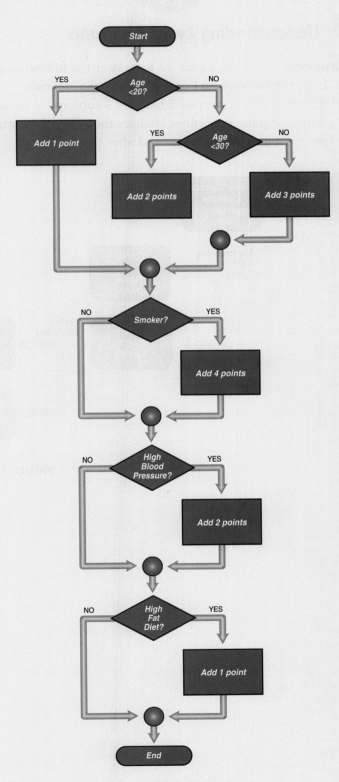

FIGURE 12

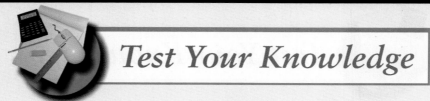

Test Your Knowledge

4 Understanding Event Diagrams

Instructions: Refer to Figure 13 to answer the following questions.

1. List each message and operation pair that follows.
2. Which of these operations includes a subsequent message? List any pairs of operations and their message.
3. Which of these operations changes the value of an attribute of an object? List the operation, attribute, and the attribute's value before and after the operation.

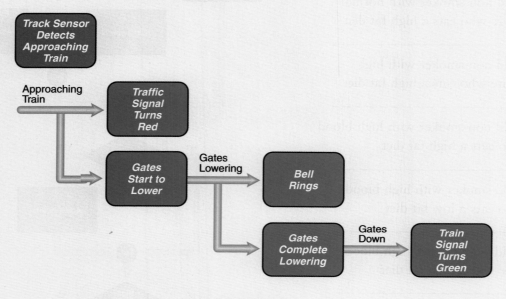

FIGURE 13

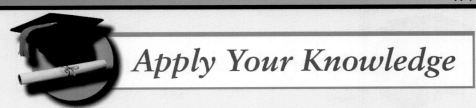

Apply Your Knowledge

1 Creating a Generalization Hierarchy

Instructions: Pick any class of objects that interests you (for example, clothes, musical instruments, physical fitness equipment, etc.). Create a generalization hierarchy showing at least four levels of subclasses and superclasses. For each subclass, identify several attributes inherited from each of its superclasses.

2 Creating a Flowchart

Instructions: Draw one flowchart that enables the mechanical man to accomplish the objectives efficiently in both Phase 1 and Phase 2, as illustrated in Figure 14.

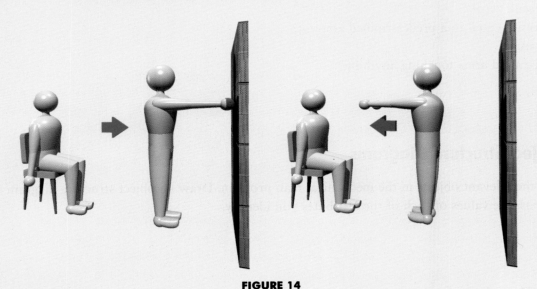

FIGURE 14

The mechanical man possesses the following properties:
1. He is restricted to a limited set of operations.
2. He is event-driven (doing nothing unless given a specific instruction).
3. He must carry out instructions one at a time.
4. He understands the following instructions:
  a. Physical movement:
    (1) Stand
    (2) Sit
    (3) Take one step forward
    (4) Raise arms straight ahead
    (5) Lower arms to sides
    (6) Turn right (90 degrees without taking a step)

(continued)

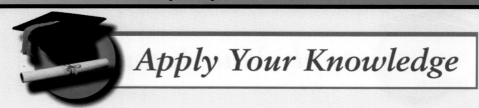

Apply Your Knowledge

Creating a Flowchart *(continued)*

   b. Arithmetic:
   (1) Add one to a running total
   (2) Subtract one from a running total
   (3) Store a total (any number of totals can be stored)
   c. Logic – the mechanical man can decide what instruction he will carry out next on the basis of answers to the following questions:
   (1) Arithmetic results
       (a) Is the result positive?
       (b) Is the result negative?
       (c) Is the result zero?
       (d) Is the result equal to a predetermined amount?
   (2) Physical status
       (a) Are the raised arms touching anything?

3 Creating Object Structure Diagrams

Instructions: Identify the relevant objects in the mechanical man problem. Draw an object structure diagram for each one. List all the possible values of each of the attributes you identify.

4 Designing a User Interface

Instructions: Based on your previous experience with Windows applications, draw a picture of a user interface for an application that will convert any amount of dollars into the equivalent amount in an international currency. The currencies should include Yen, Lire, Marks, and Francs. Describe the events and methods (the exact exchange rates and calculations are not necessary). Referring to the user interface you designed, what mistakes could a user make? What will your application do in response to those mistakes?

In the Lab

1 Identifying Events and Methods

Instructions: Start any software application available to you. On your own paper, briefly describe what the application generally allows the user to do. Identify five specific events in the application and their corresponding methods (operations). Write your name on the paper and hand it in to your instructor.

2 Principles of Interface Design

Instructions: Start any software application available to you. On your own paper, briefly describe what the application generally allows the user to do. Identify one example of each of the interface design principles discussed in this introduction. Write your name on the paper and hand it in to your instructor.

3 Interface Consistency

Instructions: Explore three different software applications created by at least two different companies. Briefly describe each one on your own paper. List at least five things that all three applications have in common. Write your name on the paper and hand it in to your instructor.

4 User Mistakes

Instructions: Start any software application available to you. On your own paper, briefly describe what the application generally allows the user to do. Intentionally make at least five user mistakes. Describe what you did and how the application responded. Write your name on the paper and hand it in to your instructor.

Microsoft **Visual Basic 6**

Microsoft Visual Basic 6

Building an Application

PROJECT

1

You will have mastered the material in this project when you can:

OBJECTIVES

- Start Visual Basic
- Select SDI Development Environment options
- Start a new Visual Basic project
- Change the size and location of a form
- Add controls to a form
- Describe the functions of the Label, TextBox, and CommandButton controls
- Move and resize controls on a form
- Set properties of controls
- Set a form's Name property
- Write an event procedure
- Use the Val function and SetFocus method within code statements
- Document code with comment statements
- Save a Visual Basic project
- Print an application's form and code
- Open an existing Visual Basic project
- Use Visual Basic Help

Gift Giving

A New Way of Looking
at an Old Tradition

Planning a wedding and expecting a baby are two of the more exciting, yet stressful, events in the lives of many couples. Part of the process involves registering for gifts for the special occasions and having friends and relatives purchase these articles. Whether it is housewares for the bride and groom or a stroller for the newborn, selecting the ideal product can be a daunting task.

Not so, if the bridal pair or the parents-to-be shop at Service Merchandise. According to corporate officials, the experience is a *no-hassle, fun way* to register. This positive process is due in part to the PC-based Gift Registry touch-screen and scanning system, which uses a Microsoft Visual Basic application developed

GIFT
Registry

Weddings

BABY

Special Occasions

by software engineers at NCR, a consulting firm and hardware vendor in Georgia.

NCR built the application using the same three-step process of creating the interface, setting properties, and writing code that you will learn in this project. Its programmers produced the system based on surveys stating that shoppers want to reduce frustration and time as they select gifts for the occasion. Using Visual Basic, they designed a graphical user interface that uses a combination of text and graphics to guide registrants and consumers.

The system works like this: registrants visit one of Service Merchandise's stores nationwide and locate the Gift Registry kiosk. Using the touch-screen keyboard developed with Visual Basic, they first select whether they are registering for a wedding, baby, or other special event, such as a retirement, birthday, or anniversary. They then enter their name, address, and event date. After inputting this pertinent information, their records are assigned specific gift registry numbers in the store's main computer processor, and they proceed to the store's information desk.

There they receive a hand-held, radio-frequency scanning gun. They walk through the store and scan the bar codes found on tags attached to specific products. As they enter their gift choices, their records are updated with the item number, description, price, and quantity desired. Once they have

selected their items, they return the scanning gun to the information desk. The sales associate then prints a list of the items and announcement cards. This entire process can be accomplished in less than 20 minutes.

Next, these records are transmitted by a roof-mounted satellite dish to Service Merchandise's mainframe located at the corporation's headquarters in Nashville, Tennessee, and added to the database of all registrants.

At this point, relatives and friends throughout the country can visit one of Service Merchandise's more than 300 stores and use the Gift Registry kiosk. They locate the registrant's record by entering the gift registry number or the registrant's name on the touch-screen. The system prints a complete listing of the registrant's gifts, indicating the item number and description, price, number desired, number purchased, and where the item appears in the corporation's catalog. When this customer selects an item on the list, this information is transmitted to the mainframe, and the database is updated immediately.

More than 100,000 individuals register annually for their special events using this system, which makes it one of the country's most popular gift registries. Certainly this no-hassle application calls for a celebration in the eyes of registrants and friends.

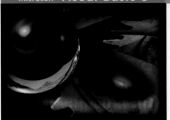

Microsoft **Visual Basic 6**

Microsoft Visual Basic 6

Building an Application

P R O J E C T

1

C A S E   P E R S P E C T I V E

MG's Auto Sales sells pre-owned automobiles on a percentage commission for its salespersons. Because much of MG's sales staff consists of temporary employees, it is difficult for management to avoid errors in manually keeping track of the sales and the proper commission for each salesperson. Management has decided to contract out for a PC-based transaction processing system, which will provide complete recordkeeping of the sales transactions at MG's. Due to the recommendation of one of your satisfied customers, they have approached your company to build the needed system.

As a part of the system proposal, your project team is building a prototype system, for which Visual Basic was chosen as the most appropriate development environment. You are responsible for building a prototype for a Windows-based calculator module for the application. The ability for the user to identify a specific salesperson, enter multiple sales transactions, or change the commission rate will be added later and are not required for the demonstration prototype.

Introduction

The way in which you give instructions to a computer and receive feedback from the computer is called a **user interface**. Microsoft Windows is called a **graphical user interface (GUI)** because it allows you to use both text and graphical images to communicate with the computer. **Applications software**, or **applications**, are computer programs that perform a specific function such as a calendar, word processing, or spreadsheet.

Numerous application software packages are available from computer stores, and several applications are included when you purchase the Microsoft Windows operating system. Although many of these Windows applications are created by different companies or individuals, they have a similar *look and feel* to the computer user. They *look* similar because they contain many of the same graphical images, or objects. Different Windows applications *feel* similar because they respond to the same kinds of user actions, such as clicking or dragging with a mouse. A typical Windows application containing common Windows objects is WordPad, as shown in Figure 1-1.

Visual Basic is itself a Windows application. Its function, however, is to help you build your own special-purpose applications and application components for the Windows operating system. With Visual Basic, professional-looking applications using the graphical user interface of Windows can be created by individuals who have no previous training or experience in computer programming. Because of the ease with which the user interface can be created, Visual Basic is especially useful for prototyping and rapid application development.

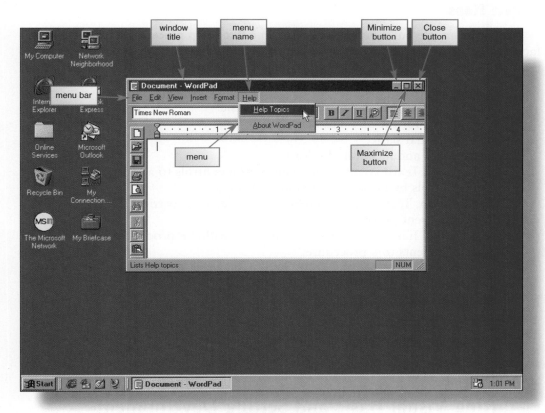

window title

menu name

Minimize button

Close button

menu bar

menu

Maximize button

FIGURE 1-1

Project One – Calculating Sales Commission

To learn the major features of application development with Microsoft Visual Basic, you will complete a series of projects using Visual Basic to build Windows applications. In this project, you will use Visual Basic to build the sales commission application shown in Figure 1-2. In this application, the user enters a number in the SALES text box. When the user clicks the CALCULATE button, the sales commission is calculated and displays in the COMMISSION text box. The Calculating Sales Commission application has some of the common features of Windows applications. It occupies a window that the user can move on the desktop, it can be maximized or minimized, and it has a Close button.

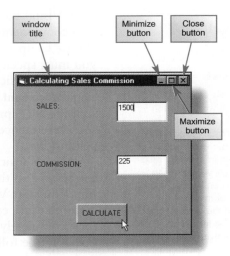

window title

Minimize button

Close button

Maximize button

FIGURE 1-2

Because you are responsible for building only one module of the prototype information system, you will not need to make the application stand-alone. A **stand-alone application**, also called an **EXE**, is one which runs independently of the Visual Basic system. You will learn how to make EXE applications in later projects. In addition, because the application is a prototype it need not contain all of the features and functionality that might be desired in the final application.

Project Steps

Applications are built with Visual Basic in a **three-step process:** creating the interface, setting properties, and writing code. You will follow this three-step process to build the sales commission application. You will complete the following tasks in this project.

1. Start a Standard EXE project in Visual Basic.
2. Set options for the SDI interface.
3. Restart Visual Basic.
4. Set the size and location of a form.
5. Add Label, TextBox, and CommandButton controls to a form.
6. Add controls by drawing and double-clicking.
7. Set Caption, Text, Locked, TabStop, and Name properties.
8. Write an event procedure.
9. Use the Val function and SetFocus method within a procedure.
10. Add comments to a procedure.
11. Save a project.
12. Open and run an existing project.
13. Print a project.
14. Quit Visual Basic.

The following pages contain a detailed explanation of each of these steps.

Starting Visual Basic and Setting Development Environment Options

More About

Multiple Document Interface

The Multiple Document Interface (MDI) was new with version 5 of Visual Basic. With the MDI option, all of the Visual Basic windows are contained within a single, resizable parent window. The windows can be docked on any side of the parent window, and the docking capabilities can be turned off or on for any individual window.

With Visual Basic 6, not only can you build desktop applications, but also application components and Internet applications. When you start Visual Basic, you can choose to open a recent, existing, or new project. When you select a new project, you must specify which type of project you will be creating.

Visual Basic 6 has an option for either a **multiple document interface (MDI)** or a **single document interface (SDI)**. The SDI presents independent windows on the desktop; the MDI presents windows within windows. The interface you use is one of personal preference; however, the MDI is better suited to larger monitors with higher resolutions.

Visual Basic records the size and location of all of these windows when you close the project so that its **integrated development environment (IDE)** displays the same each time you start Visual Basic. This can be a problem for a student working in a public computer lab, especially a student who is new to Visual Basic, because the IDE may look completely different every time the student comes to the lab and starts Visual Basic. In the following two sets of steps, you will open a new Standard EXE project and make the one IDE arrangement that is used in all of the projects in this book.

Starting Visual Basic and Setting Option Preferences

Whether you use the MDI or SDI, Visual Basic requires a lot of *real estate* on the desktop. Generally, you should minimize or close all other windows on the desktop before starting Visual Basic. This will make it easier for you to work with the Visual Basic windows. The currency conversion is a desktop application, or **Standard EXE**, project type. Perform the following steps to start Visual Basic, open a new Standard EXE project, and set option preferences.

 ### To Start Visual Basic and Set Option Preferences

1 **Click the Start button on the taskbar and then point to Programs on the Start menu. Point to Microsoft Visual Basic 6.0 on the Programs submenu, and then point to Visual Basic 6.0.**

The default menu structure for Visual Basic 6.0 is shown in Figure 1-3. Your system may have a different set of menus.

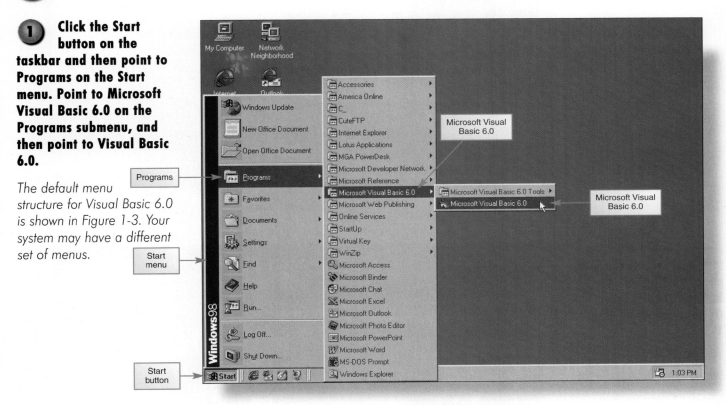

FIGURE 1-3

2 **Click Microsoft Visual Basic 6.0. If necessary, click the New tab and then point to the Standard EXE icon.**

The New Project dialog box displays (Figure 1-4).

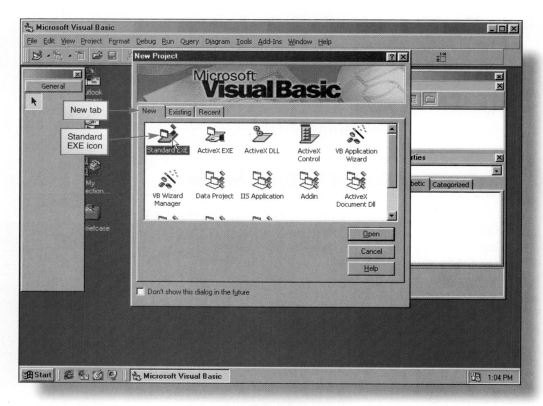

FIGURE 1-4

3 **Double-click the Standard EXE icon, click Tools on the menu bar and then point to the Options command (Figure 1-5).**

The Visual Basic IDE on your desktop may look different from Figure 1-5.

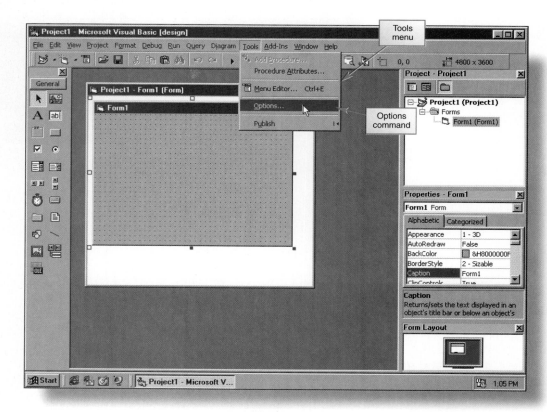

FIGURE 1-5

4 Click Options, click the Advanced tab, and then point to SDI Development Environment.

The Options dialog box displays. It contains six tab sheets (Figure 1-6).

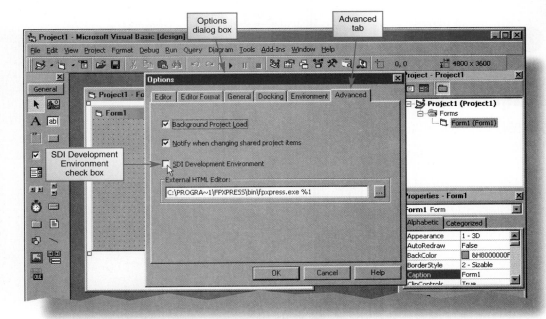

FIGURE 1-6

5 If necessary, click SDI Development Environment to select it. Click the Editor tab. Point to Default to Full Module View in the Window Settings area.

If SDI Development Environment was not selected, the MDI to SDI change does not take effect until VB is restarted. The Editor tab in the Options dialog box is shown in Figure 1-7.

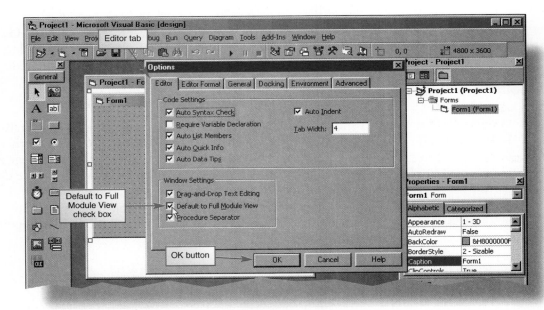

FIGURE 1-7

6 If necessary, click Default to Full Module View to remove the check mark so that the Default to Full Module View option is not selected. Click the OK button. Point to the Visual Basic Close button.

The Options dialog box closes (Figure 1-8).

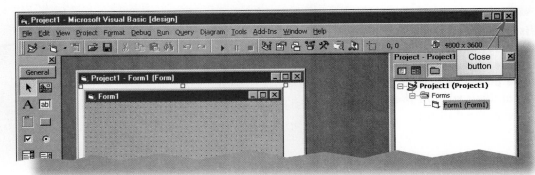

FIGURE 1-8

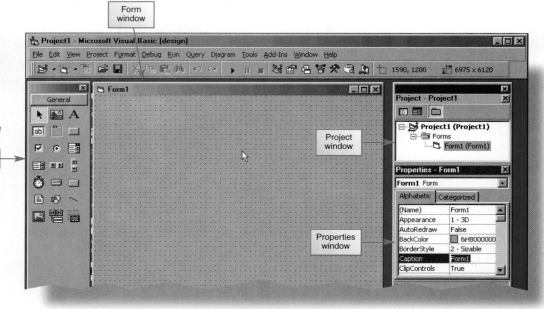

(7) **Click the Close button. Repeat Step 1 through Step 3 to restart VB and open a new Standard EXE project.**

The SDI interface is activated (Figure 1-9)

FIGURE 1-9

More About

Customizing Toolbars

The Toolbars tab in the Custom dialog box allows you to create, rename, delete, and reset your toolbars. The Options tab allows you to change the appearance of your menu bar and toolbars. The Commands tab allows you to add controls and modify existing controls on the menu bar or any toolbar.

When you start Visual Basic, several windows are added to the desktop. It is possible to work with Visual Basic without clearing the desktop. If other windows already are open, however, the desktop becomes cluttered.

Arranging Visual Basic Toolbars and Windows

The Visual Basic **integrated development environment (IDE)** contains nine different windows, all of which can be **docked**, or *anchored*, to other windows that are dockable and four toolbars that can be docked or float in their own windows. All of the windows can be resized and located anywhere on the desktop. To ensure the windows dock as shown in Figure 1-9, all the Dockable check boxes except Object Browser must be selected on the Docking sheet in the Options dialog box. Perform the following steps to establish a Visual Basic IDE arrangement similar to the one used in this book.

Steps **To Arrange Visual Basic Toolbars and Windows**

(1) **With the exception of the Visual Basic menu bar and toolbar window, click the Close button on each Visual Basic window that is open on the desktop.**

Only the menu bar and toolbar window remains open (Figure 1-10).

FIGURE 1-10

2 **Click View on the menu bar and then point to Project Explorer.**

The View menu displays (Figure 1-11).

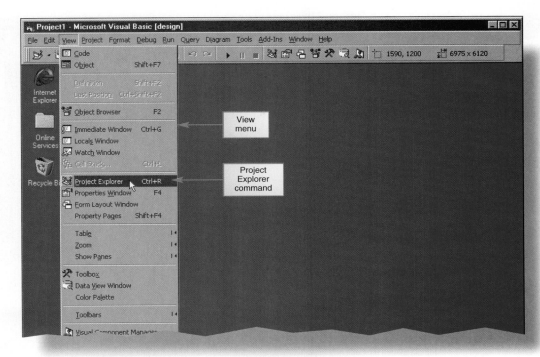

FIGURE 1-11

3 **Click Project Explorer. Click View on the menu bar and then click Properties Window. Click View on the menu bar and then click Toolbox. Double-click Form1 (Form1) in the Project window to open the Form window. Right-click the Properties window and then click Description to deselect it. Drag the windows to the locations shown in Figure 1-12 and drag each window's borders to resize the windows to the sizes shown in Figure 1-12.**

Five Visual Basic windows are open on the desktop (Figure 1-12).

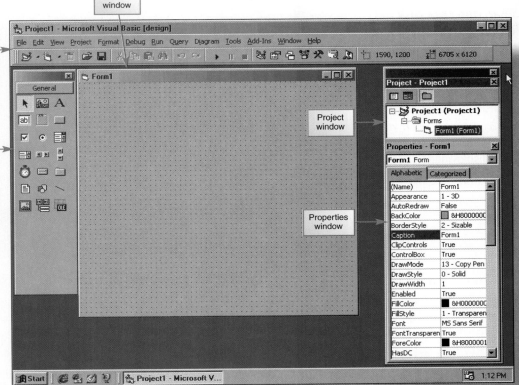

FIGURE 1-12

4 **Right-click the Visual Basic menu bar to the right of the Help menu.**

The shortcut menu displays (Figure 1-13). Your toolbar settings may be different from those shown in Figure 1-13.

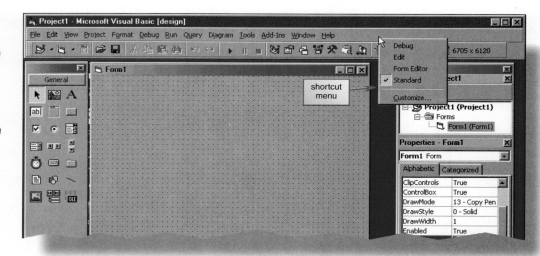

FIGURE 1-13

5 **If necessary, click Standard on the shortcut menu to display the Standard toolbar. Right-click the Standard toolbar, and then click any other toolbars that display with a check mark to the left of their names to deselect them.**

Your desktop should display similarly to Figure 1-14, with the Standard toolbar the only toolbar displaying.

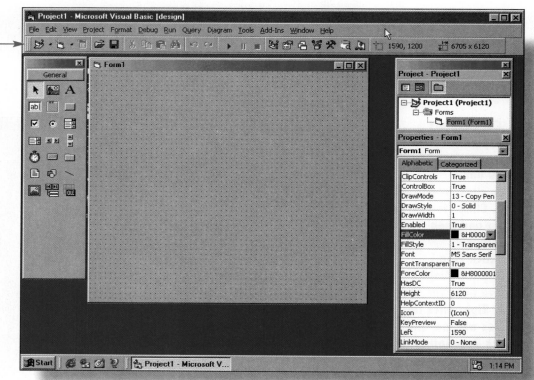

FIGURE 1-14

You can arrange the Visual Basic windows on the desktop in many different ways without affecting Visual Basic's functions. As you become more experienced, you may prefer to work with a different arrangement. Each project in this book uses the sizes and arrangement of the Visual Basic windows shown in Figure 1-14.

Setting the Size and Location of Forms

The time during which you build an application with Visual Basic is called **design time**. In contrast, the time during which you use an application for its intended purpose is called **run time**. In Visual Basic, the applications you build are called projects. A **project** always begins with a form. At run time, a **form** becomes the window the application occupies on the desktop. You will begin building the Calculating Sales Commission application shown in Figure 1-2 on page VB 1.7 by specifying the size and location where you want the application's window to display on the desktop during run time.

Setting the Size of a Form

The size of an application's window on the desktop during run time is specified by adjusting the size of the form during design time. Adjustments to the form's size can be made at any time during design time.

Perform the following steps to set the size of the Calculating Sales Commission form.

 To Set the Size of a Form

 Click the Form window's title bar.

The Form window becomes the active window (Figure 1-15). This can be seen by the color of the title bar and the Form window moving on top of the Project and Properties windows (only if the Project or Properties windows previously obscured the Form window – as has been done here for illustration purposes).

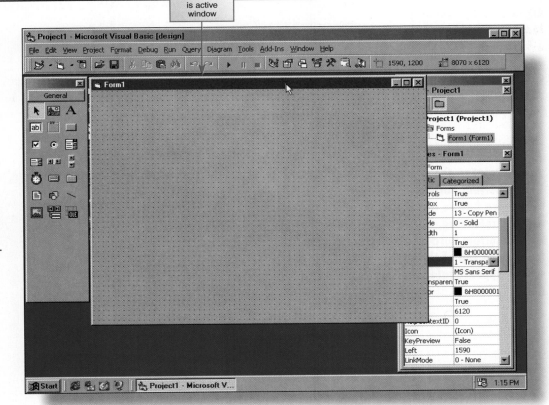

Form window is active window

FIGURE 1-15

Point to the form's right border.

The mouse pointer changes to a double horizontal arrow indicating the form can be sized (Figure 1-16).

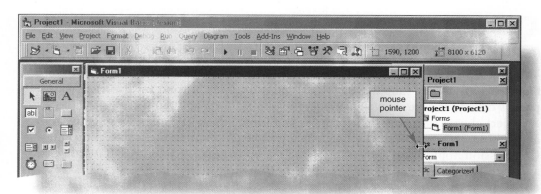

FIGURE 1-16

3 **Click the mouse button and without releasing, drag the form's right border toward the left side of the screen approximately three inches. Release the mouse button.**

During the drag operation, the form's right border moves to the new location (Figure 1-17). The Project and Properties windows again become visible (if they were previously obscured).

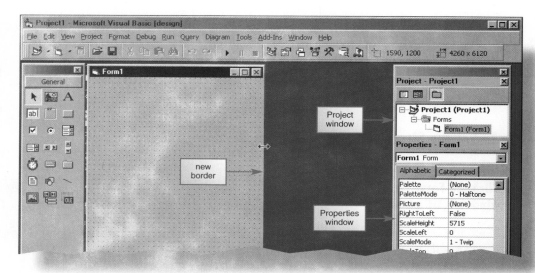

FIGURE 1-17

4 **Point to the Form's bottom border. Click the mouse button and without releasing, drag the form's bottom border toward the top of the screen approximately one inch.**

The mouse pointer changes to a double vertical arrow indicating the form can be sized (Figure 1-18).

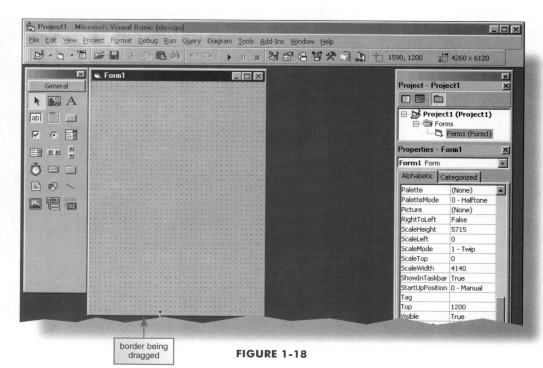

FIGURE 1-18

5 **Release the mouse button.**

The form's bottom border moves to the new location (Figure 1-19).

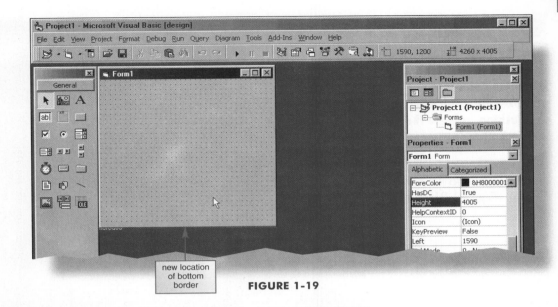

new location of bottom border

FIGURE 1-19

In the preceding steps, you set the form's **Width** and **Height** properties by dragging the form's right and bottom borders. You can drag each of the form's four borders in either an inward or outward direction to change its size. The form's width and height are measured in units called twips. A **twip** is a printer's measurement equal to 1/1440 inch. The width of a twip, however, can vary slightly from one computer monitor to another.

Positioning a Form

The location of an application's window on the desktop during run time is specified by adjusting the location of the form during design time. Adjustments to the form's location can be made at any time during design time. Perform the following steps to set the location on the desktop for the Calculating Sales Commission window.

More About

Twips

A twip is a unit of screen measurement equal to 1/20 of a printer's point. There are approximately 1440 twips to a logical inch or 567 twips to a logical centimeter (the length of a screen item measuring one inch or one centimeter when printed).

 To Position a Form

1 **Point to the Form window title bar (Figure 1-20).**

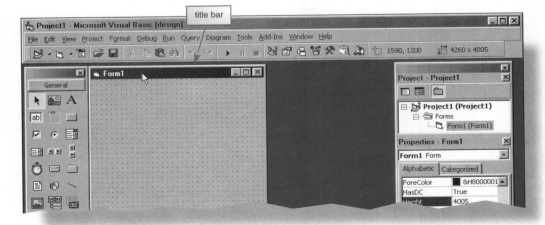

title bar

FIGURE 1-20

2 **Without releasing the mouse button, drag the Form window down and to the right. When the Form is approximately centered on the desktop, release the mouse button.**

During the drag operation, the form moves to the new location (Figure 1-21).

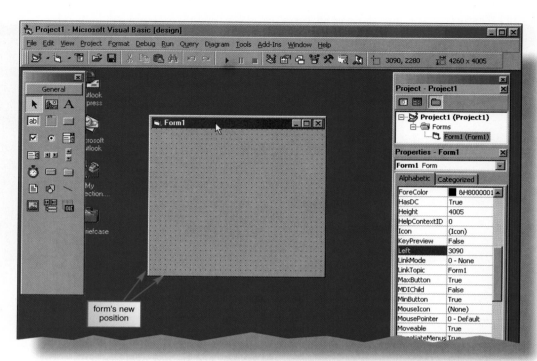

FIGURE 1-21

In the preceding steps, you set the form's location by dragging the form to the desired position. The form's location is given as two numbers. The first number is the value of the Left property. The **Left** property is the distance in twips between the left side of the desktop and the left border of the form. The second number is the value of the Top property. The **Top** property is the distance in twips between the top of the desktop and the top border of the form. The form's location can be changed as often as desired during design time. Sometimes, it is useful to move the form temporarily to work more easily in the other Visual Basic windows.

Adding and Removing Controls

Figure 1-1 on page VB 1.7 shows some of the graphical images, or objects, common to many Windows applications. In Visual Basic, these objects are called **controls**. The Calculating Sales Commission application contains three different types of controls (Figure 1-22). These controls and their functions are described as follows.

LABEL – A **Label control** is used to display text on a form. At run time, the person using the application cannot change the text on a label, such as SALES.

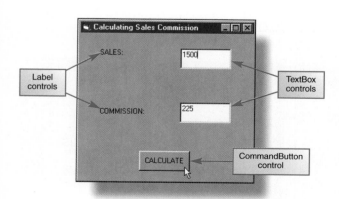

FIGURE 1-22

TEXTBOX – A **TextBox control** also is used to display text on a form, but its contents can be changed at run time by the person using the application. It frequently is used as a way for the user to supply information to the application.

COMMANDBUTTON – A **CommandButton control** is used during run time to initiate actions called **events**.

Adding Controls to a Form

Controls are added to a form using tools in the Visual Basic window called the **Toolbox**. To use a tool, you click its respective button in the Toolbox. Although you can add additional controls to the Toolbox, the Toolbox contains twenty **intrinsic** controls. More than 2,000 additional controls are available from Microsoft and from third-party vendors. Specific controls and their functions will be discussed as they are used throughout the projects in this book. Figure 1-23 identifies the intrinsic tools in the Toolbox.

Complete the following steps to use the Toolbox to add controls to the form.

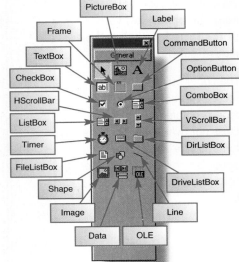

FIGURE 1-23

 To Draw Label Controls on a Form

1 **Point to the Label button in the Toolbox (Figure 1-24).**

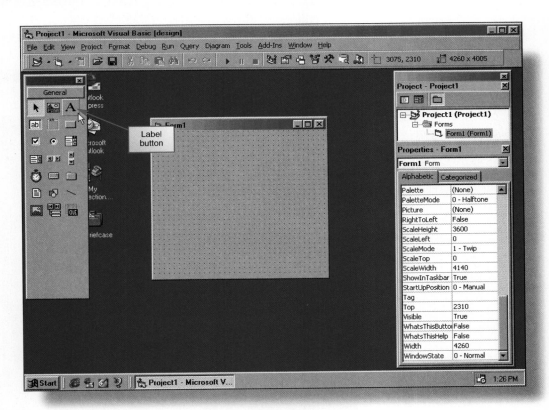

FIGURE 1-24

2 **Click the Label button. Position the cross hair mouse pointer near the upper-left corner of the form by moving the mouse pointer.**

The Label button in the Toolbox is recessed, and the mouse pointer changes to a **cross hair** when it is over the form (Figure 1-25). The upper-left corner of the Label control will be positioned here.

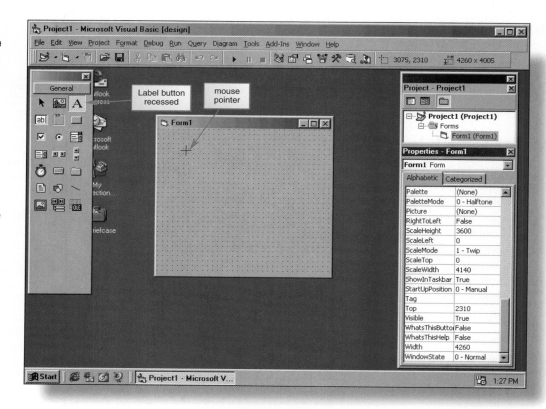

FIGURE 1-25

3 **Drag down and to the right.**

A gray outline of the Label control displays (Figure 1-26).

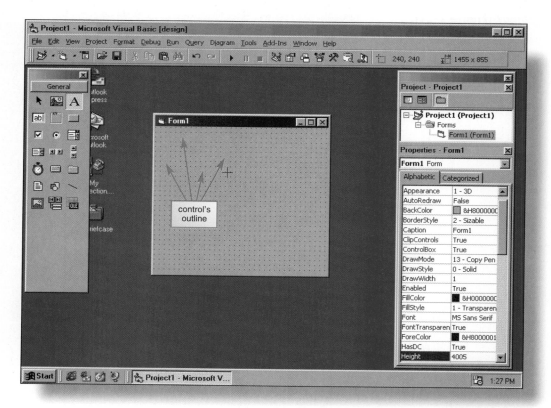

FIGURE 1-26

4 When the Label control outline is the desired size, release the mouse button.

The gray outline changes to a solid background. The name of the Label control (Label1) displays on the control. Small **sizing handles** *display at each corner and in the middle of each side of the Label control (Figure 1-27).*

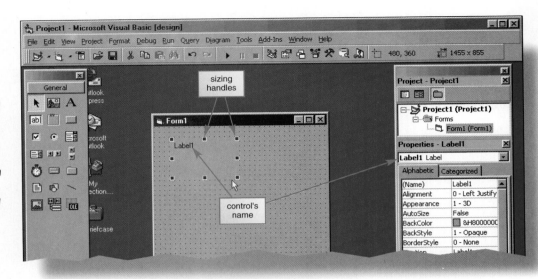

FIGURE 1-27

5 Repeat Step 1 through Step 4 to draw a second Label control on the form in the size and position shown in Figure 1-28 and then click any blank area on the form.

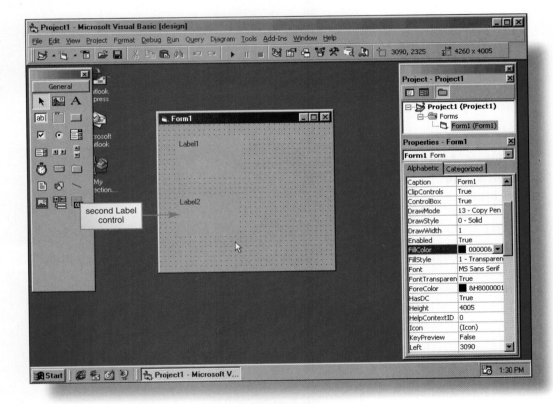

FIGURE 1-28

Two Label controls now have been added to the form by drawing them with the Label tool selected from the Toolbox. Complete the steps on the next page to add two TextBox controls to the form.

To Draw TextBox Controls on a Form

1 **Point to the TextBox button in the Toolbox (Figure 1-29).**

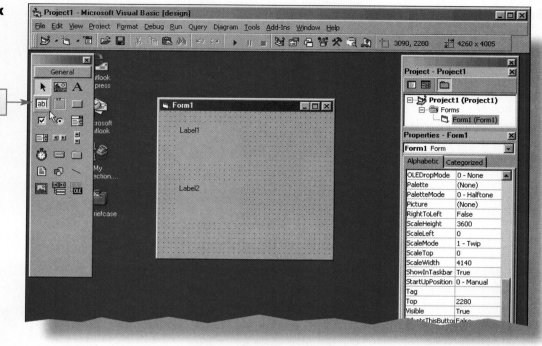

FIGURE 1-29

2 **Click the TextBox button. Position the cross hair mouse pointer toward the middle-right side of the form.**

The TextBox button is recessed in the Toolbox and the mouse pointer changes to a cross hair (Figure 1-30). The upper-left corner of the TextBox control will be positioned here.

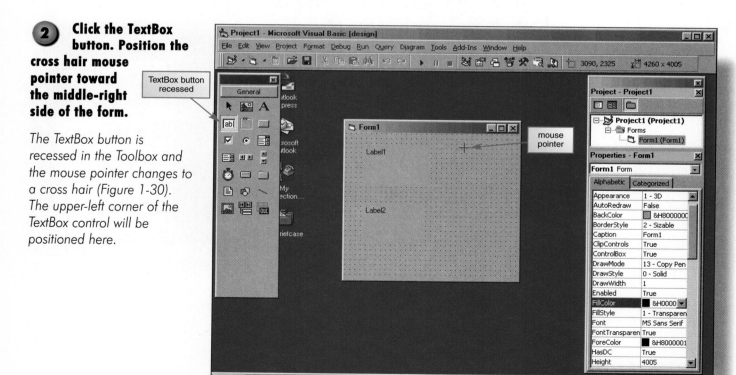

FIGURE 1-30

3 **Drag down and to the right.**

*A gray outline of the TextBox control displays (Figure 1-31). If you pause while drawing the TextBox control, a ToolTip displays indicating the width and height. A **ToolTip** is a small pop-up window that displays a single line of text that describes the purpose of a tool in an application.*

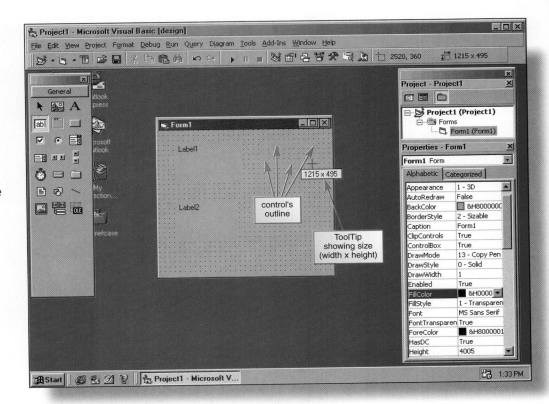

FIGURE 1-31

4 **When the TextBox control outline is the desired size, release the mouse button.**

The gray outline changes to a solid background. The name of the TextBox control (Text1) displays on the control. Sizing handles display at each corner and in the middle of each side of the TextBox control (Figure 1-32).

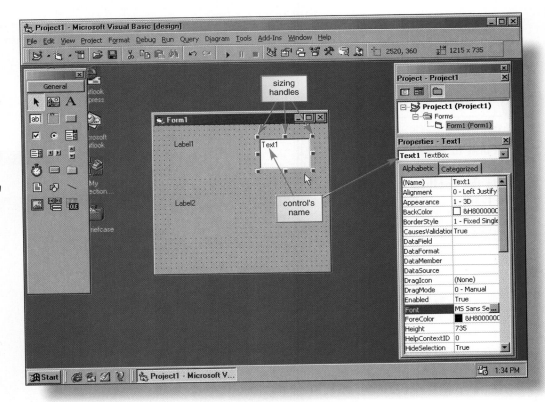

FIGURE 1-32

5 Repeat Step 1 through Step 4 to place a second TextBox control on the form as shown in Figure 1-33.

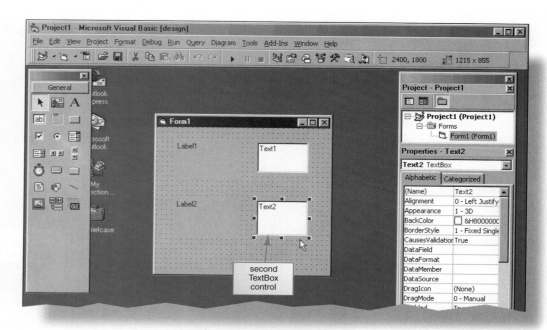

FIGURE 1-33

Two TextBox controls were added to the form in the same way as the two Label controls by clicking the button in the Toolbox and then drawing the control's outline on the form. This method can be used for adding any of the controls in the Toolbox to a form. This method, however, is not the only way to add controls to a form. The following steps use an alternative method to add a CommandButton control to the Calculating Sales Commission form.

 To Add Controls by Double-Clicking

1 Point to the CommandButton button in the Toolbox (Figure 1-34).

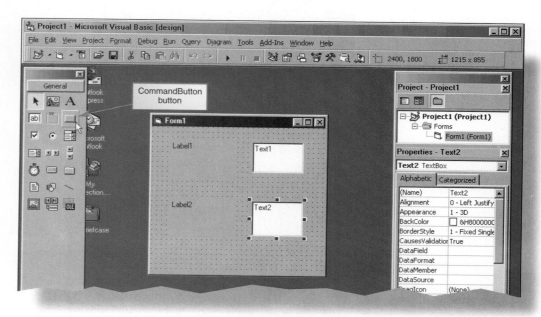

FIGURE 1-34

2 **Double-click the CommandButton button.**

The CommandButton control displays in the center of the form. The control's name, Command1, displays on the control. Sizing handles display around the Command-Button control (Figure 1-35).

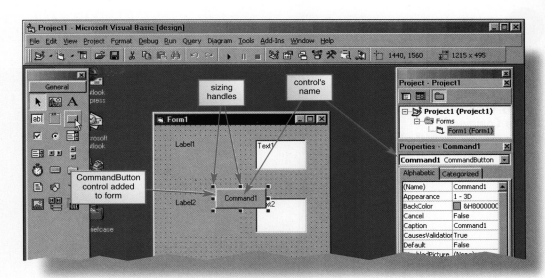

FIGURE 1-35

As you have just seen, double-clicking a button in the Toolbox adds a default-sized control to the center of the form. If another control already is located in the center of the form, this method will add the new control on top of the previous control.

Removing Controls

If you click the wrong button in the Toolbox or want to modify the project, controls can be removed from the form at any time during design time. Use the following steps to remove a control.

TO REMOVE A CONTROL

1 Point to the control you want to remove.

2 Click the control to select it.

3 Press the DELETE key.

Changing the Location and Size of Controls

If you add a control to a form by double-clicking a button in the Toolbox, you will need to move the control from the center of the form, and frequently, you will want to change its size from the default. The location and size of any of the controls on a form can be changed at any time during design time.

Moving a Control on a Form

A control can be moved by dragging it to a new location. Perform the steps on the next page to move the CommandButton control from the center of the Calculating Sales Commission form.

To Move a Control on a Form

1 Point to a location in the interior (not on any of the handles) of the Command1 CommandButton control (Figure 1-36).

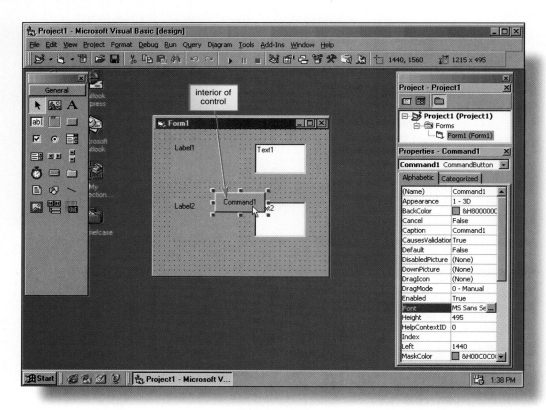

FIGURE 1-36

2 Drag the Command1 control toward the bottom of the form.

A gray outline of the CommandButton control displays (Figure 1-37).

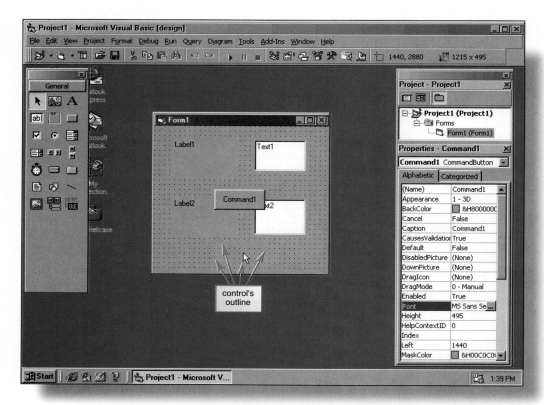

FIGURE 1-37

3 **Position the gray outline at the desired location on the form, and then release the mouse button.**

The control moves to the location of the outline (Figure 1-38).

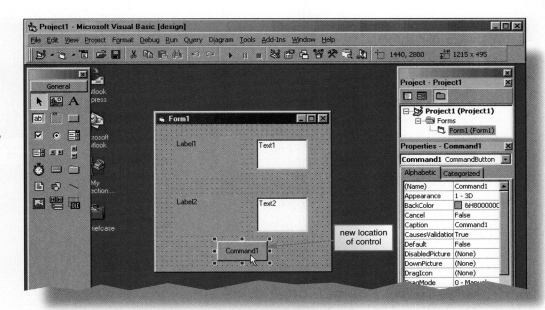

FIGURE 1-38

The location given to a control by dragging during design time is where the control will display at the beginning of run time. Dragging the control changes the values of its Top and Left properties. A control does not have to remain in its original location during run time. Changing a control's location during run time will be covered in a later project.

Changing the Size of a Control

Controls can be made larger or smaller by dragging the sizing handles located around the control. Perform the following steps to make the Text1 control smaller.

More About

Control Location

The Top property is the distance between the internal top edge of a control and the top edge of its container. The Left property is the distance between the internal left edge of a control and its container. A container is any control that can contain other controls, such as a Form control.

Steps **To Change the Size of a Control**

1 **Click the Text1 TextBox control.**

Sizing handles display around the control (Figure 1-39).

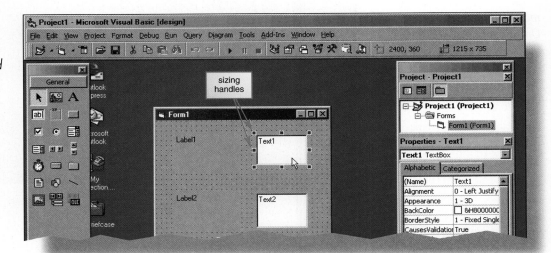

FIGURE 1-39

2 **Point to the handle located at the center of the bottom border of the control.**

The mouse pointer changes to a double vertical arrow (Figure 1-40).

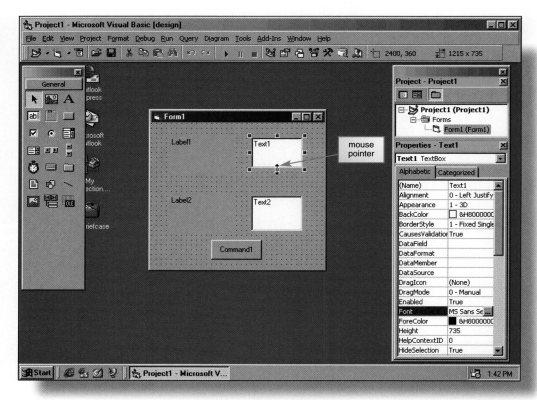

FIGURE 1-40

3 **Drag the border toward the top of the screen approximately one-quarter inch.**

The new position of the bottom border displays as a shaded gray line (Figure 1-41). Dragging a handle located in the center of one of the borders of a control moves that one border. Dragging one of the handles located at the corner of a control simultaneously moves the two borders that form the corner.

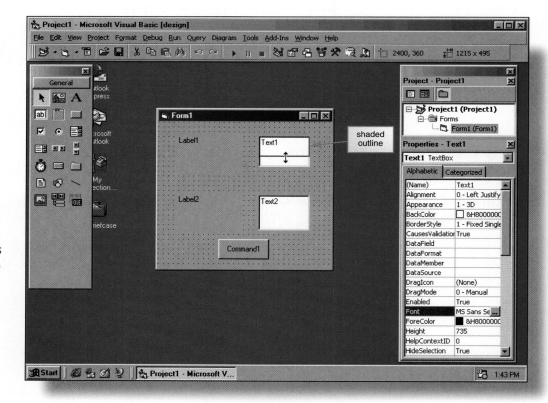

FIGURE 1-41

4 **Release the mouse button.**

The bottom border of the Text1 TextBox control moves to the location of the outline (Figure 1-42).

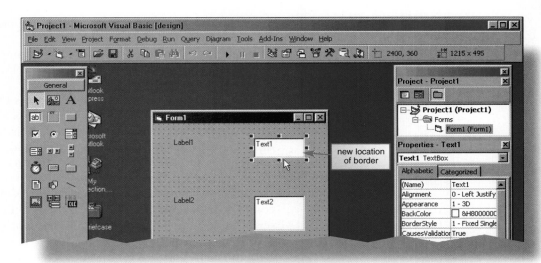

FIGURE 1-42

5 **Repeat Step 1 through Step 4 to resize the Text2 TextBox control to the size shown in Figure 1-43.**

The Form window now resembles the one shown in Figure 1-43.

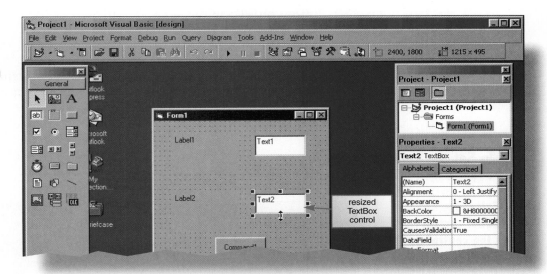

FIGURE 1-43

You may have noticed how similar the procedures are for setting the location and size of the form and for setting the locations and sizes of the Label, TextBox, and CommandButton controls on the form. This similarity should not be surprising, because a Visual Basic form also is a type of control. You will work more with Form controls in Project 3.

Setting Properties

Now that controls have been added to the form, the next step in the Visual Basic application development is to set the controls' properties. **Properties** are characteristics, or attributes, of a control, such as its color or the text that displays on top of it. Properties are set at design time by using the **Properties window** (Figure 1-44 on the next page).

Microsoft **Visual Basic 6**

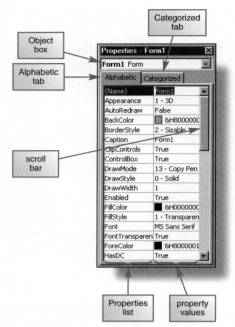

FIGURE 1-44

The Properties window consists of the following elements.

OBJECT BOX — The **Object box** displays the name of the currently selected object, or control, whose properties are being set.

PROPERTIES LIST — The **Properties list** displays the set of properties belonging to the control named in the Object box and the current value of those properties. The Properties list has two tab sheets. The **Alphabetic tab sheet** lists the properties in alphabetical order. The **Categorized tab sheet** groups the properties by category.

Different controls have different sets of properties. Because some controls' Properties lists are very long, the Properties window has a scroll bar to move through the list. It is not necessary to set every property of each control because Visual Basic assigns initial values for each of the properties. You need to change only the properties that you want to differ from their initial values, called **default** values. The major properties of controls will be discussed as they are used throughout the projects in this book.

The Caption Property

The **Caption property** of a control contains the text to be displayed on the control. Complete the following steps to set the Caption property of the Label1 control.

 To Set the Caption Property

1 **Select the Label1 Label control by clicking the control on the form.**

Handles display around the selected control. The control's name (Label1) displays in the Object box of the Properties window. The currently selected property (ForeColor) is highlighted in the Properties list (Figure 1-45). Another property may be highlighted on your screen.

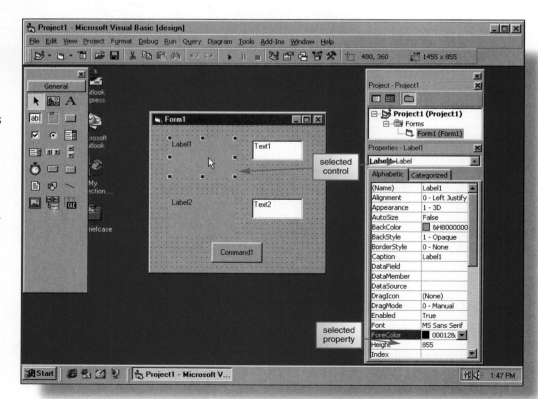

FIGURE 1-45

2   **Scroll the Properties list until the Caption property is visible in the list and then double-click the Caption property.**

The Caption property is highlighted in the Properties list. The current value of the property, Label1, is highlighted (Figure 1-46).

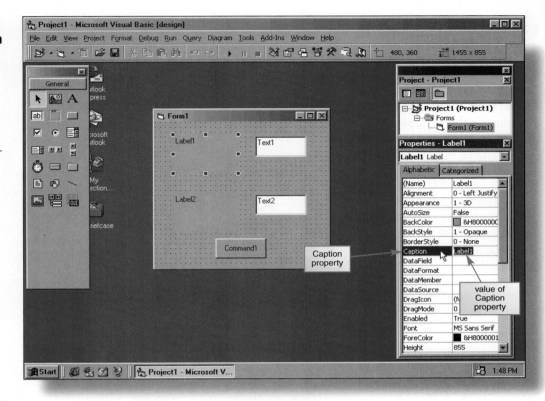

FIGURE 1-46

3   **Type** SALES: **as the new value.**

When you type the first character, the old value of the caption is replaced by that character. As you continue typing characters, they display in the Properties list and on the Label control on the form (Figure 1-47). If you make a mistake while typing, you can correct it by using the BACKSPACE key or the LEFT ARROW and DELETE keys.

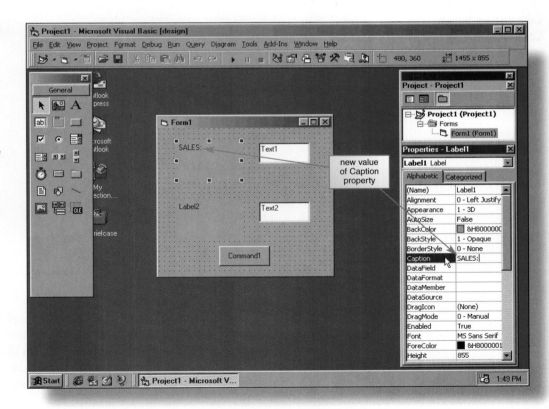

FIGURE 1-47

4 Repeat Step 1 through Step 3 to change the caption of the second Label control from Label2 to COMMISSION:. Repeat Step 1 through Step 3 to change the caption of the CommandButton control to CALCULATE.

5 Select the Form1 control by clicking an empty area of the form that does not contain any other controls.

The form should display as shown in Figure 1-48.

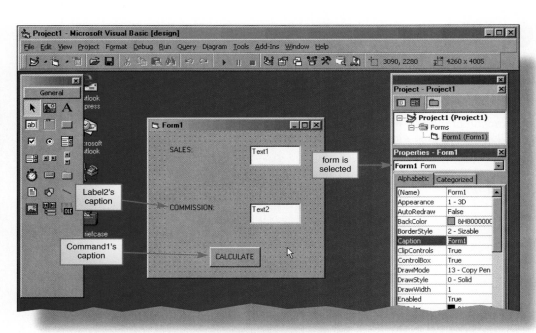

FIGURE 1-48

6 Repeat Step 1 through Step 3 to change the Form control's caption from Form1 to Calculating Sales Commission.

The form's caption displays in the title bar (Figure 1-49).

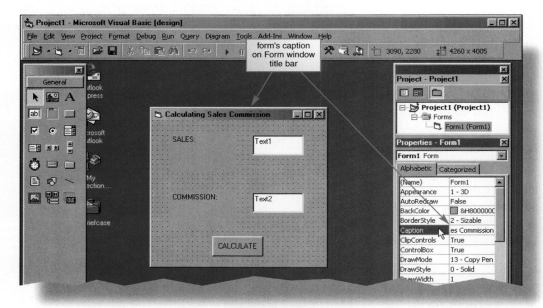

FIGURE 1-49

In the preceding steps, you changed the Caption property of four different types of controls. The caption of a Label control displays as text in the Label control's location. This control frequently is used to place text in different locations on a form. The Caption property of a form displays as text on the title bar of the form.

An alternative method of selecting the control whose properties you want to change is to click the Object box arrow (Figure 1-50), and then click the control's name from the list box that displays. This list expands as you add more controls to a form.

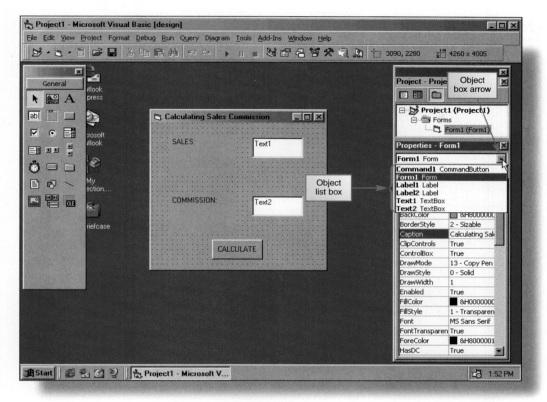

FIGURE 1-50

The Text, Locked, TabStop, and TabIndex Properties

The **Text property** of a text box is similar to the Caption property of a label. That is, whatever value you give to the Text property of a TextBox control displays in the text box at the beginning of run time. Later in this project, you will see how to change the Text property during run time.

The default value of a text box's Text property (the text that displays within its borders) is the name of the control. In the Calculating Sales Commission application, the two text boxes should be empty when the application begins, so you will set their Text property to be blank. In addition, the user should not be able to edit the contents of the text box that displays the resulting commission amount. This is accomplished by changing the text box's **Locked property** value from False to True.

It is common in Windows applications for the user to be able to move the focus from one control to another by pressing the TAB key. The order in which the control gets the focus by tabbing is determined by the control's **TabIndex property**. You can cause the focus to skip a control by changing its **TabStop property** value from True to False.

Perform the steps on the next page to set the text boxes' text values to blank, prevent the COMMISSION text box's text from being changed by the user, and disable tabbing in the application.

Tab Order

By default, Visual Basic assigns a tab order to controls as you draw them on a form. If you change the value of a control's TabIndex property to adjust the tab order, Visual Basic automatically renumbers the TabIndex of the other controls to reflect insertions and deletions.

To Set Text, Locked, and TabStop Properties

1 **Click the Text1 TextBox control on the form.**

The selected control's name displays in the Object box of the Properties window (Figure 1-51).

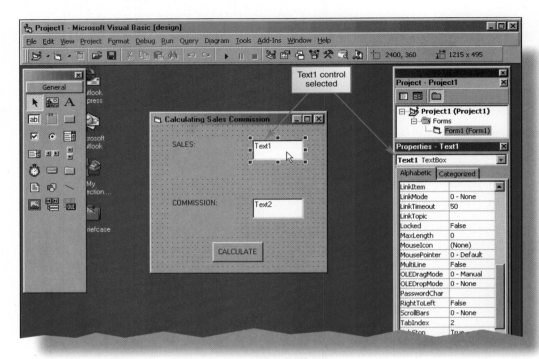

FIGURE 1-51

2 **Scroll the Properties window Properties list to display the Text property and then double-click the Text property.**

The Text property is highlighted in the Properties list, and the current value of the property, Text1, is highlighted (Figure 1-52).

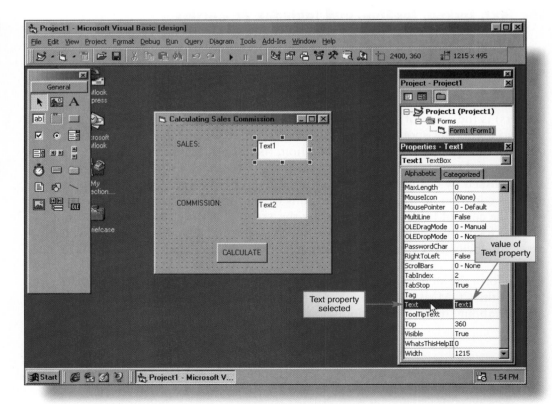

FIGURE 1-52

3 **Delete the value of the TextBox control by pressing the DELETE key.**

The selected text box is blank (Figure 1-53).

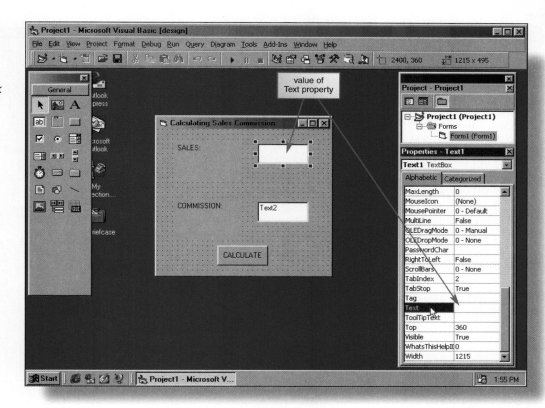

FIGURE 1-53

4 **Repeat Step 1 through Step 3 for the Text2 TextBox control and then point to the Locked property in the Properties list.**

The form displays as shown in Figure 1-54.

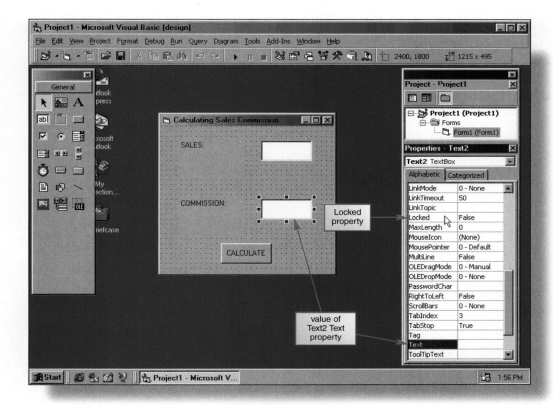

FIGURE 1-54

5 **Double-click the Locked property. Scroll the Properties list and then double-click the TabStop property.**

The value of the Text2 control's Locked property changes from False to True and the value of the Text2 control's TabStop property changes from True to False (Figure 1-55).

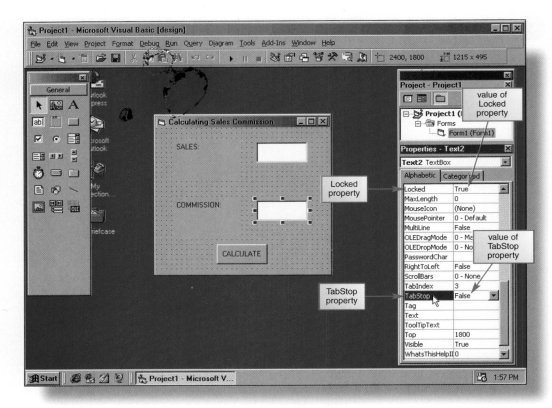

FIGURE 1-55

6 **Select the CommandButton control and then double-click its TabStop property in the Properties list.**

The CommandButton control's TabStop property is now False (Figure 1-56).

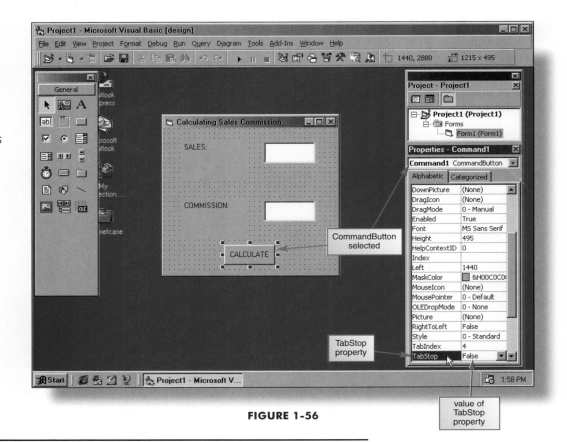

FIGURE 1-56

You used the same procedure for setting the Text property of the text boxes and for setting the Caption property of the labels. This same basic procedure is used for setting most of the properties of any type of control during design time. Label controls never have the capability of receiving the focus on a form and therefore do not have a TabStop property. They do, however, have a TabIndex property used internally by Visual Basic for other purposes.

Naming Controls

Visual Basic assigns unique default names to controls, such as Form1, Label1, Label2, Text1, and Command1. These names are reflected in the control's **Name property**. Although Visual Basic initially sets the caption of some controls to be equal to the name of the control, the name of a control and the caption of a control are two different properties. For example, the caption of the command button in your application is CALCULATE; its name is Command1.

Each control has its own unique name to distinguish it from another instance of the same class of objects. For example, the Calculating Sales Commission form has more than one text box. It is very important in the application to distinguish which text box gets what text printed in it. Many times, it is useful to give a different name to a control. This renaming often is beneficial with forms, which are themselves a type of control.

You will see in Project 3 that a single Visual Basic project can have more than one form and that forms created in one project can be used in other projects. For these reasons, it is advisable to give each form you create a unique name. Forms are named by setting the Name property of the form control. Perform the steps on the next page to change the Name property of the Form1 control.

More About

Control Names

An object's Name property must start with a letter and can be a maximum of 40 characters. It can include numbers and underline (_) characters but cannot include punctuation or spaces.

 To Set the Name Property of a Control

1 Select the Form1 control by clicking an area of the form that does not contain any other control.

The form's name displays in the Object box of the Properties window. Clicking an empty area allows you to select the form instead of one of the controls on the form (Figure 1-57).

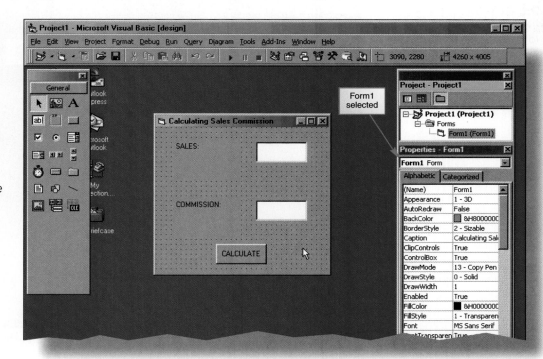

FIGURE 1-57

2 Scroll the Properties list and then double-click the Name property (the first property in the list) in the Properties list.

The Name property and its value, Form1, are highlighted in the Properties list (Figure 1-58).

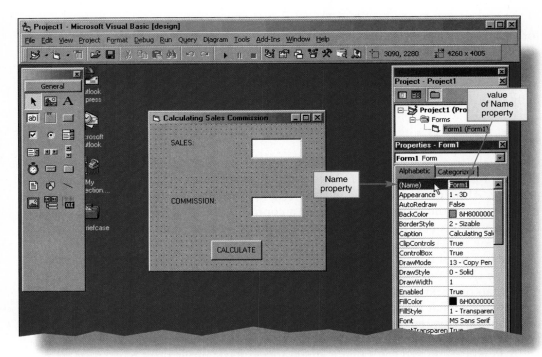

FIGURE 1-58

3 Type SLSCOMSN as the new value and then press the ENTER key.

The value of the form's name in the Object box and the Project window is changed to SLSCOMSN (Figure 1-59). Notice that the form's caption in the title bar is unchanged because the Caption property is different from the Name property.

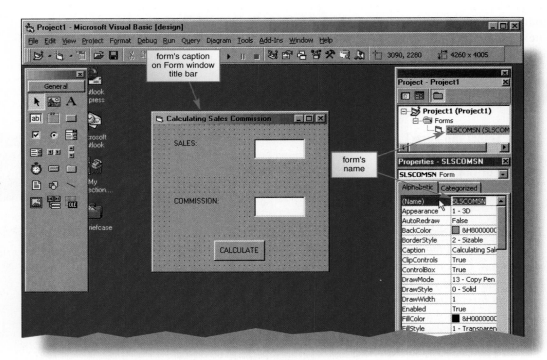

FIGURE 1-59

When you save a Visual Basic project, forms are saved as separate files with a file extension **.frm**. The default file name for the form is the current value of the form's Name property. You can, however, assign a file name different from the form's Name property.

Writing Code

You began the development of the Calculating Sales Commission application by building the user interface, which consisted of a form and controls. You then set the properties of the controls. The remaining step in developing the application is to write the **code**, or *actions*, that will occur within the application in response to specific events.

Events are messages sent to an object when the application runs. Events can be initiated by the user, such as clicking or dragging a control. Events also can be initiated by the application itself. Events trigger **procedures**, which are groups of code statements, sometimes simply called code. **Code statements** are instructions to the computer written at design time for the computer to execute at run time. Visual Basic has its own language, which are the words and symbols used to write these instructions. This language is very similar to Beginner's All-Purpose Symbolic Instruction Code (BASIC).

In Visual Basic, certain controls are capable of recognizing certain events. For example, the **Click** event, which is clicking the left mouse button, is recognized by most types of Visual Basic controls. CommandButton controls are one type of control that can recognize the Click event. A control's name is used to associate an event with a specific control on a form in order to initiate the procedure or code statements you write. For example, when the mouse is clicked with its pointer positioned on a specific CommandButton control, such as Command1, the **Command1_Click event procedure** is executed.

Many times, the actions you want to occur in response to events can be expressed as changes in the values of the properties of objects on the form. The generalized code statement would be

controlname.propertyname = propertyvalue

Functions and methods are additional types of procedures within Visual Basic. A **function** is code that transforms one or more values into a new value. For example, the **Val** function takes whatever value is given and converts it to a number. If it cannot convert the value to a number, it returns a zero. For example, `val(8)` returns 8 and `val("hello")` returns 0. **Methods** are code statements that can be applied to an object to change its attributes or behavior. For example, the **SetFocus** method causes the focus to be changed to a specific control on a form. The code statement, `Text1.SetFocus` applies the SetFocus method to the Text1 control. Visual Basic has many predefined functions and methods that you can use in your code. You will learn more about these in later projects.

Programmers often add comments within their code statements as a form of **internal documentation**. A **comment** is text added within a procedure that explains how the code in the procedure works. Each comment line must begin with an apostrophe (') or the letters **Rem**.

The sales commission application has an event procedure that is triggered when the user clicks the command button. The procedure should take the sales amount entered by the user, calculate the commission and display the result. If the user enters text instead of a number, the answer should be zero. The procedure should contain a statement of explanation. Perform the steps on the next page to write the Command1_Click event procedure.

More) *About*

Writing Code

Code in a Visual Basic application is divided into blocks called procedures. You write code for the Visual Basic application in a separate window, called the Code window. Using the Code window, you can view and edit any of the code quickly. You can choose to display all code procedures in the same Code window, or display a single procedure at a time.

Steps To Write an Event Procedure

1 Point to the Command1 CommandButton control.

Although you changed the CommandButton control's caption to CALCULATE (Figure 1-60), its name is still Command1, which is the name supplied by Visual Basic when you added the control to the form. If you had more than one command button on the form, you might want to change the control's name to cmdCalculate or something that more clearly identifies its function.

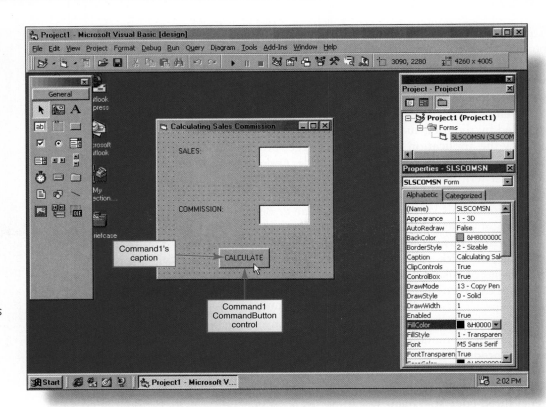

FIGURE 1-60

2 Double-click the CommandButton control on the form.

The Code window opens on the desktop (Figure 1-61). The name of the control you selected displays in the Object box in the Code window. Two lines of code for the Click event procedure display in the Code window.

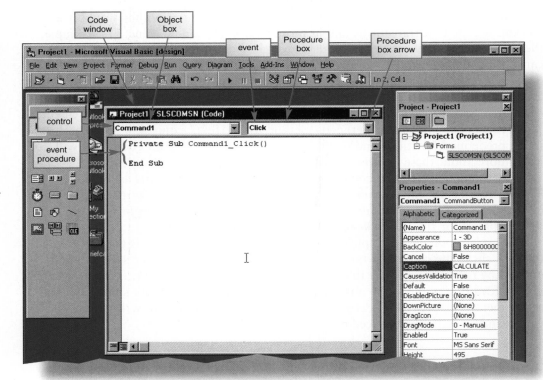

FIGURE 1-61

3 **Click the Procedure box arrow.**

The Procedure list box displays, containing all the event procedures that can be associated with the Command1 control (Figure 1-62).

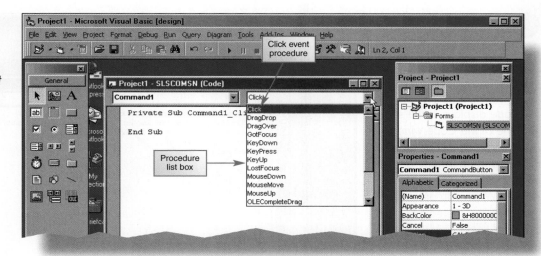

FIGURE 1-62

4 **Click the Click event procedure in the list.**

The insertion point displays at the beginning of a blank line in between the two code statements (Figure 1-63).

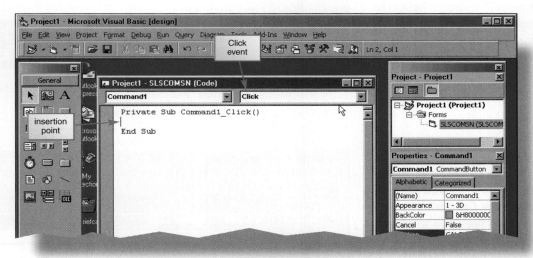

FIGURE 1-63

5 **Type** 'Display Commission Amount as Value of User Input * Rate **and then press the ENTER key. If necessary, resize the Code window by dragging its right border so the entire code statement displays as shown in Figure 1-64.**

The insertion point moves to the next line. The statement changes color because Visual Basic recognizes it as a comment and not a code instruction.

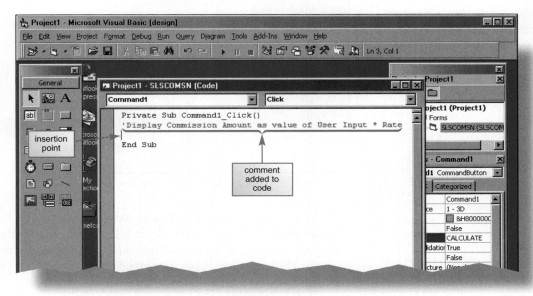

FIGURE 1-64

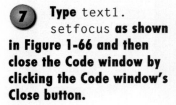

6 Type `text2.text = val(text1.text) * 0.15` **on one line and then press the ENTER key.**

*The code displays in the second line of the Code window. As you typed the code statement a **pop-up list box** of properties and methods displayed. When you pressed the ENTER key, the editor changed some characters to uppercase (Figure 1-65). This code statement changes the value of the Text property of the Text2 control to equal the value of the Text property of the Text1 control times 0.15, the rate of commission on sales.*

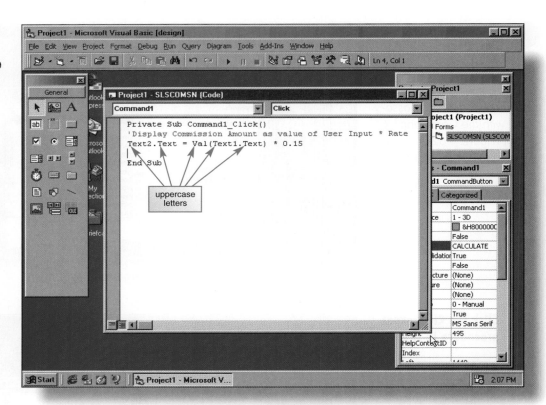

FIGURE 1-65

7 Type `text1.setfocus` **as shown in Figure 1-66 and then close the Code window by clicking the Code window's Close button.**

As you type the period after a control's name, a pop-up list box of that control's properties and methods display depending on your option settings (Figure 1-66).

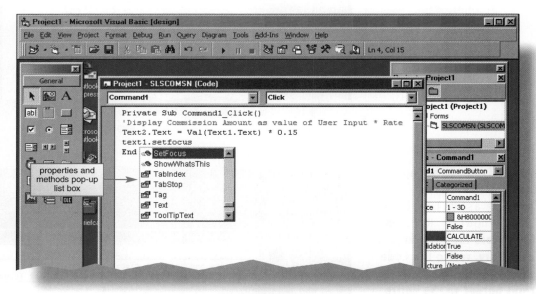

FIGURE 1-66

Other Ways

1. Double-click property or method in pop-up window to insert in code statement

The event procedures in Visual Basic are written in blocks of code called **subroutines**. Each block begins with a statement that includes the subroutine's name and ends with a statement that indicates no further instructions are within that subroutine. These first and last statements are supplied by Visual Basic when you begin a new event procedure subroutine.

The Code window functions as a text editor for writing your code statements. You can add and change text within the window in the same manner as you would with a text editor such as WordPad.

Saving a Project

The Calculating Sales Commission application now is complete. Before starting a new Visual Basic project or quitting Visual Basic, you should save your work. You also should save your project periodically while you are working on it and before you run it for the first time.

Visual Basic projects are saved as a set of files. Forms are saved as files with a file name and an **.frm** (form) **extension**. If the form contains graphics, an additional file with an **.frx** (form extension) **extension** is saved. In addition to form files, Visual Basic creates an overall project file. This file has a file name and a **.vbp** (Visual Basic project) **extension**. You specify the path and file name for these files using the Save and Save As dialog boxes, similarly to other Windows applications. Perform the following steps to save the form and project files for this project on a formatted floppy disk in drive A.

More About

File Extensions

The .vbp, .frm, and .frx file extensions are the most common Visual Basic design mode file extensions you will encounter. In earlier versions of Visual Basic, the project file had an .mak rather than a .vbp extension. Visual Basic version 6 has 25 design mode file extensions whose use depends on the type of project or component you are creating.

Steps To Save a Project

1 Click the Save Project button on the toolbar.

The Save File As dialog box opens (Figure 1-67). The default file name in the dialog box is the name you gave to the form previously.

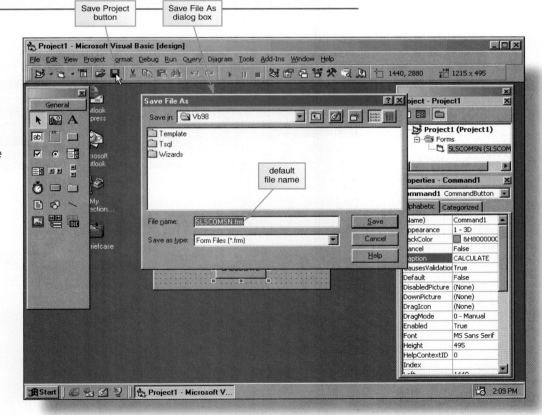

FIGURE 1-67

2 Click 3½ Floppy (A:) in the Save in list box and then point to the Save button.

The Save File As dialog box displays as shown in Figure 1-68.

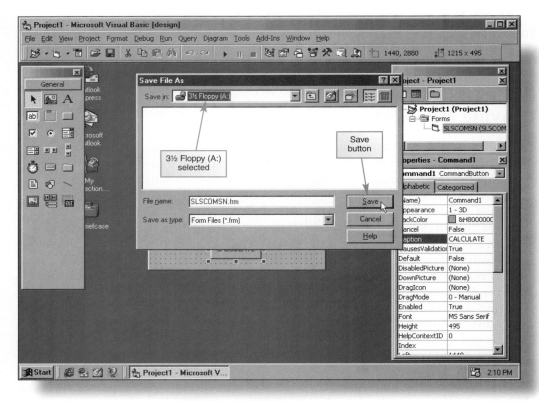

FIGURE 1-68

3 Click the Save button in the Save File As dialog box.

The form is saved as the file SLSCOMSN.frm, and the Save Project As dialog box displays (Figure 1-69). The default project name, Project1.vbp, displays in the File name box.

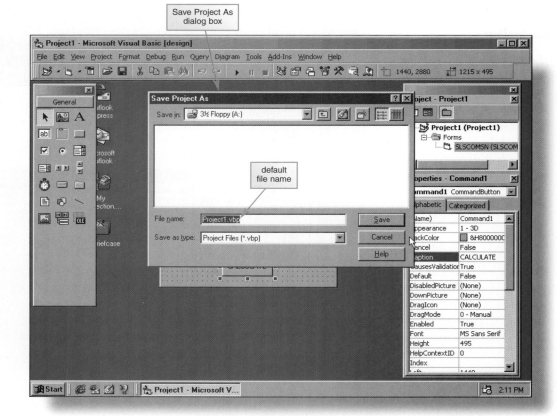

FIGURE 1-69

④ Type Commission **in the File name box and then point to the Save button.**

The default name for the project is replaced in the File name box with the characters you typed (Figure 1-70). If you make an error while typing, you can use the BACKSPACE key or the LEFT ARROW and DELETE keys to erase the mistake and then continue typing.

⑤ Click the Save button in the Save Project As dialog box.

The project is saved as Commission.vbp and the dialog box closes.

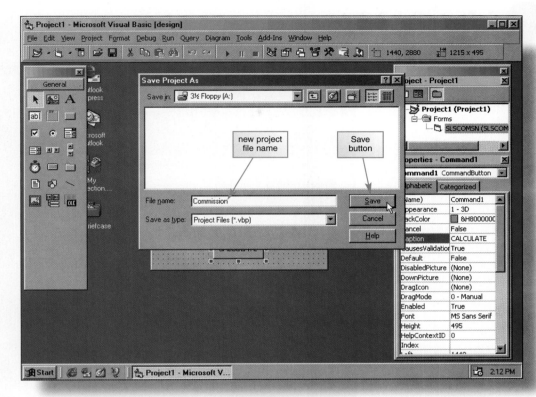

FIGURE 1-70

In the Save File As dialog box you specified the drive used to save the form file, but you did not need to change the drive in the Save Project As dialog box. After you change a drive or folder in any of the common dialog boxes, it remains current in all the dialog boxes until you change it again.

You can resave your work without opening the common dialog box by clicking the Save Project button on the Standard toolbar. If you want to save your work with a different file name, folder, or drive, you must click Save File As after clicking File on the menu bar.

Starting, Opening, and Running Projects

In the next sets of steps you will start a new project, open an existing project, and run a project within the Visual Basic environment.

Starting a New Project

When you started Visual Basic, you selected a Standard EXE project from the New tab sheet. The form had no controls or event procedures, and all properties had their default values. It is not necessary to restart Visual Basic each time you want to build a new application. Before beginning a new application, however, you should be certain that you have saved any work you do not want to lose. Because you already have saved the Calculating Sales Commission application, perform the steps on the next page to begin another project.

Steps ## To Start a New Project

1 **Click File on the menu bar and then point to New Project.**

The File menu displays (Figure 1-71).

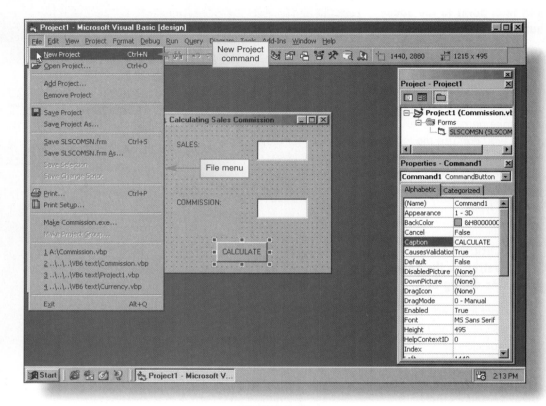

FIGURE 1-71

2 **Click New Project and then point to the Standard EXE icon.**

The New Project dialog box displays (Figure 1-72).

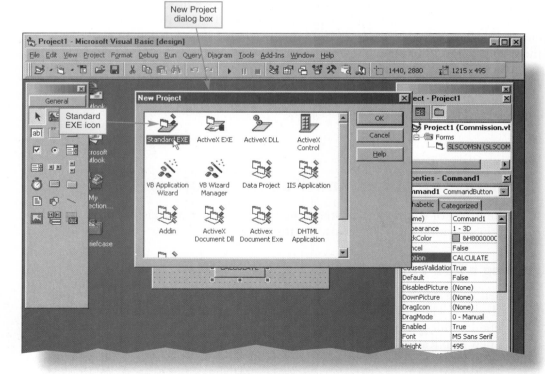

FIGURE 1-72

Double-click the Standard EXE icon.

A new Standard EXE project is opened on the desktop (Figure 1-73).

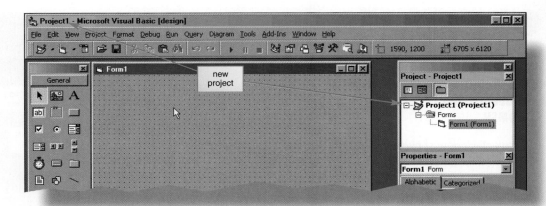

FIGURE 1-73

The new form has the default form name, Form1, and the project has the default project name, Project1. If you attempt to open a new project before saving the current project, Visual Basic will display a message box asking if you want to save the previous work.

Opening a Project

Once a project has been saved, you can return to that project and make changes. You instruct Visual Basic which project you want to use in the Open Project dialog box that contains two tab sheets. The first tab sheet, Existing, is similar to the Save File As dialog box. The second tab sheet, Recent, displays a list and location of recently opened projects. Perform the following steps to open the Calculating Sales Commission application you completed previously.

 To Open an Existing Project

1 **Click the Open Project button on the Standard toolbar. If necessary, click the Existing tab.**

The Open Project dialog box displays (Figure 1-74). If 3½ Floppy (A:) is not the selected drive, you can change it in the same way you changed the selected drive when you saved the form file.

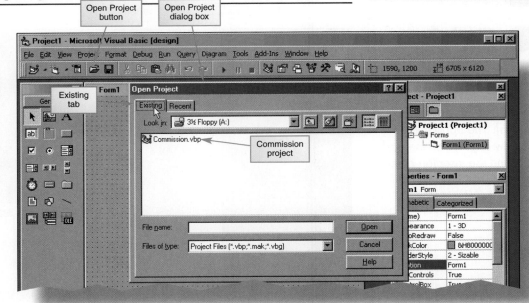

FIGURE 1-74

> ### More About
>
> ### Opening Projects
>
> The names of the four most recently used projects also are displayed on the bottom of the File menu. You can open any of these projects by clicking its name on the File menu. The Recent tab in the Open Project dialog box displays a much longer list of recent projects.

2 **Double-click the project's name, Commission.vbp, in the File list box. Double-click Forms in the Project window and then double-click SLSCOMSN.**

The Project window shows a tree list view of all of the files that are part of the project (Figure 1-75). The Properties window is empty until a form is selected.

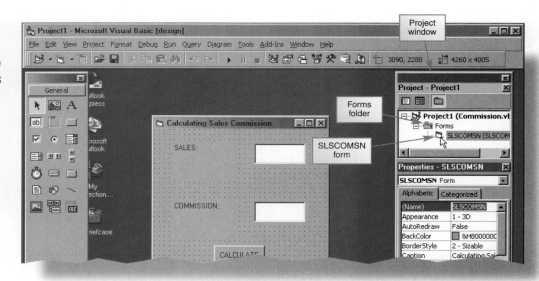

FIGURE 1-75

When you save a project, you can save a form file and project file individually. When you open a project, you only have to open the project file. Any other files associated with that project are opened automatically. All of these files are listed in the Project window.

Running an Application

Perform the following steps to run the Calculating Sales Commission application from within the Visual Basic environment.

Steps **To Run an Application**

1 **Click the Start button on the Standard toolbar.**

The word, [design], on the Visual Basic title bar changes to [run]. The application's window displays on the desktop, and the insertion point moves to the first text box (Figure 1-76).

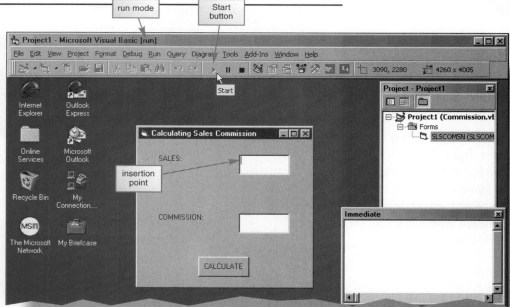

FIGURE 1-76

2 Type 1500 **text box and then point to the CALCULATE button.**

The number displays in the first text box (Figure 1-77). You can change or edit your entry using the BACKSPACE *key or the* LEFT ARROW *and* DELETE *keys.*

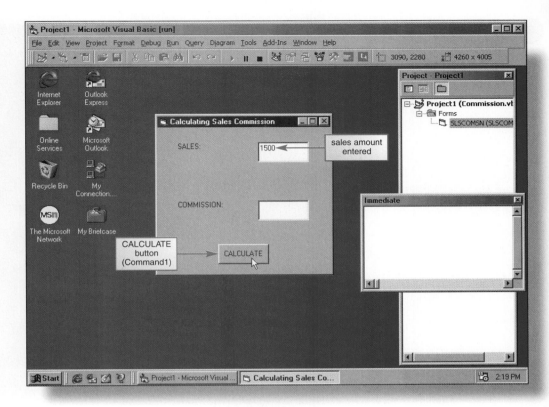

FIGURE 1-77

3 **Click the CALCULATE button and then point to the End button on the Standard toolbar.**

The number 225 displays in the second text box (Figure 1-78). Thus, 1500 dollars in sales = 225 dollars at 15% commission.

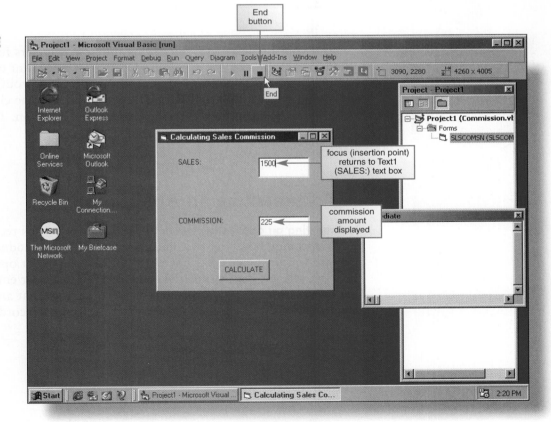

FIGURE 1-78

Click the End button.

Visual Basic returns to design mode (Figure 1-79).

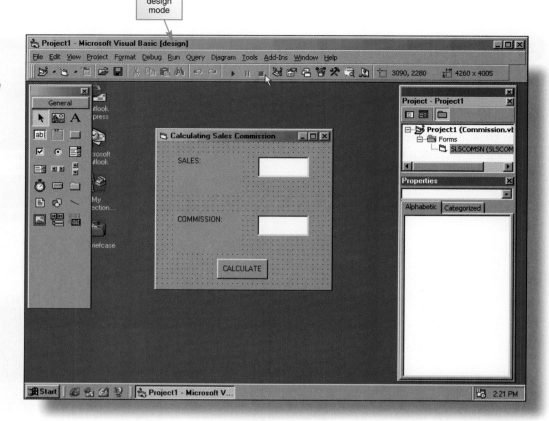

FIGURE 1-79

1. On Run menu click Start
2. Press F5

Run your application again, trying different numbers for the sales amount. You do not need to restart the application each time you want to perform another conversion. Press the BACKSPACE key several times to erase your entry, and then type a new number. Click the CALCULATE button. Enter some characters or a word in the SALES: text box and then click the CALCULATE button. Try to change the amount in the COMMISSION: text box.

Documenting an Application

Documenting an application refers to producing a printed record of the application. In the Print dialog box, you first must select the current module (form) or the entire project. You then can select any or all of the Print What options. **Form Image** prints the form images; **Code** prints the code for the module or entire project; and **Form As Text** prints a list of all controls and property settings that are different from their default values. Perform the following steps to print a record of the Calculating Sales Commission application.

Steps **To Print a Record of an Application**

1 **Click File on the menu bar and then point to Print.**

The File menu displays (Figure 1-80).

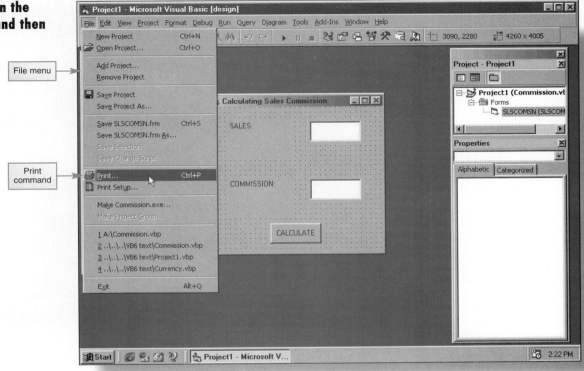

FIGURE 1-80

2 **Click Print. When the Print dialog box opens, click all the check boxes in the Print What area (Figure 1-81). Point to the OK button.**

The Print dialog box displays (Figure 1-81).

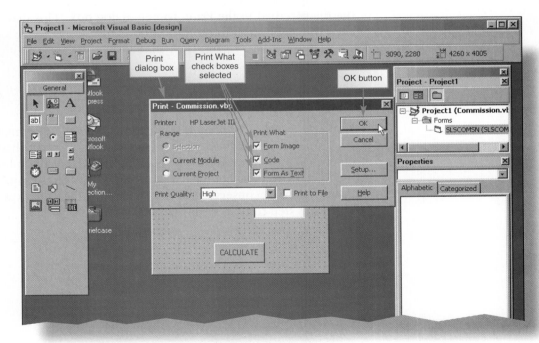

FIGURE 1-81

Click the OK button.

The form, properties listing, and code are printed. The Print dialog box closes (Figure 1-82).

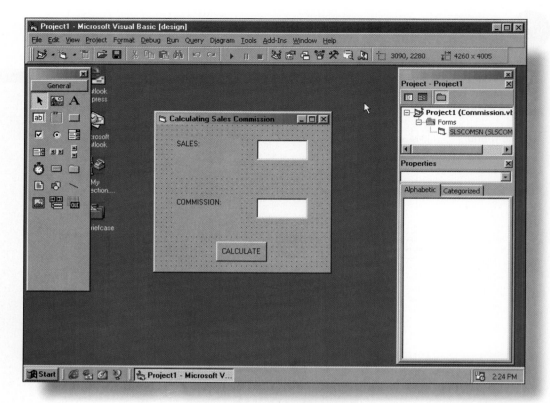

FIGURE 1-82

If the Print to File check box is selected in the Print dialog box, print is sent to the file specified in the Print To File dialog box. This dialog box displays after you click the OK button in the Print dialog box.

Quitting Visual Basic

Similarly to other Windows applications, you can minimize Visual Basic to work with another application temporarily, such as a spreadsheet or word processing document. You then can return by clicking the Visual Basic button on the taskbar.

When you have completed working with Visual Basic, you should quit the Visual Basic system to conserve memory space for other Windows applications. Perform the following step to quit Visual Basic.

To Quit Visual Basic

Step 1 **Click the Visual Basic Close button.**

If you made changes to the project since the last time it was saved, Visual Basic displays the Microsoft Visual Basic dialog box (Figure 1-83). If you click the Yes button, you can resave your project and quit. If you click the No button, you will quit without saving the changes. Clicking the Cancel button will close the dialog box.

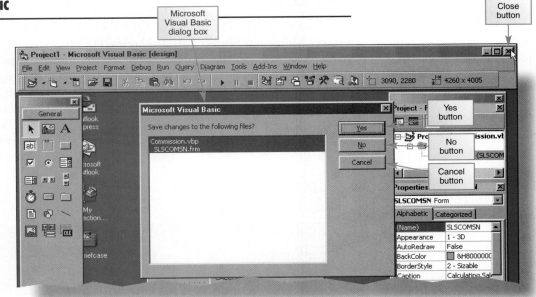

FIGURE 1-83

Visual Basic Help

The Visual Basic programming system includes an extensive online Help system. You can access **Help** any time you are working with Visual Basic by clicking Help on the menu bar and then clicking one of the Help menu commands (Figure 1-84).

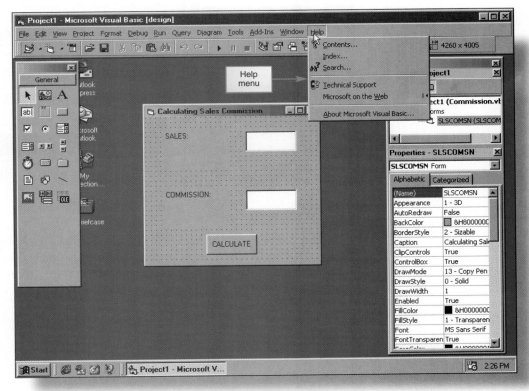

FIGURE 1-84

MSDN Library

Clicking Contents, Index, or Search on the Help menu opens the MSDN Library Viewer for Visual Studio 6.0, displaying HTML help files in a three-paned browser-like Help window. The top pane contains the toolbar, the left pane contains the navigation methods, and the right pane displays the topic. The navigation pane contains a drop-down list box, which allows you to limit help to an Active Subset of the Visual Studio collection. The navigation pane also contains the **Contents**, **Index**, **Search**, and **Favorites** tabs. The Contents sheet (Figure 1-85) displays a series of online books with topics organized by category, similarly to the table of contents in a book.

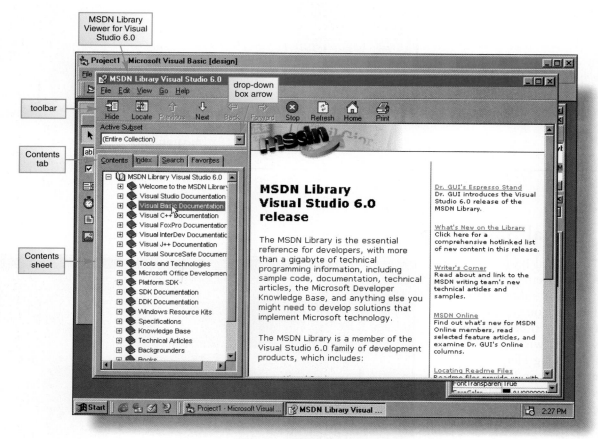

FIGURE 1-85

The Index sheet (Figure 1-86) displays words and phrases similarly to the index in a book along with a text box for entering the keyword to find. Double-clicking a topic displays a Topics Found dialog box from which selected topics can be displayed.

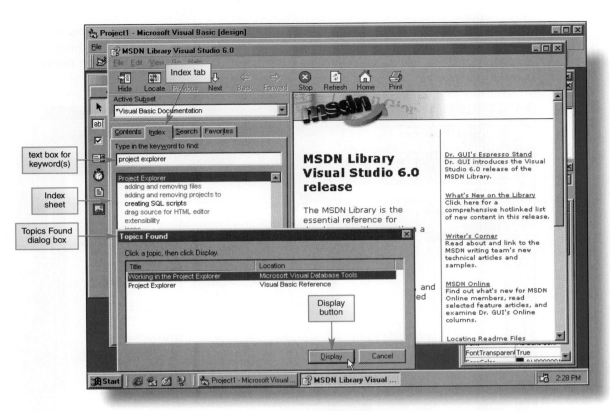

FIGURE 1-86

The Search sheet (Figure 1-87) provides a text box in which you can type the keyword(s) or phrase you want to find. Click the List Topics button to initiate the search. It will locate every occurrence of a word or phrase that may be contained in any topic where the search phrase was found and will display the selected topics in a scrollable list box. When searching for topics, Boolean operators may be used to refine your search.

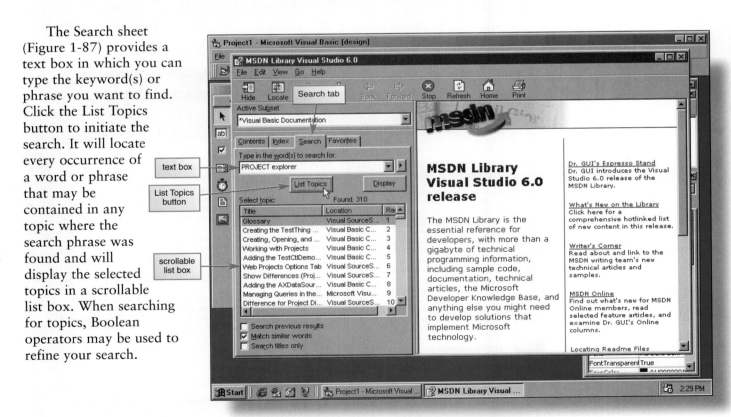

FIGURE 1-87

The last tab, Favorites (Figure 1-88), allows you to add the current topic to a list of your favorites so that such topics can be accessed directly without searching again. To access help for using the MSDN Library, select MSDN Library Help on the Help menu in the Library Viewer (Figure 1-89).

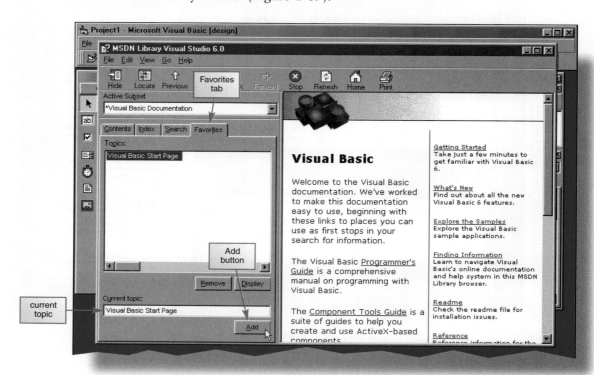

FIGURE 1-88

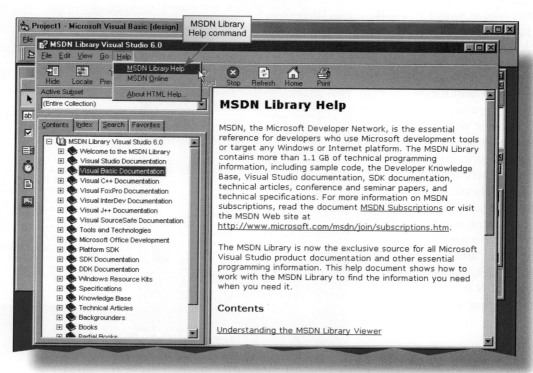

FIGURE 1-89

Context-Sensitive Help

Help on many areas of the Visual Basic screen can be accessed without using the Help menu. This feature, called **context-sensitive Help**, is available by pressing the F1 key. For example, to get Help about Project Explorer, click the Project window title bar and then press the F1 key. The MSDN Library window opens (Figure 1-90), displaying information on Project Explorer (the Project Explorer window). The Tab sheet displayed is the one last used. To close the Library window and return to the design environment, click the Close button on the Library window title bar.

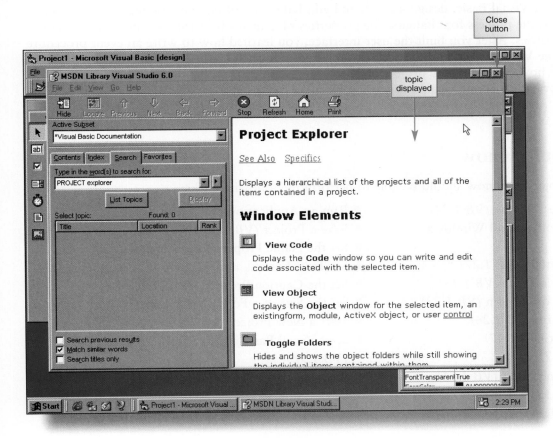

FIGURE 1-90

Project Summary

Project 1 introduced the major elements of Visual Basic by developing a Windows application. The process to build the application consists of three steps.

1. Creating the interface — Drawing the form and controls
2. Setting properties — Setting the values of properties for the controls added to the form
3. Writing code — Creating the event procedures that will occur when the application runs

You learned how to start Visual Basic, design a form, and add Label, TextBox, and CommandButton controls to a form. You learned the process for changing the properties of controls by setting Caption, Text, Name, Locked, and TabStop properties. After you built the user interface, you learned how to write an event procedure that included comments, the Val function, and the SetFocus method. You then learned how to run, save, and print your application and how to start a new project or open an existing project. Finally, in Project 1 you learned how to access information about Visual Basic using Help.

What You Should Know

Having completed this project, you now should be able to perform the following tasks:

▶ Add Controls by Double-Clicking *(VB 1.24)*

▶ Arrange Visual Basic Toolbars and Windows *(VB 1.12)*

▶ Change the Size of a Control *(VB 1.27)*

▶ Draw Label Controls on a Form *(VB 1.19)*

▶ Draw TextBox Controls on a Form *(VB 1.22)*

▶ Move a Control on a Form *(VB 1.26)*

▶ Open an Existing Project *(VB 1.47)*

▶ Position a Form *(VB 1.17)*

▶ Print a Record of an Application *(VB 1.51)*

▶ Quit Visual Basic *(VB 1.53)*

▶ Remove a Control *(VB 1.25)*

▶ Run an Application *(VB 1.48)*

▶ Save a Project *(VB 1.43)*

▶ Set the Name Property of a Control *(VB 1.37)*

▶ Set Text, Locked, and TabStop Properties *(VB 1.34)*

▶ Set the Caption Property *(VB 1.30)*

▶ Set the Size of a Form *(VB 1.15)*

▶ Start a New Project *(VB 1.46)*

▶ Start Visual Basic and Set Option Preferences *(VB 1.9)*

▶ Write an Event Procedure *(VB 1.40)*

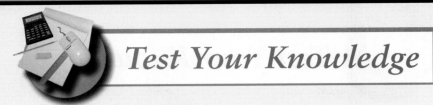

Test Your Knowledge

1 True/False

Instructions: Circle T if the statement is true or F if the statement is false.

T F   1. A GUI allows you to use both text and graphical images to communicate with the computer.

T F   2. An individual must have previous training or computer programming experience to create Windows applications using Visual Basic.

T F   3. When opened, Visual Basic consists of only one window.

T F   4. A form can be positioned by clicking its title bar, dragging it to a new location, and dropping it.

T F   5. Controls must be added to the form by selecting them in the Toolbox and drawing them individually.

T F   6. The only method of changing the location of a control on a form is by dragging the control to the new location.

T F   7. The Object box of the Properties window is where you enter a value for a specific property.

T F   8. In Visual Basic code, the NUM function is used to return the numbers contained in a string.

T F   9. Comments provide a written record of how your code works.

T F   10. The Form Image of a project cannot be printed.

2 Multiple Choice

Instructions: Circle the correct response.

1. Computer programs that perform specific tasks are _____ software.
   a. system
   b. application
   c. utility
   d. multimedia

2. You must use the _____ to set the size of a form in Visual Basic.
   a. edges
   b. sides
   c. rims
   d. borders

3. A _____ control that is used to display text cannot be changed by the user at run time.
   a. Label
   b. Caption
   c. TextBox
   d. Font

4. The area that displays the name of the control whose properties are being set is called the _____.
   a. Properties list
   b. Object box
   c. Toolbox
   d. Form

5. The _____ property of a TextBox control contains text that will display on the control.
   a. Name
   b. Caption
   c. Text
   d. Label

6. Actions that occur when an application runs are called _____.
   a. codes
   b. commands
   c. responses
   d. events

(continued)

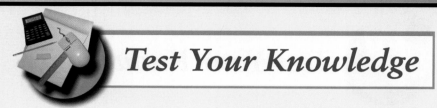

Test Your Knowledge

Multiple Choice *(continued)*

7. Point to a control and double-click it to open the _____ for that control.
   a. Object box
   b. Properties list
   c. Code window
   d. Save As dialog box

8. A project always should be _____ before it is run.
   a. printed
   b. saved
   c. closed
   d. reviewed

9. Once Help is opened, selecting _____ on the Help menu will display information on how to use Help.
   a. MSDN Library Help
   b. About HTML Help
   c. Contents
   d. Library Viewer Help

10. Visual Basic includes online _____ to improve your Visual Basic skills.
   a. tutorials
   b. guides
   c. lessons
   d. books

3 Understanding the Visual Basic Environment

Instructions: In Figure 1-91, arrows point to the windows of the Visual Basic environment. Identify the various windows in the spaces provided.

4 Understanding the Visual Basic Toolbar and Toolbox

Instructions: In Figure 1-92, arrows point to buttons on the Standard toolbar and in the Toolbox. Identify the various buttons in the spaces provided.

Test Your Knowledge

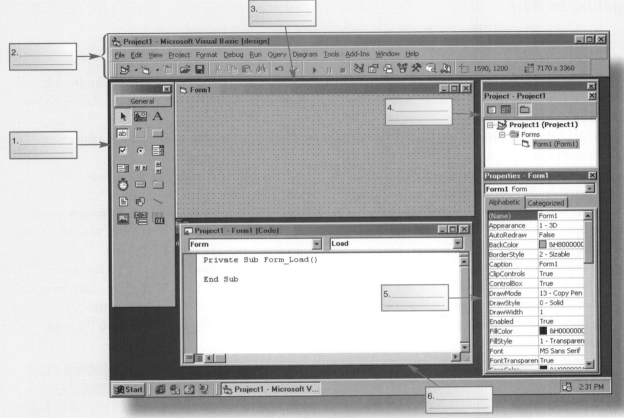

FIGURE 1-91

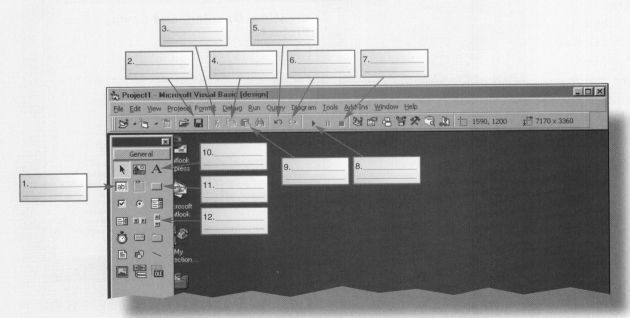

FIGURE 1-92

Use Help

1 Navigating in Help

Instructions: Perform the following tasks using a computer.

1. Start Visual Basic.
2. Click Help on the menu bar and then click Contents. The MSDN Library Viewer for Visual Studio 6.0 will display with the Contents tab selected. If necessary, select Visual Basic Documentation as the Active Subset in the drop-down list box.
3. Double-click the MSDN Library Visual Studio 6.0 book. Double-click the Visual Basic Documentation book. Click the Visual Basic Start Page. Click the Programmer's Guide underlined link. Read and print the information in the topic area. Hand in the printout to your instructor.
4. Click the Visual Basic Basics underlined link. Scroll down to find the link to the Managing Projects book and click the link. Scroll down to find the Creating, Opening, and Saving Projects link. Click the link. Read and print the information in the topic area. Hand in the printout to your instructor.
5. Click View on the menu bar and click the Locate Topics in Contents selection (Figure 1-93). Resize the navigation pane to view the nested topics list. Move the scroll bar to the top to view the hierarchy of topics.
6. Click the Index tab. Type Run menu commands in the keyword text box. Click the Display button. Read and print the information in the topic area. Click the Start link. Read and print the information in the topic area. Scroll down to the design time link and click it. Read and print the information in the topic area. Click the Back button. Click the run time link. Read and print the information in the topic area. Hand in the printouts to your instructor. Close the MSDN Library.

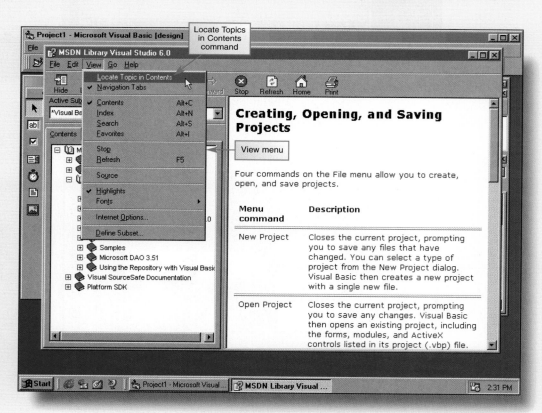

FIGURE 1-93

Use Help

2 Learning More of the Basics

Instructions: Use Visual Basic Help to understand the topics and answer the questions listed below. Answer the questions on your own paper to hand in to your instructor.

1. Click Help on the menu bar and then click Contents. The MSDN Library Viewer for Visual Studio 6.0 will display with the Contents tab selected (Figure 1-94). If necessary, select Visual Basic Documentation as the Active Subset in the drop-down list box.

2. In the Navigation area under this tab, double-click MSDN Library Visual Studio 6.0 to open the books. Double-click the Visual Basic Documentation book. Click the Visual Basic Start Page. Click the Programmer's Guide

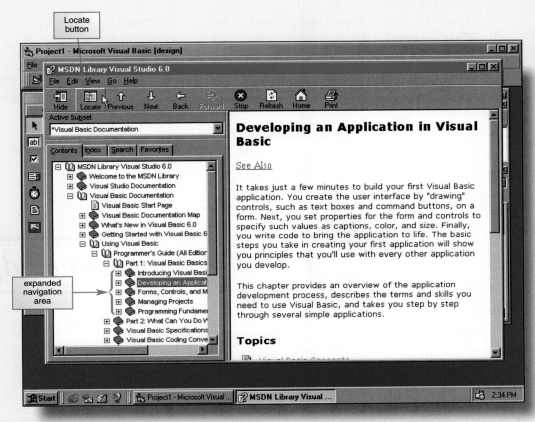

FIGURE 1-94

underlined link. Click the Part 1: Visual Basic Basics underlined link. Click the Developing an Application in Visual Basic link. Read the information in the topic area. Click Visual Basic Concepts under Topics in the topic area. As you read the text in the topic area, answer the following questions. Once you have answered the questions, click the Locate button on the toolbar.

a. What are the three key concepts of the inner workings of Windows?

b. What is a window?

c. What is an event?

d. What is a message?

e. How do event-driven applications differ from traditional applications?

(continued)

Use Help

Learning More of the Basics (continued)

3. Click the Forms, Controls, and Menus book in the navigation area. Read the information in the topic area and then answer the following questions.
   a. What is a form?
   b. How are a form's appearance, behavior, and events defined?
   c. What are controls?
   d. How is the purpose of a control determined?
4. Scroll down and then click the Understanding Properties, Methods and Events topic in the topic area. Read the information and answer the following questions. After you answer the questions, close the MSDN Library.
   a. What can an object's properties include?
   b. What kind of methods or actions might an object perform?
   c. What kind of object response can external events cause?

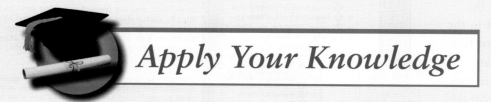

Apply Your Knowledge

1 Writing Code in a Visual Basic Application

Instructions: Start Visual Basic and open the project, Moving Shape, from the Student Data Disk (see inside back cover for instructions on how to obtain a copy of the Data Disk). This application consists of a form that contains one square Shape control and four CommandButton controls (Figure 1-95).

1. One at a time, change the Caption property of each of the four CommandButton controls. The caption for Command1 is Move Up, for Command2 is Move Down, for Command3 is Move Left, and for Command4 is Move Right.
2. Open the Code window for the CommandButton control captioned Move Up. Add a comment to indicate what the code for this button is accomplishing. Type the code statement shape1.top = shape1.top - 50 and then close the Code window.

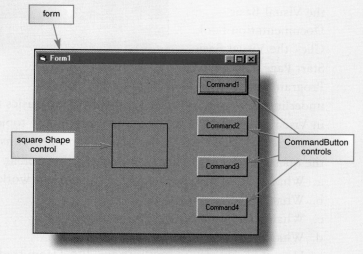

FIGURE 1-95

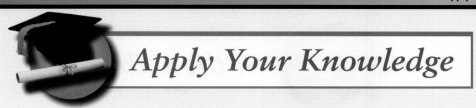

Apply Your Knowledge

3. Click the Start button on the Standard toolbar to run the application. Click the Move Up command button several times. Click the End button on the Standard toolbar. If necessary, make corrections to the code statement.

4. Open the Code window for the CommandButton control captioned Move Down. Type an appropriate comment and then type the code statement `shape1.top = shape1.top + 50` for the command button.

5. Click Command3 in the Object list box. Type an appropriate comment and then type the code statement `shape1.left = shape1.left - 50` for the Move Left command button. Click Command4 in the Object list box. Type an appropriate comment and then type the code statement `shape1.left = shape1.left + 50` for the Move Right command button.

6. Save the form and the project using the file name, Moving Square.

7. Click the Start button on the Standard toolbar to run the application. Click the command buttons several times. Click the End button on the Standard toolbar, make any necessary corrections to the comments and code statements, and save the project again using the same file name.

8. Print the Form Image, Code, and Form As Text.

In the Lab

1 Kilometer Converter

Problem: You want an application to convert the number of miles you enter into the corresponding number of kilometers. Whenever you click the command button, the miles in the first text box should be converted to the appropriate kilometers and displayed in the second text box. Use the conversion of 1 mile equals 1.61 kilometers.

Instructions: Build an application with a user interface that resembles the one shown in Figure 1-96.

1. Open a new project in Visual Basic.

2. One by one, add two Label controls, two TextBox controls, and a CommandButton control by double-clicking their respective buttons in the Toolbox.

3. Drag the Command1 control to the lower-center portion of the form.

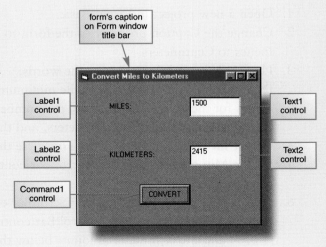

FIGURE 1-96

(continued)

In the Lab

Kilometer Converter *(continued)*

4. Change the form's Caption property to Convert Miles to Kilometers. Change the Caption property of the Label1 control to MILES and the Label2 control to KILOMETERS.
5. Remove the text from the Text1 and Text2 controls by deleting the existing text.
6. Change the Caption property of the Command1 control to the word, CONVERT.
7. Open the Code window for the Command1 control. Type an appropriate comment to explain the purpose of the code. Type the code statement text2.text = val(text1.text) * 1.61 for the Command1 control.
8. Save the form and the project using the file name, Convert Miles to Kilometers.
9. Run the application to make certain no errors exist. If any errors are encountered, correct them, and save the form and the project again using the same file name.
10. Print the project Form Image, Code, and Form As Text.

2 Equivalency Application

Problem: The fabric and notions department of Melman's needs a simple method of converting measurements of inches to centimeters. Create an application that will convert a number of inches beginning at a minimum of zero up to and including a maximum of 100.

Instructions: Perform the following tasks to build an application similar to the one shown in Figure 1-97.

1. Open a new project in Visual Basic.
2. Change the Caption property of the form to Inches to Centimeters.
3. Place Label controls to display the words, INCHES and CENTIMETERS, the minimum values for inches and centimeters, the number of inches selected with the HScrollBar control, the corresponding number of centimeters, and the maximum values for inches and centimeters.
4. Center the form on the desktop. *Hint:* Use the StartUpPosition property.
5. Set the Min property for the HScrollBar control to 0 and set the Max property for the HScrollBar control to 100.
6. Open the Code window for the HScrollBar control. Type label5.caption = hscroll1.value to display the inch amounts above the HScrollBar control. On the next line, type label6.caption = hscroll1.value * 2.54 and the centimeter amounts below the HScrollBar control.
7. Save the form and the project using the file name, Inches to Centimeters.
8. Print the project Form Image, Code, and Form As Text.

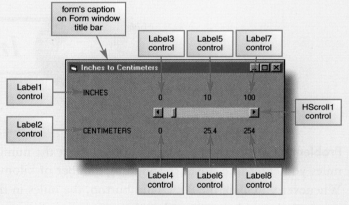

FIGURE 1-97

3 Maturity Calculator

Problem: You are planning to invest money and would like to know what your investment will be worth within a specified period of time. You have decided to develop an application that will allow entry of different amounts, different annual interest rates, and different numbers of years. This will aid you in determining how much you would like to invest. When a command button is clicked, the application displays the maturity value of the investment based on quarterly compounding.

Instructions: Perform the following tasks to create the maturity calculator as shown in Figure 1-98.

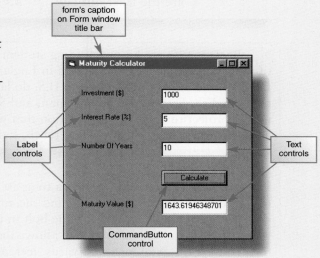

FIGURE 1-98

1. Open a new project in Visual Basic.
2. Size the form appropriately and center it by setting the StartUpPosition property.
3. Add four Label controls, four TextBox controls, and one CommandButton control to the form.
4. Set the form's Caption property to Maturity Calculator.
5. Set the Caption property of each of the four Label controls.
6. Set the Text property of each of the four TextBox controls to be blank.
7. Set the CommandButton control's Caption property.
8. Save the form and the project using the file name, Maturity Calculator.
9. Write the Click event for the Command1 control. *Hint:* Use Text1 for investment, Text2 for rate, Text3 for years, and Text4 for maturity value. Type the code statement `text4.text = val(text1.text) * (1 + val(text2.text)/400) ^ (4 * val(text3.text))` for the CommandButton control.
10. Save the form and the project using the file name, Maturity Calculator.
11. Print the project Form Image, Code, and Form As Text.

Cases and Places

The difficulty of these case studies varies:
▶ are the least difficult; ▶▶ are more difficult; and ▶▶▶ are the most difficult.

1 ▶ Because you are an outstanding student, a local civic organization has awarded you a generous sum of money to pursue your education in England. You also plan to do some sightseeing while you are in Europe. The money currently is in U.S. dollars and you want to know what one U.S. dollar will convert to in English, French, Italian, German, and Spanish currency. Use the concepts and techniques presented in this project to create an application that will accept the U.S. dollar amount, convert the U.S. dollar amount, and display the English, French, Italian, German, and Spanish equivalents.

2 ▶ A Stitch In Time has hired you to assist with taking inventory at its fabric store. Most of the bolts of fabric have been used partially and the amounts remaining are no longer even yards. The clerks will measure the remaining fabric on the bolt in inches and report the number of inches to you. It is up to you to develop an application that allows the entry of amounts in inches. Create the application and then convert the total inches to yards, feet, and total inches of fabric. This application also will have to store a total as the amounts are reported by the clerks and added together. *Hint:* Use Help to find out how to add up the inches and store a total number of inches.

3 ▶▶ To earn some extra spending money, you have taken a part-time position at the Xpress Mart convenience store. Many of the beverages sold by the store are measured in liters. Customers would like to know the equivalent in gallons, quarts, or pints. You have decided to use the knowledge gained in this project to develop an application to perform these conversions.

4 ▶▶ You are an intern at radio station, KNOYZ. The disc jockeys announce the current temperature in both Fahrenheit and Celsius every half-hour. They would like an easy way to display both the Fahrenheit and the Celsius temperatures quickly at the same time. They have requested that you develop such an application for their use and suggest that a scroll bar may be the best solution.

Cases and Places

5 ▶▶ As a consultant for the local telephone company, you determine it requires an application to respond to customer requests. The current customer information system does not permit representatives to supply customers with information regarding competitor's long-distance telephone rates. Your new application will display the telephone companies and rates as shown in the table below.

TELEPHONE COMPANY NAME	TELEPHONE COMPANY ABBREVIATION	RATE FOR FIRST TEN MINUTES BEFORE 7:00 P.M.	RATE FOR FIRST TEN MINUTES AFTER 7:00 P.M.
Canter	Canter	.10	.10
Local Telephone Exchange	LTE	.12	.09
Pacific Telephone & Telegraph	PTT	.15	.13
Regional Communication Interchange	RCI	.11	.08

6 ▶▶▶ As a new employee in the computer information department of The Northwest Indiana Railroad, you have been assigned the task of developing an application to display ticket rates. The railroad makes five different stops along the line with the final destination Chicago, Illinois. Different ticket prices have been established for each stop and different ticket categories. Single-ride ticket prices are South Bend, $8.10, Dunes, $7.30, Gary, $4.60, East Chicago, $4.00, and Hammond, $3.75. The ten-ride ticket costs are the same as ten single ride tickets less two percent of the total cost of ten single ride tickets. The monthly ticket costs are the same as thirty single ride tickets less five percent of the total cost of thirty single ride tickets. The application should display the stops and the rates for each type of ticket for each stop as well as the yearly cost for each category.

7 ▶▶▶ Collecting model cars is among your hobbies. As a collector, it has come to your attention that model cars could be a reasonable investment as well. For your own use, you decide to develop an application that will allow you to enter the current value of a model, a rate of appreciation, and the amount of time you estimate you will keep the model. After these amounts are entered, you want the application to calculate and display the future value of the investment. *Hint:* Refer to Help for assistance in calculating a future value.

Microsoft **Visual Basic 6**

Microsoft Visual Basic 6

P R O J E C T

2

Working with Intrinsic Controls and ActiveX Controls

You will have mastered the material in this project when you can:

O B J E C T I V E S

- Describe the differences between intrinsic controls and ActiveX controls
- Use a ListBox control in an application
- Use a Shape control in an application
- Use a CheckBox control in an application
- Use an OptionButton control in an application
- Build an OptionButton group
- Use a Frame control in an application
- Use the CommonDialog control in an application
- Copy controls on a form
- Add ActiveX controls to the Toolbox
- Set the Locked, MultiLine, FontSize, and ScrollBars properties of TextBox controls
- Set the AutoSize and BackStyle properties of Label controls
- Name controls
- Copy code between procedures in the Code window
- Use code to concatenate text
- Use the AddItem and ShowColor methods within code
- Declare a variable
- Use variables and constants within code
- Use arithmetic and comparison operators in code
- Use the If...Then...Else code structure
- Incorporate the ENTER key in applications
- Save and run an application

Moviemaking!

Create Blockbusters with Your Personal Computer

Hollywood film executives spend millions of dollars predicting how their movies will fare with today's audiences. They use their experience, talent, and instincts to ascertain how much money the films will make for the studio and whether the actors will win awards.

Now the venue for predicting movie success can move from Hollywood to your personal computer.

With Hollywood Mogul™, an interactive business simulation program created with Microsoft Visual Basic, you can run a movie studio in this Hollywood movie production game.

The object is to make as much money as possible by releasing 100 movies throughout the world. You begin with $1 billion and then decide which books and scripts to buy that ultimately will become the next blockbuster films. Next, you plan a budget, select your producers, directors, and stars, who are called *creatives* in Hollywood lingo, and decide when and where to release the films.

Carey DeVuono used his experience as a screenwriter to develop the initial version of the game in 16 months. It contains 35,000 lines of Visual Basic code, two forms, and a variety of controls. These controls resemble the ones you will create in this project as you build complex applications with multiple events.

Hollywood Mogul™ game players use a control to select one of five source ideas for the film: original screenplay, novel, stage play, sequel, or the players' own ideas. All the source ideas except the screenplay require the players to hire screenwriters to write the screenplay. Other Visual Basic controls involve obtaining ownership of the idea so it can be made into a film, hiring the creatives, and producing the film.

Producing the film includes filming, editing, adding music, and special effects.

The creatives' salaries are above-the-line expenses. In contrast, the physical elements used in film production are termed below-the-line expenses and are added to the total production costs. They include materials to build the movie sets, food, transportation, and lodging. Users add these expenses through more Visual Basic controls. When the film is complete, added expenditures include the print cost to duplicate the movie for theaters worldwide and advertising expenses.

Now, the game players wait for revenues to roll in based on box office receipts worldwide. These results are determined by a probabilities algorithm using 500 variables tracked for each film, such as the major stars, number of special effects, release date, and genre. Additional ancillary revenue is generated by video sales and merchandising, such as clothing and toys.

Awards for Hollywood Mogul™ include Top 100 Games Of The Year, *Games* magazine; Special Award, *Computer Game Review* magazine; and *Computer Gaming World* gave Hollywood Mogul™ a 4-Star rating out of 5 possible. You can visit Hollywood Mogul™ online at www.hollywood-mogul.com.

If you decide to use your creative talents and business savvy playing Hollywood Mogul,™ you soon will realize the many facets of filmmaking. As an added benefit, you will begin to appreciate the intrinsic capabilities of Visual Basic to produce a variety of applications. And while your applications may not become big moneymakers, your biggest victory may be seeing your name appear in the credits.

Microsoft Visual Basic 6

Working with Intrinsic Controls and ActiveX Controls

P R O J E C T

2

CASE PERSPECTIVE

The ANC Theater Corporation is upgrading its box office ticket vending technology. Your development team has been assigned the task of developing a prototype of the user interface. For the prototype, you have decided to use a PC running the Windows operating system.

The ANC theaters have two ticket prices - a regular price and a matinee discount price for early show times. Children under 10 years old and seniors receive the matinee price for all show times. The prototype should provide an intuitive way for the salesperson to select the name of the show, indicate a matinee price when applicable, select the number of tickets, calculate the amount due, and record the transaction.

The final system will allow the theater manager to change the show list and ticket prices, and will write the transactions to a file, but these features are not required for this prototype. Although the user will not be able to select the color of the interface, you want to include a way to show different color possibilities when you demonstrate the prototype.

Introduction

In Project 1, you built a Windows application that converted a sales amount into its corresponding commission amount. The application consisted of one event and three types of controls: Label, TextBox, and CommandButton. In this project, you will begin building more complex applications with additional controls and multiple events.

In Project 1, you learned how to add basic controls to your application by drawing them on a form using a corresponding button in the Toolbox. This is the way that all controls are added to applications during design time (you also can add controls at run time through code statements). The controls you used in Project 1 belong to a group called built-in, or intrinsic, controls. The **intrinsic controls** are the basic set of twenty controls in the Toolbox. These controls exist within the Visual Basic .exe file. You do not have to add these controls to the Toolbox, nor can you remove them from the Toolbox.

In this project, you will use several more intrinsic controls, as well as an ActiveX control. **ActiveX controls** exist as separate files. In earlier versions of Visual Basic, these were called VBXs (Visual Basic Extensions) and later OCXs (OLE Control Extensions). Beginning with VB5, ActiveX controls are separate files with an **.ocx** extension. You can include these controls in your applications by adding them to the Toolbox and then using them the same way you use the intrinsic controls. Microsoft includes a number of ActiveX controls with the Professional and Enterprise editions of VB. Thousands of ActiveX controls are available from software vendors. Visual Basic offers the capability of building your own ActiveX controls. This will be covered in a later project.

Application developers often build routines and functions into an application that are not designed for the end user, but exist to help the developer in troubleshooting and revising the application. Sometimes, these functions are available in the end-user version of the product, but they are not documented and they are accessed in a way in which the user is unlikely to notice. In this project, you will include a *hidden* way for you to demonstrate different color choices to the ANC management, even though the end user will not have a color selection option.

Project Two – Theater Box Office

The application in this project is shown in Figure 2-1. This application simulates a ticket vending operation at a theater. For each transaction, the name of the show is selected, whether a matinee discount is available, and the number of tickets to be purchased. When the number of tickets is selected, the total price displays in the Amount Due box. After the money has been accepted, the Enter button is chosen by clicking it, or by pressing the ENTER key on the keyboard. This action adds the name of the show and number of tickets sold to the transaction list and clears the previous settings.

The Theater Box Office application uses the Label, TextBox, and CommandButton controls presented in Project 1. In addition to learning about some additional properties of these controls, you will learn how to use the ListBox, CheckBox, Shape, and Frame intrinsic controls and the CommonDialog ActiveX control. The intrinsic controls used in this project are identified in Figure 2-2.

To use an ActiveX control in an application, you first must add it to the Toolbox. In this project, you will learn how to add ActiveX controls to the Toolbox. In addition to writing several event procedures, you will learn some new features of the Code window.

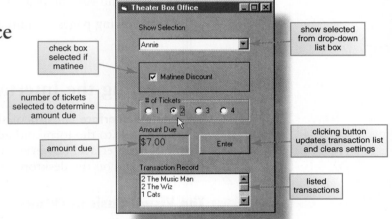

FIGURE 2-1

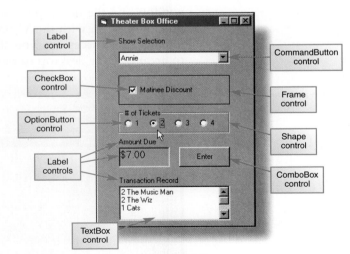

FIGURE 2-2

Project Steps

Applications are built with Visual Basic in the three-step process of creating the interface, setting properties, and writing code. You will follow this three-step process to build the Theater Box Office application. The tasks on the next page will be completed in this project.

1. Start a Standard EXE project in Visual Basic.
2. Set the form's size and position.
3. Add labels and set the AutoSize and BackStyle properties.
4. Copy controls.
5. Add ListBox and ComboBox controls.
6. Add Shape, Frame, and CheckBox controls.
7. Create an OptionButton group.
8. Set the alignment of controls on the form.
9. Name controls and set Caption properties.
10. Set the Style property of the ComboBox control.
11. Set the Locked, MultiLine, and ScrollBars properties of the TextBox control.
12. Set BorderStyle, FontSize, Visible, and Default properties.
13. Declare a variable and use variables and constants in code.
14. Copy and paste code.
15. Use the If...Then...Else code structure.
16. Save and run the project.

The following pages contain a detailed explanation of each of these steps.

Creating the Interface

Creating the interface consists of sizing and locating the form and then adding each of the controls to the form and adjusting their sizes and positions. Before you begin creating the interface, however, you need to start Visual Basic and arrange the Visual Basic windows on the desktop.

The Visual Basic Desktop

Begin this project by starting Visual Basic as described on page VB 1.9 in Project 1 or by opening a new Standard EXE project if you already are running Visual Basic. In Project 1, you learned you could change the sizes and positions of the Visual Basic windows on the desktop to whatever arrangement you prefer. All of the projects in this book begin with the Visual Basic windows in the sizes and positions shown in Figure 2-3. If necessary, you should complete the steps on page VB 1.12 in Project 1 to arrange your desktop to resemble Figure 2-3.

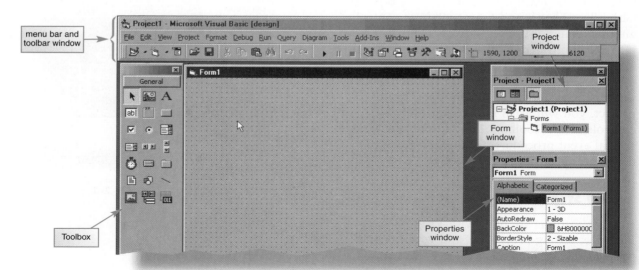

FIGURE 2-3

Form Size and Position

You can resize a form during design time by changing the values of its **Height** and **Width properties** in the Properties window, and you can change a form's location on the desktop by changing the values of its **Top** and **Left properties**. You also can resize a form by dragging its borders and change its location by dragging and dropping. Perform the following steps to set the size of the form by dragging its borders and set its location by dragging and dropping.

 To Set the Size and Location of a Form

1 **Point to the form's lower-right corner. Without releasing the mouse button, drag its corner down and to the left as shown in Figure 2-4.**

Dragging a corner of the form moves the two adjacent borders at the same time (Figure 2-4).

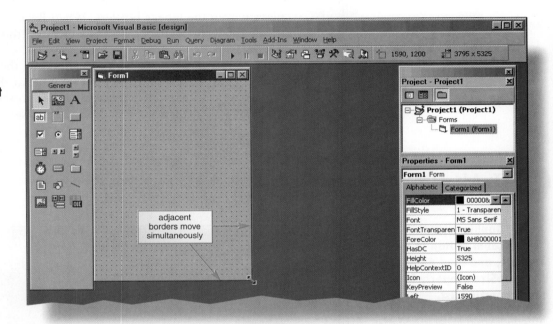

FIGURE 2-4

2 **Release the mouse button and then drag the form to the location shown in Figure 2-5. Release the mouse button.**

The form's size and position should display as shown in Figure 2-5.

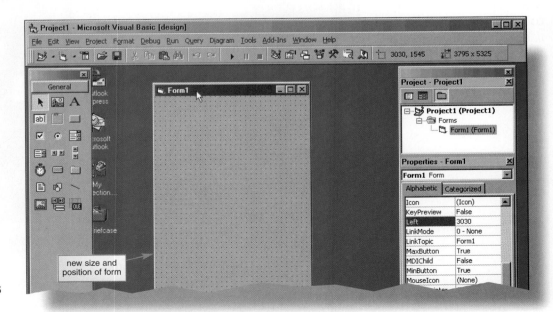

FIGURE 2-5

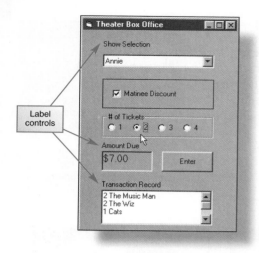

FIGURE 2-6

Label Controls and the AutoSize and BackStyle Properties

Next, you will add the three Label controls in the Theater Box Office application shown in Figure 2-6. Recall that unlike a text box, the contents of a Label control cannot be directly changed by the user of the application at run time. For example, the words Show Selection only can be changed with code statements at run time because those words are the caption of one of the Label controls.

When you set the **AutoSize property** of a label to True, the label's size automatically adjusts to the size of the label's caption. Because you will be changing the color of the form later, you will change the value of the label's BackStyle property from opaque to transparent. When a label's **BackStyle property** is **opaque**, the label's **BackColor property** displays within the label's borders. When BackStyle is set to **transparent,** the color of the control below the label (in this case the form) displays within the label's borders.

Although normally you set properties after building the interface, you will set the AutoSize and BackStyle properties of the first label at this time so when you copy the control these property values will be applied to the copies. Perform the following steps to add one Label control to the form and set its AutoSize and BackStyle properties.

Steps **To Add a Label Control and Set its AutoSize and BackStyle Properties**

1 **Double-click the Label button in the Toolbox, and then point to the AutoSize property in the Properties list.**

A default-sized label is added to the center of the form. The Label1 control is the selected control. Its properties display in the Properties window (Figure 2-7).

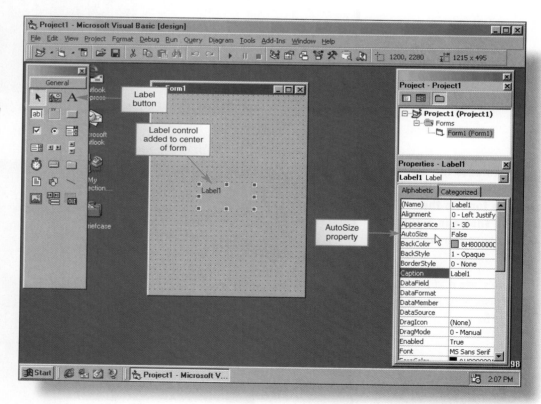

FIGURE 2-7

2 **Double-click the AutoSize property in the Properties list.**

The value of the label's AutoSize property is changed from False to True in the Properties window, and its size is adjusted on the form (Figure 2-8).

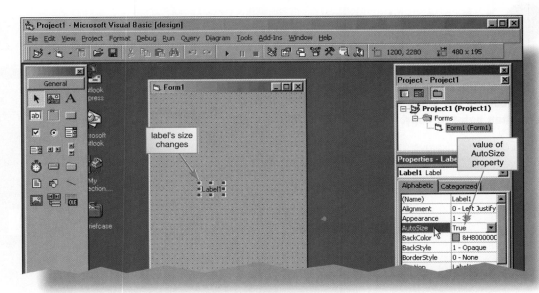

FIGURE 2-8

3 **Double-click the BackStyle property in the Properties list and then drag the Label1 control to the position shown in Figure 2-9.**

The value of the label's Back-Style property size is changed from 1 - Opaque to 0 - Transparent in the Properties window, and its location is changed on the form (Figure 2-9).

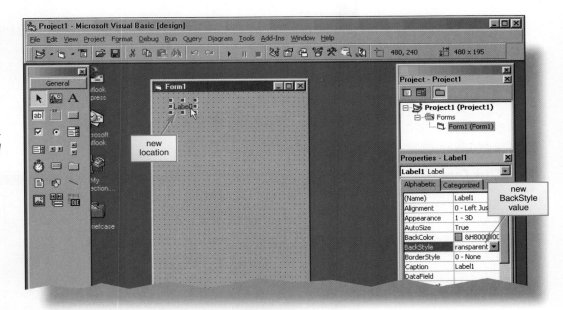

FIGURE 2-9

When a property has fixed values, such as the False/True values of the AutoSize property and the Opaque/Transparent values of the BackStyle property, you can switch between those values by double-clicking the name of the property in the Properties list.

Copying Controls

The two additional Label controls identified in Figure 2-6 are similar to the one that was just added. When you want to add multiple, similar controls to a form, it often is easier to **copy** the control to the Clipboard and then paste copies of it from the Clipboard to the form. Perform the steps on the next page to add two copies of the Label1 control to the form.

Steps To Copy Controls

1 **Click the Label1 control to select it. Click Edit on the menu bar and then point to Copy.**

The Edit menu displays (Figure 2-10).

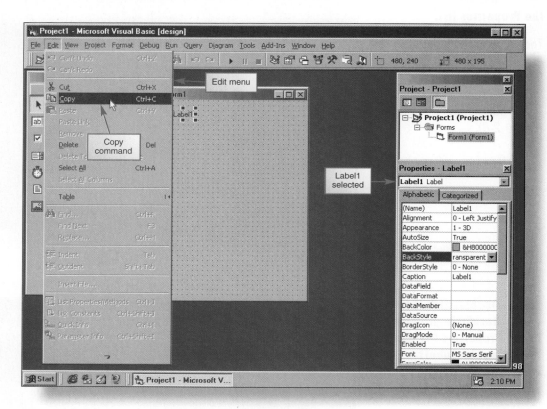

FIGURE 2-10

2 **Click Copy.**

The selected control (Label1) is copied to the Clipboard, and the Edit menu closes (Figure 2-11). The selected control changes to Form1 in the Properties window.

FIGURE 2-11

3 **Click Edit on the menu bar and then click Paste. Point to the No button.**

The Microsoft Visual Basic dialog box displays (Figure 2-12).

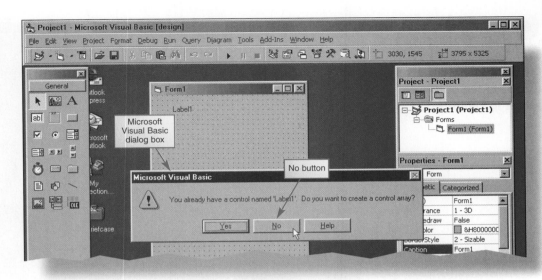

FIGURE 2-12

4 **Click the No button.**

The dialog box closes, and a copy of the control is added to the form (Figure 2-13). The control's Name property automatically is named Label2 and is the selected control. The Caption property (Label1) will be changed later.

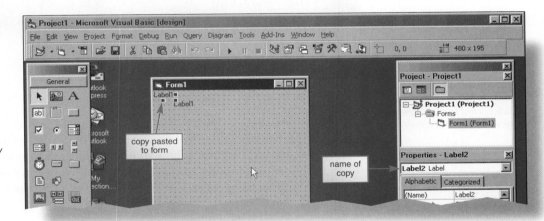

FIGURE 2-13

5 **Drag the new Label control to the position shown in Figure 2-14.**

The label's name shown in the Properties window is Label2, but its caption is Label1 (Figure 2-14).

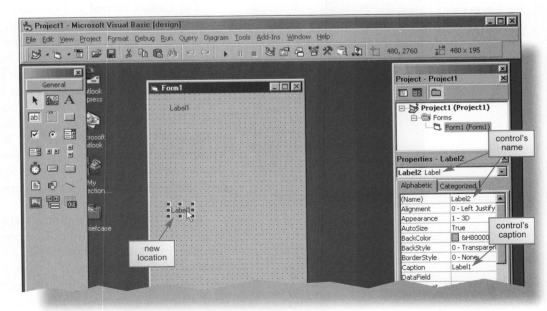

FIGURE 2-14

6 Repeat the procedures shown in Step 3 and Step 4 to add the third label, and then drag it to the position shown in Figure 2-15.

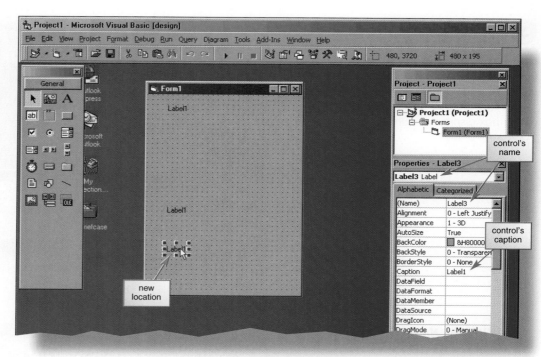

FIGURE 2-15

Other **Ways**

1. Click control to copy, press CTRL+C, then press CTRL+V

When you copy a control, the pasted control has a new name but has all of the other properties of the control you copied. Thus, both additional controls are AutoSized, have transparent BackStyles and have the same caption, Label1. The captions will be changed later in this project. Once a control is copied to the Clipboard, multiple copies can be pasted without having to copy the control to the Clipboard each time.

The ListBox and ComboBox Controls

The **ListBox control** and **ComboBox control** are used in applications to present lists of choices. In a list box, part or all of the list of choices displays. When the list of choices is longer than can display in the list box, a scroll bar automatically is added to move the list up or down. When an item is selected from the list by clicking it, the item displays in a highlighted color.

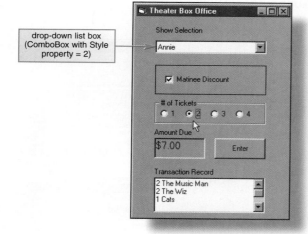

FIGURE 2-16

The Theater Box Office application contains a ComboBox control with properties set so the show names display in a drop-down list of choices (Figure 2-16). With a drop-down list, the list of choices displays only when you click the list box arrow. When you select an item from the list by clicking it, the drop-down list closes, and only the selected item displays in the list box.

At run time, ListBox controls always have one way to select an item from the list. ComboBox controls can have different selection methods and can display differently, depending on the value of its **Style property**. The appearance of ListBox controls and ComboBox controls and the method of selecting an item from these controls at run time are summarized in Table 2-1.

Perform the following steps to add a ComboBox control to the Theater Box Office form. Later, you will set its Style property to 2 (see Table 2-1) to make it a drop-down list.

Table 2-1

CONTROL	APPEARANCE OF LIST	SELECTION FROM LIST
ListBox	List always shows, scroll bar added if list is longer than control's size	Click item in list
ComboBox (Style = 0)	Drop-down list	Click item in list or type item directly in ComboBox's text box
ComboBox (Style = 1)	List always shows, scroll bar added if list is longer than control's size	Click item in list or type item directly in ComboBox's text box
ComboBox (Style = 2)	Drop-down list	Click item in list

 To Add a ComboBox Control

1 **Double-click the ComboBox button in the Toolbox.**

A default-sized ComboBox control is added to the form (Figure 2-17).

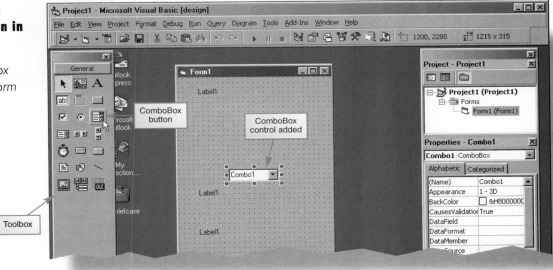

FIGURE 2-17

2 **Drag the combo box to the position shown in Figure 2-18. Point to the right center sizing handle.**

The combo box is moved, and the pointer points to the right center sizing handle.

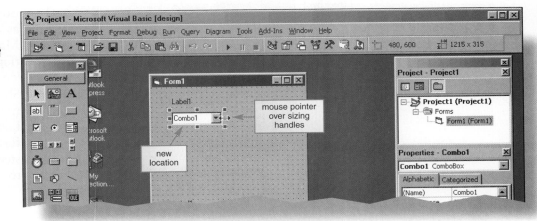

FIGURE 2-18

Drag the sizing handle on the right center side of the combo box to the position shown in Figure 2-19.

The outline of the control displays on the form.

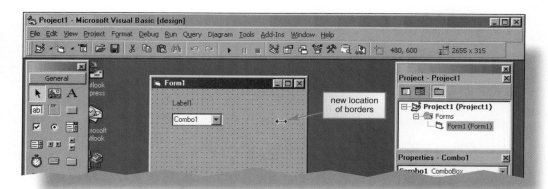

FIGURE 2-19

4 **Release the mouse button.**

The combo box is resized on the form (Figure 2-20).

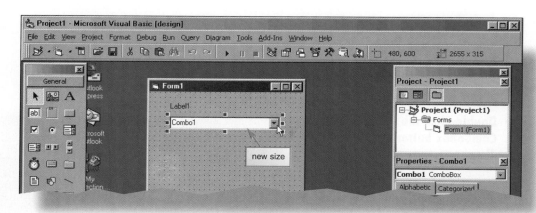

FIGURE 2-20

You will add the names of the shows to the drop-down list box later in this project.

 About

Shape Controls

You can draw a Shape control in a container, but it cannot act as a container. If you draw additional controls inside a Shape control and then drag the Shape control to a new position, the positions of the other controls will not change.

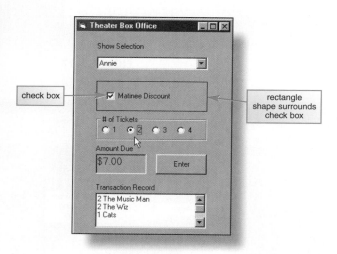

FIGURE 2-21

The Shape Control

The **Shape control** is used to add a rectangle, square, oval, or circle to a form. The Theater Box Office application uses a rectangular shape as a border surrounding the Matinee Discount check box (Figure 2-21).

The only purpose of the Shape control in this application is to enhance the visual balance of the controls on the form. Perform the following steps to add the Shape control to the form.

Steps To Add a Shape Control

1 **Click the Shape button in the Toolbox, and then move the mouse pointer under the lower-left corner of the ComboBox control, which is where the top-left corner of the shape will display (Figure 2-22).**

The Shape button is recessed in the Toolbox, and the mouse pointer changes to a cross hair.

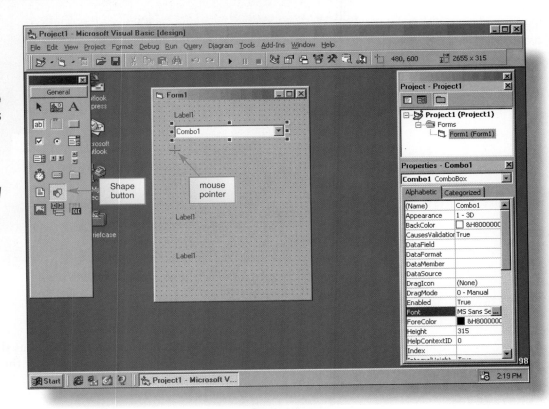

FIGURE 2-22

2 **Drag down and to the right as shown in Figure 2-23.**

A shaded outline of the control displays on the form.

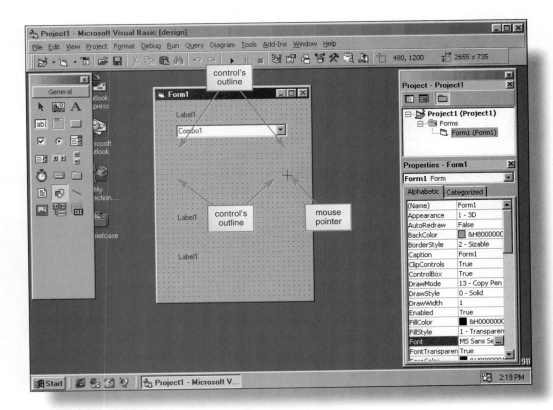

FIGURE 2-23

3 **Release the mouse button.**

The control is sized to fit the area of the shaded outline (Figure 2-24).

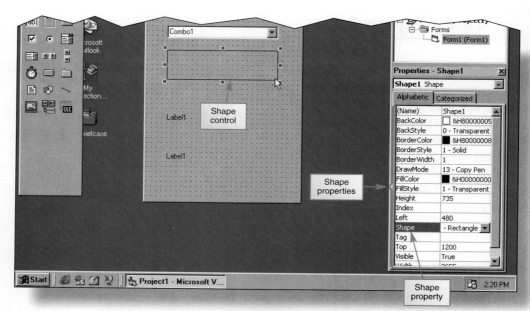

FIGURE 2-24

The different properties of the Shape control, such as the Shape property, display in the Properties list (Figure 2-24). The default value of the **Shape property** of a Shape control is Rectangle.

The CheckBox Control

A **CheckBox control** is used in applications to turn options on or off, such as the Matinee Discount (Figure 2-21 on page VB 2.14). Clicking an empty check box places a check mark in the check box to indicate the option is selected. Clicking a selected check box removes the check mark to indicate the option is not selected. Perform the following steps to add a CheckBox control to the form.

 *More About*

CheckBoxes

You can use CheckBox controls in groups to display multiple choices from which the user can select one or more. You also can set the value of a check box in code by changing its Value property.

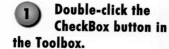 **To Add a CheckBox Control**

1 **Double-click the CheckBox button in the Toolbox.**

A default-sized CheckBox control is added to the form (Figure 2-25).

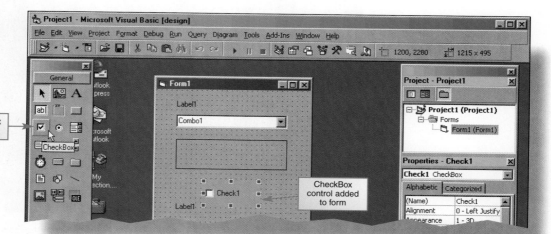

FIGURE 2-25

2 Drag the CheckBox control to a position inside the Shape control. Drag the sizing handle on the right of the control to extend its width, as shown in Figure 2-26.

The CheckBox control is positioned inside the Shape control, and its width is extended.

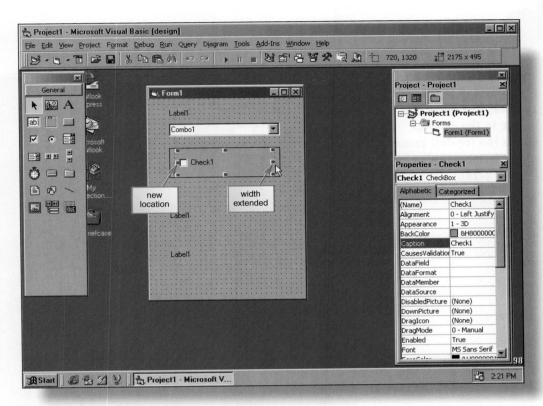

FIGURE 2-26

Check boxes are used to indicate the selection or deselection of individual options. For this reason, any number or combination of check boxes on a form can be selected at the same time. In the Theater Box Office application, the check box is used to switch between the two different prices of the tickets purchased. The two prices will be established later in the code for the application.

The Frame Control

The **Frame control** is used as a container for other controls, as shown in Figure 2-27. It has several properties similar to the Shape control, but it has some important differences:

▶ A frame can have only a rectangular shape.
▶ A frame can have a caption.
▶ When option buttons are added inside a frame, only one can be selected at a time during run time.

Perform the steps on the next page to add the Frame control to the form.

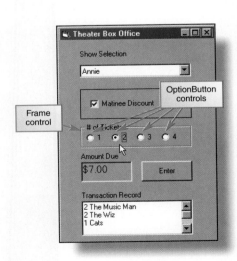

FIGURE 2-27

Steps **To Add a Frame Control**

1 **Click the Frame button in the Toolbox, and move the mouse to the position where the top-left corner of the frame will display (Figure 2-28).**

The Frame button is recessed in the Toolbox, and the mouse pointer changes to a cross hair.

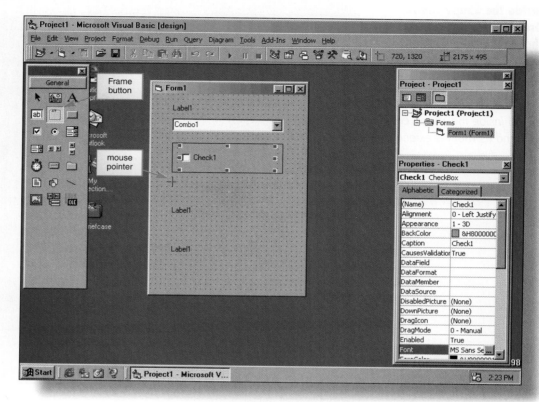

FIGURE 2-28

2 **Drag down and to the right as shown in Figure 2-29.**

A gray outline of the control displays on the form.

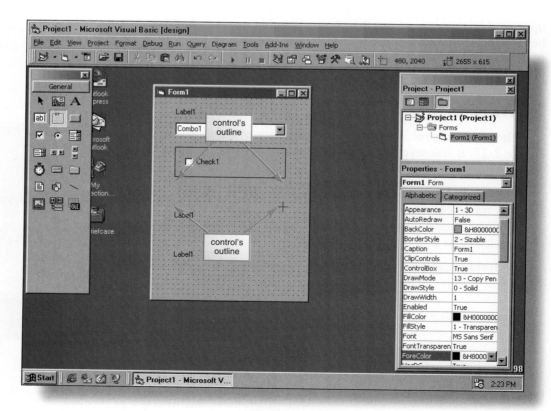

FIGURE 2-29

Release the mouse button.

The control is sized to fit the area of the shaded outline (Figure 2-30).

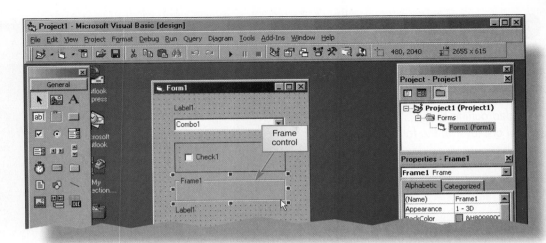

FIGURE 2-30

When controls have been added by drawing them inside a Frame control, dragging the frame to a new position causes the controls inside to be moved as well.

The OptionButton Control

The **OptionButton control** presents a set of choices, such as the number of tickets bought in a single box office transaction (Figure 2-27 on page VB 2.17). Option buttons are placed in **groups** that allow the user to make only one selection from a group, such as the number of tickets sold. All of the option buttons on a form function as one group unless they are placed inside a frame. Multiple groups of option buttons can be created by adding another frame to the form for each option button group. For an option button to be part of a group, it must be added directly inside the frame. You cannot add an option button to the form and then drag it inside a frame if you want it to be part of the group formed by that frame.

The application in this project offers four options for the number of tickets sold (1, 2, 3, or 4). Perform the following steps to create a group of five option buttons within the Frame control already added. The reason for the fifth button will be explained later in this project.

 To Build an OptionButton Group

 **Click the OptionButton button in the Toolbox, and then move the mouse to the position where the top-left corner of the option button will display (Figure 2-31).**

The OptionButton button is recessed in the Toolbox, and the mouse pointer changes to a cross hair.

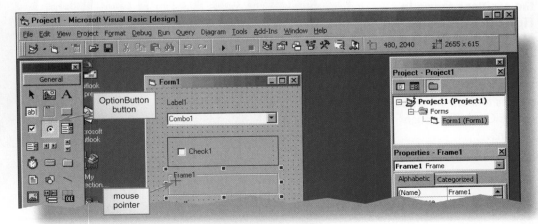

FIGURE 2-31

2 **Drag down and to the right. If necessary, drag the borders to size the control as shown in Figure 2-32.**

A shaded outline of the control displays on the form.

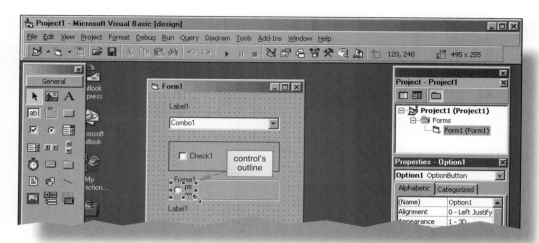

FIGURE 2-32

3 **Release the mouse button.**

The control is sized to fit the area of the shaded outline (Figure 2-33). Only part of the option button's caption, Option1, is visible on the form because of the size of the control.

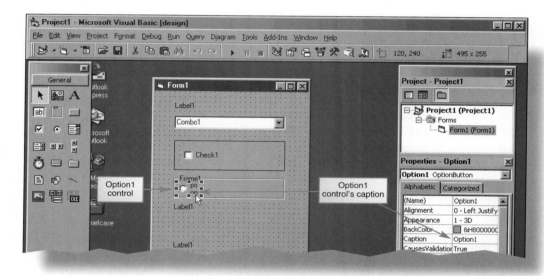

FIGURE 2-33

4 **Repeat Step 1 through Step 3 four times to add four more OptionButton controls in the positions shown in Figure 2-34. Click any blank area of the form.**

As the OptionButton controls are added, Visual Basic assigns to them the default names Option2 through Option5.

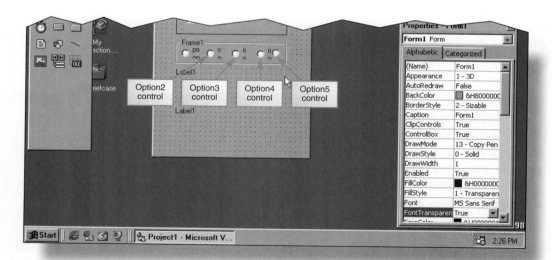

FIGURE 2-34

You may have wondered why Step 4 did not use the cut and paste method or the double-click method to add the last four option buttons. The reason is that both of these methods would have added the option buttons to the form, not to the Frame control. To add the option buttons to a Frame control, the preceding procedure must be used. The option buttons were added to the form inside the Frame control in order to form an OptionButton group.

Label, CommandButton, and TextBox Controls

Three intrinsic controls remain to be added to the form: one additional Label control, a CommandButton control, and a TextBox control as shown in Figure 2-35. You should be familiar with working with these controls from Project 1.

The Theater Box Office application uses a Label control with borders around it to contain the total cost of the transaction (number of tickets times the ticket price). The Command-Button control is used to clear the amount displayed in the label and to add the number of tickets purchased and the name of the show to a list contained in the Transaction Record TextBox control. Perform the following steps to add these controls to the Theater Box Office form.

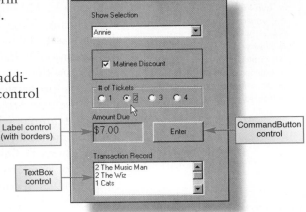

FIGURE 2-35

TO ADD LABEL, COMMANDBUTTON, AND TEXTBOX CONTROLS

1 Click the Label button in the Toolbox, and then draw a Label control on the form in the location and size shown in Figure 2-36.

2 Double-click the CommandButton button in the Toolbox and then drag and drop the command button in the location shown in Figure 2-36.

3 Double-click the TextBox button in the Toolbox. Drag and drop the text box under the third Label control and resize it by dragging its borders to the size shown in Figure 2-36.

The locations and sizes of the Label4, Command1, and Text1 controls should display as shown in Figure 2-36.

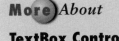

More About

TextBox Controls

At run time, the Microsoft Windows operating system automatically implements a standard keyboard interface to allow navigation in TextBox controls. The user can enter, edit, and delete text with the arrow keys (UP ARROW, DOWN ARROW, LEFT ARROW, and RIGHT ARROW), and the DELETE, BACK-SPACE, HOME and END keys.

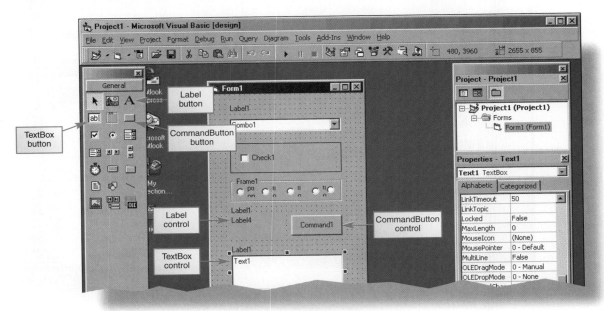

FIGURE 2-36

More About

ActiveX Controls

Over 2,000 ActiveX controls are available today. In addition, version 5 was the first version of Visual Basic that enabled you to create your own controls. You can create controls from scratch, customize controls, or combine controls to make new controls.

The CommonDialog Control

You can add the Open, Save As, Color, Print, and Font dialog boxes easily to your applications with the **CommonDialog control**. The CommonDialog control is an ActiveX control and must be added to the Toolbox before you can add it to an application. Although the CommonDialog control displays as a small icon on the form during design time, it never is visible on the form during run time. You cause a dialog box to be opened during run time by applying one of the **Show** methods to the CommonDialog control through code. When a user interacts with the dialog box during run time by selecting a file or clicking a check box, the user is changing values of the properties of the CommonDialog control. You can write code that then uses those new property values.

For example, when the CommonDialog control is used to display the Color dialog box, any color selection the user makes is captured as the value of the CommonDialog control's **Color property**. You then can set (through a code statement) the BackColor property of some other control to be equal to the Color property of the CommonDialog control. The actions from the user's perspective are: (1) the Color dialog box displayed, (2) a color was selected and the OK button was clicked, and (3) the color selected was applied to some other control(s).

The theater salesperson will not be able to change the Theater Box Office application's color. You will, however, use the Color dialog box to demonstrate different color possibilities to the ANC management when you present the prototype interface. Perform the following steps to add a CommonDialog control to the Toolbox and then add it to the form.

 To Add a CommonDialog Control

1 **Right-click the Toolbox and then point to Components on the shortcut menu.**

The shortcut menu displays (Figure 2-37).

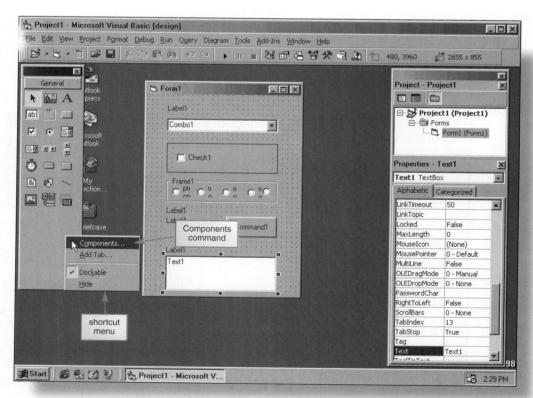

FIGURE 2-37

2 **Click Components on the shortcut menu. If necessary, when the Components dialog box displays, click the Controls tab. Scroll down the list and then click the Microsoft Common Dialog Control 6.0 check box (double-clicking the entry also will select the check box). Point to the OK button.**

The Components dialog box displays. The list of ActiveX controls available on your PC may be different from the list shown in Figure 2-38.

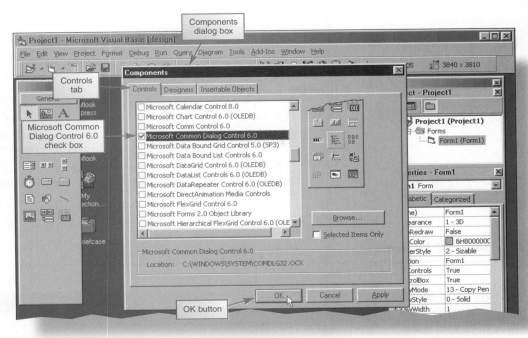

FIGURE 2-38

3 **Click the OK button.**

The Components dialog box closes and the CommonDialog button is added to the Toolbox (Figure 2-39).

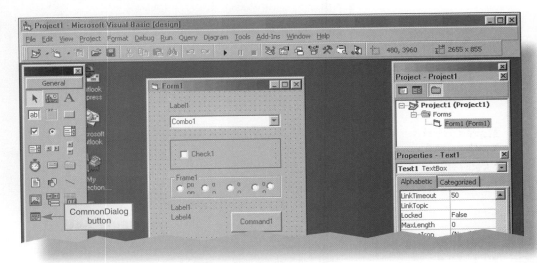

FIGURE 2-39

4 **Double-click the CommonDialog button in the Toolbox. Drag and drop the CommonDialog control to the position shown in Figure 2-40.**

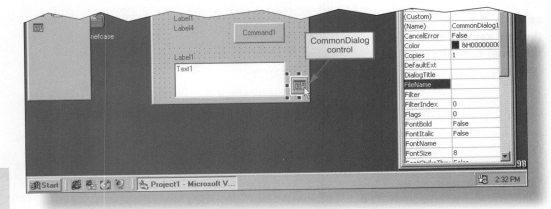

FIGURE 2-40

1. On Project menu click Components
2. Press CTRL+T

More About

The Form Editor Toolbar

The Form Editor toolbar contains buttons that are shortcuts to some commonly used Format menu items useful for working with forms. You can select the Show ToolTips option on the General tab in the Options dialog box if you want to display ToolTips for the Form Editor toolbar buttons.

You have added the CommonDialog control to the application. Later, you will write the code that activates the control during run time.

Aligning Controls

You can use either VB6's **Format menu** or **Form Editor Toolbar** to access form layout commands that adjust the alignment, spacing, and size of any group of controls on a form. The **Align** command aligns selected objects with each other using the last selected object in a group.

Perform the following steps to select a group of controls on the Form1 control and left-align the selected controls.

Steps To Align Controls

1 Drag and drop the topmost Label control to the location shown in Figure 2-41.

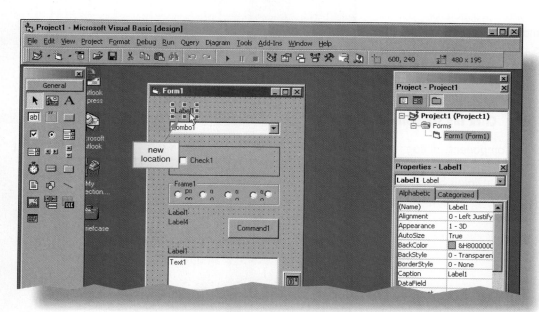

FIGURE 2-41

2 Click the TextBox control (Text1) at the bottom of the form to select it. Press and hold the CTRL key and then click the Label control above the text box.

The sizing handles around the text box display as outlines. The text box remains selected while the label also is selected. The label's sizing handles are solid (Figure 2-42).

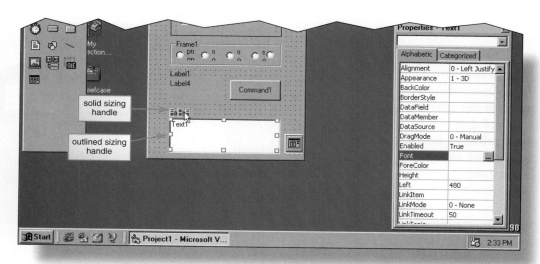

FIGURE 2-42

3 Press and hold the CTRL key and click the remaining controls to be left-aligned as shown in Figure 2-43. Select the topmost label last.

The controls selected as a group display as shown in Figure 2-43.

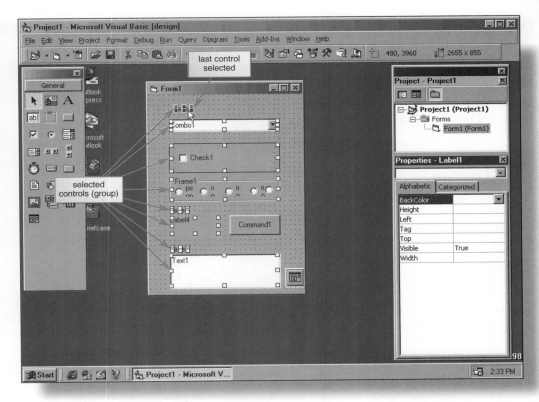

FIGURE 2-43

4 Click Format on the menu bar. Point to Align and then point to Lefts.

The Format menu and Align submenu display (Figure 2-44).

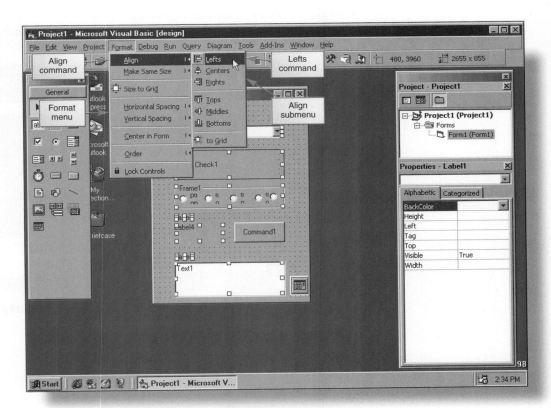

FIGURE 2-44

5 **Click Lefts.**

The left borders of all selected controls are aligned with the left border of the topmost Label1 control (Figure 2-45).

6 **Click any blank area of the form.**

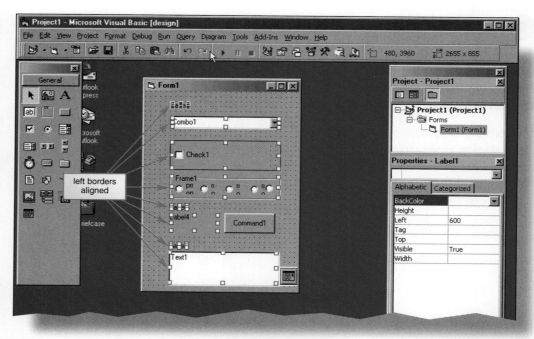

FIGURE 2-45

Other Ways

1. Press ALT+O, press A, then press L

The interface for the Theater Box Office application now is finished. The form should display as shown in Figure 2-46. Figure 2-47 shows how the form will display at run time after the properties of the controls have been set.

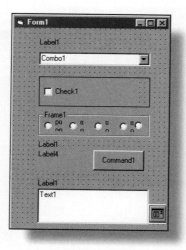

FIGURE 2-46

FIGURE 2-47

Setting Properties

In this section, you will complete the second phase of Visual Basic application development, **setting the properties** of the controls.

Naming Controls

When you add controls to a form, Visual Basic assigns a name to the control, which consists of the type of control and a number, such as Label1. It often is easier to read and edit your code if controls have names that more closely represent the purpose or function of the control within the application. The **Name** of a control is a property of a control and can be changed to whatever seems appropriate. Visual Basic has a suggested standard for naming controls. A control's name should consist of a three-letter prefix that designates the type of control followed by a unique text description. Control types and name prefixes are listed in Table 2-2.

This project follows the Visual Basic conventions for naming controls. Table 2-3 lists the current (default) name of each control (shown in Figure 2-46), its function in the Theater Box Office application, and the new name that will be assigned. Perform the following steps to assign new values of the Name property to several of the controls on the Theater Box Office form.

Table 2-2

CONTROL	PREFIX	CONTROL	PREFIX
Form	frm	Image	img
CheckBox	chk	Label	lbl
ComboBox	cbo	Line	lin
CommandButton	cmd	ListBox	lst
Data	dat	Menu	mnu
DirListBox	dir	OLE	ole
DriveListBox	drv	OptionButton	opt
FileListBox	fil	PictureBox	pic
Frame	fra	Shape	shp
Grid	grd	TextBox	txt
HScrollBar	hsb	Timer	tmr
		VScrollBar	vsb

Table 2-3

CURRENT NAME	CONTROL'S FUNCTION	NEW NAME
Combo1	Selects name of show	cboShow
Check1	Selects matinee discount price	chkMatinee
Label4	Displays purchase amount	lblAmtdue
Command1	Enters transaction in list	cmdEnter
Text1	Contains record of purchases	txtRecord
Form1	Theater Box Office form	frmTheater

Steps **To Name Controls**

① **Select the control you want to change (Combo1) by clicking it on the form or by selecting its name in the Object list box in the Properties window.**

The name of the selected control and its properties display in the Properties window (Figure 2-48).

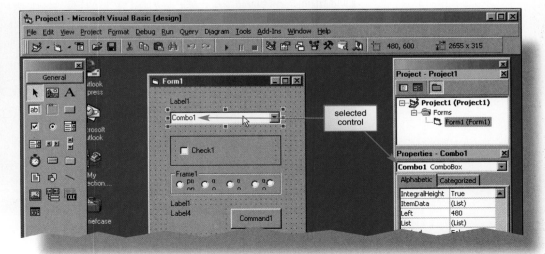

FIGURE 2-48

2 **Scroll up to the top of the Properties list. Double-click the Name property in the Properties window.**

The current name of the control (Combo1) is highlighted (Figure 2-49).

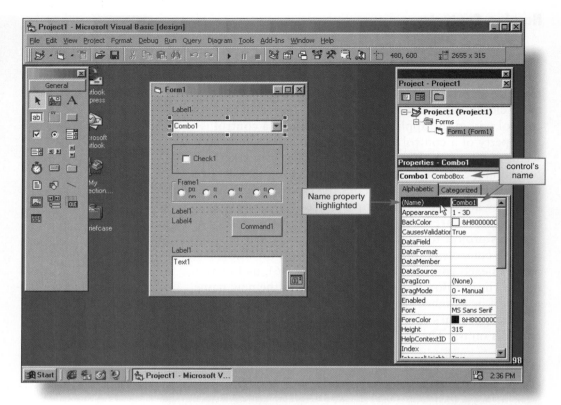

FIGURE 2-49

3 **Type** cboShow **as the new name and then press the ENTER key.**

As you type, Combo1 is replaced with the new value next to the Name property in the Properties list (Figure 2-50).

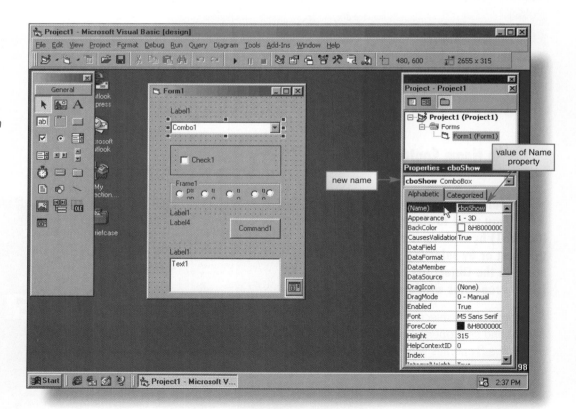

FIGURE 2-50

4 **Repeat Step 1 through Step 3 to name the Check1 control** chkMatinee. **Repeat Step 1 through Step 3 to name the Label4 control** lblAmtdue. **Repeat Step 1 through Step 3 to name the Command1 control** cmdEnter. **Repeat Step 1 through Step 3 to name the Text1 control** txtRecord. **Repeat Step 1 through Step 3 to name the Form1 control** frmTheater.

5 **Click the Object box arrow in the Properties window.**

The Object list displays showing the new names (Figure 2-51).

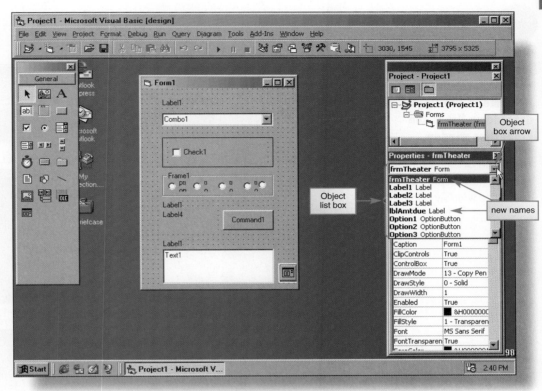

FIGURE 2-51

Changing the control names did not change their appearance on the form because the characters that display on the control are the control's caption, which is separate from the control's name.

Caption and Text Properties

Perform the following steps to add meaningful captions to the controls and clear the initial text in the ComboBox and TextBox controls as shown in Figure 2-52.

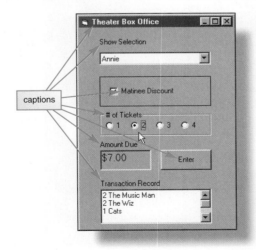

FIGURE 2-52

More About

Caption and Text Properties

The Text setting for a TextBox control is limited to 2048 characters unless the MultiLine property is True, in which case the limit is about 32K. A Label control's caption size is unlimited.

To Set Caption and Text Properties

1 **Select the Label1 control by clicking its name in the Object drop-down list in the Properties window.**

The name of the control and its properties display in the Properties window (Figure 2-53).

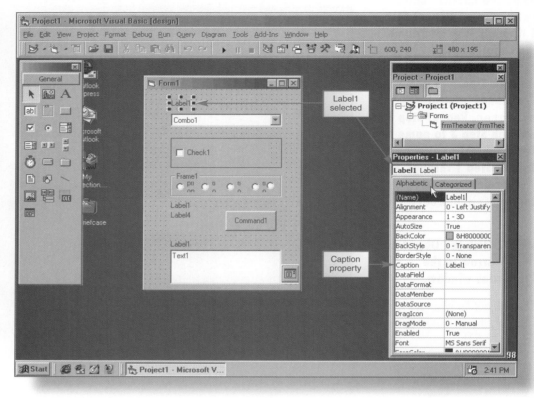

FIGURE 2-53

2 **If necessary, scroll the Properties list until the Caption property is visible. Double-click the Caption property in the Properties list.**

The current value of the control's Caption property displays highlighted (Figure 2-54).

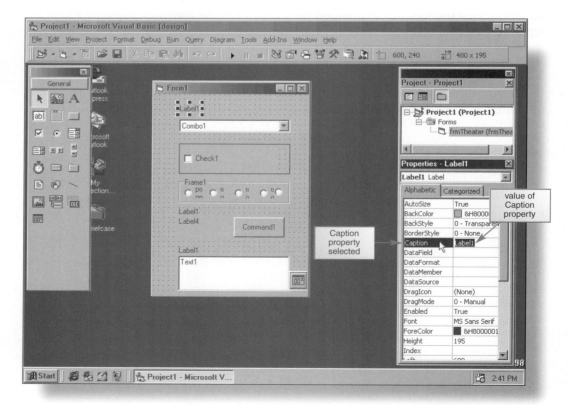

FIGURE 2-54

3 **Type** Show
Selection **as the
new caption and then press
the ENTER key.**

*As you type, the value is
replaced with the new caption and displays next to the
Caption property in the
Properties list (Figure 2-55).*

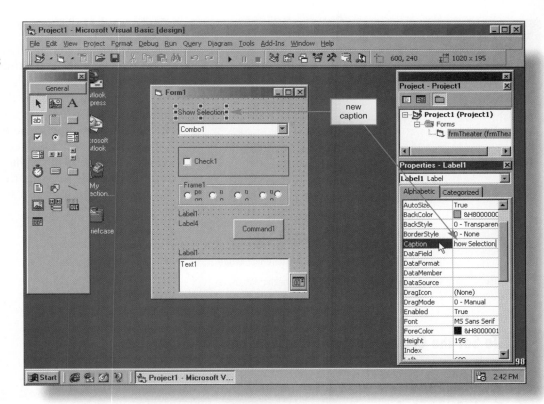

FIGURE 2-55

4 **Repeat Step 1
through Step 3 to
change the caption of each
control as listed in the New
Caption column in Table
2-4 on the next page.**

*Note that the new caption for
lblAmtdue is changed from
Label4 to be blank.*

5 **Follow the
procedure in Step 1
through Step 3 to change
the txtRecord control's Text
property to be blank and
the Combo1 (cboShow) Text
property to be blank.**

*The Theater Box Office form
(frmTheater) displays as
shown in Figure 2-56.*

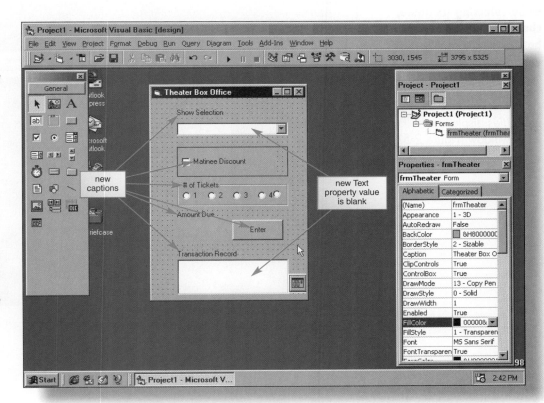

FIGURE 2-56

Table 2-4		
CONTROL	*CURRENT CAPTION*	*NEW CAPTION*
chkMatinee	Check1	Matinee Discount
Frame1	Frame1	# of Tickets
Option1	Option1	1
Option2	Option2	2
Option3	Option3	3
Option4	Option4	4
Label2	Label1	Amount Due
lblAmtdue	Label4	[blank]
cmdEnter	Command1	Enter
Label3	Label1	Transaction Record
frmTheater	Form1	Theater Box Office

Style and List Properties

The Theater Box Office application contains a drop-down list for selecting the name of the show. The ComboBox control selected in Figure 2-57 was added to the form when the other controls were added. Recall from Table 2-1 on page VB 2.13 that a **drop-down list** is one type of a ComboBox control. The type of ComboBox control is set by using the ComboBox control's **Style** property. Perform the following steps to make the ComboBox (cboShow) control a drop-down list box and add items to its list.

 Steps **To Set the ComboBox Control's Style and List Properties**

1 Select the ComboBox control by clicking it on the form or by selecting its name, cboShow, in the Object list box in the Properties window.

Sizing handles display around the control and the control's properties display in the Properties window (Figure 2-57).

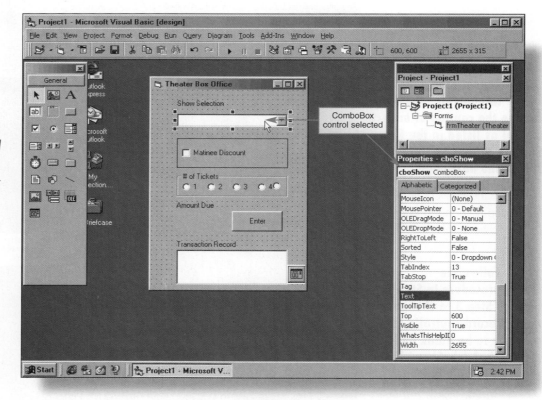

FIGURE 2-57

2 Click the Style property in the Properties list and then click the Style box arrow located on the right of the Style property value.

The default value of the Style property, 0 - Dropdown Combo, displays in the Style property values list (Figure 2-58).

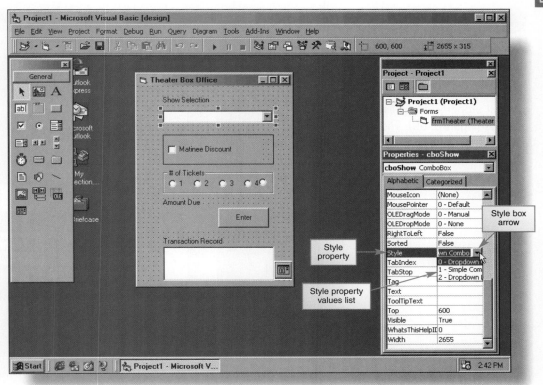

FIGURE 2-58

3 Click 2 - Dropdown List in the Property values list.

The selected value of the Style property displays. The list closes. The Text value changes to the name of the control (Figure 2-59).

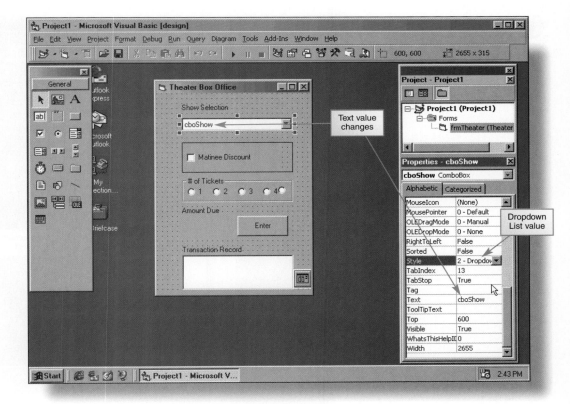

FIGURE 2-59

4 **Scroll the Properties list until the List property is visible and then double-click the List property.**

The List property values list displays (Figure 2-60). The list currently is empty.

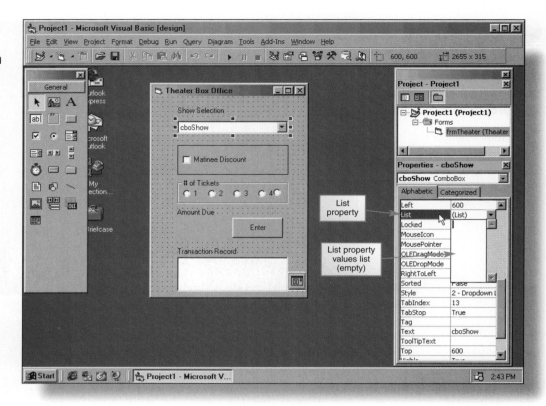

FIGURE 2-60

5 **Type** Annie **and then press** CTRL + ENTER.

The first item is added to the list (Figure 2-61).

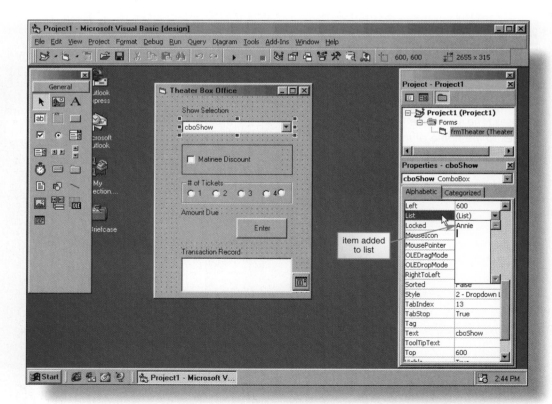

FIGURE 2-61

Repeat Step 5 four times to add Cats, The Music Man, The Wiz, **and** Phantom of The Opera **to the list.**

The list displays as shown in Figure 2-62.

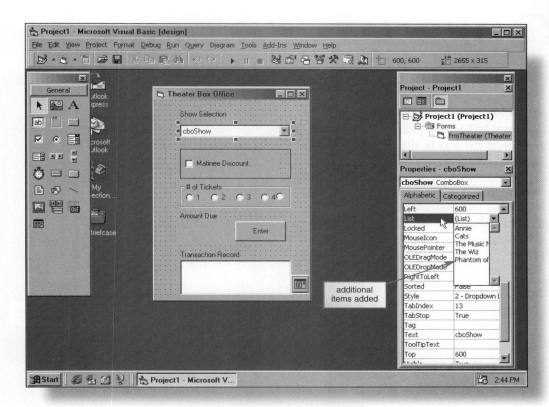

FIGURE 2-62

Although a separate Visual Basic control exists for a simple list box, the **drop-down list box** is one of three types of ComboBox controls specified by setting the Style property of the ComboBox control.

You can add items to a ComboBox or ListBox control during design time by adding to the control's List property as you just did. You can add items to a ComboBox or ListBox control during run time by using the **AddItem method** in code statements.

Locked, MultiLine, and ScrollBars Properties

The Theater Box Office application contains one TextBox control. Its appearance in Figure 2-63 is different from the TextBox controls that were used in Project 1. It contains multiple lines of text (three are visible at a time), it has a vertical scroll bar to move up and down through the text that extends beyond the borders of the control, and the user cannot change its contents. Perform the steps on the next page to add these features by setting the **Locked property, MultiLine property,** and **ScrollBars property** of the TextBox control.

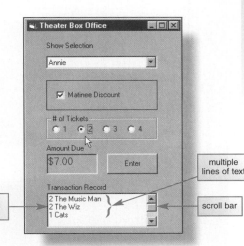

FIGURE 2-63

More About

The ScrollBars Property

On some Visual Basic controls, a scroll bar automatically displays when the control's contents extend beyond the control's borders. This is not true of text boxes. You must add scroll bars to text boxes with the ScrollBars property. Scroll bars then will always appear on the text box, even when its contents do not extend beyond its borders.

To Set the Locked, MultiLine, and ScrollBars Properties

1 Select the TextBox control by clicking it on the form or by selecting its name, txtRecord, from the Object list box in the Properties window.

Sizing handles display around the control, and the control's properties display in the Properties window (Figure 2-64).

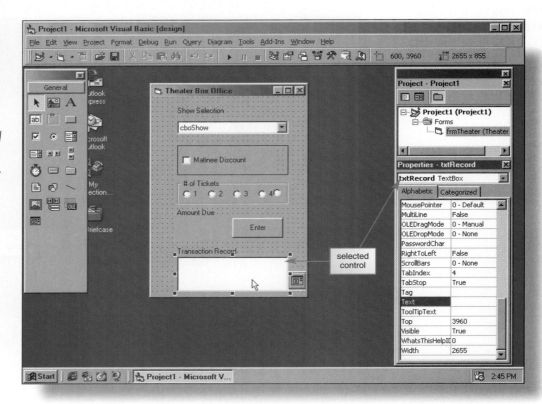

FIGURE 2-64

2 Double-click the Locked property and then double-click the MultiLine property in the Properties list.

The value of the Locked and MultiLine properties change from the default value of False to the new value, True (Figure 2-65).

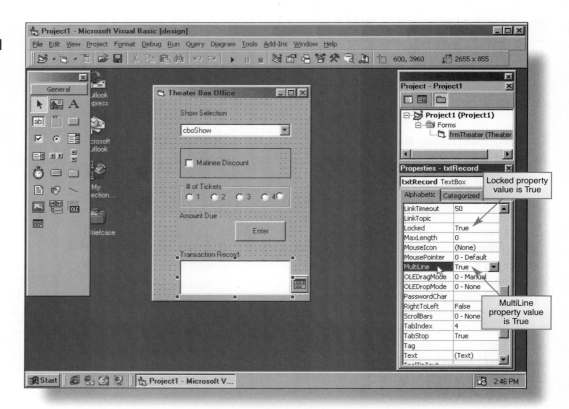

FIGURE 2-65

③ **Click the ScrollBars property in the Properties list. Click the ScrollBars property value box arrow.**

The ScrollBars property values list displays (Figure 2-66).

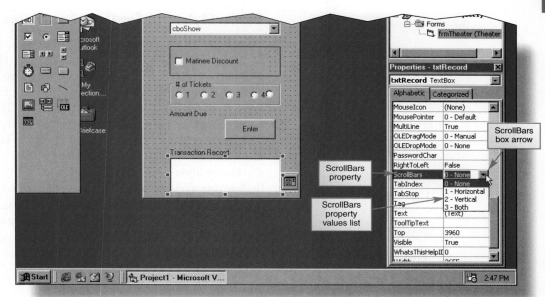

FIGURE 2-66

④ **Click 2 - Vertical in the Property values list.**

A vertical scroll bar is added to the control. The selected value of the property displays and the list closes (Figure 2-67).

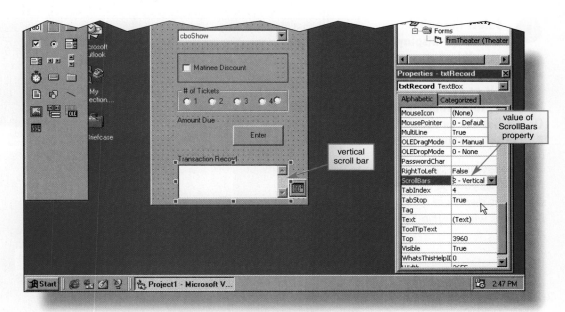

FIGURE 2-67

The ScrollBars property values list also contains values for a horizontal scroll bar or both horizontal and vertical scroll bars to be added to a text box. If the ScrollBars property is not set and the size of the TextBox control is smaller than the text you want to display, you are unable to view the text that extends beyond the borders of the text box.

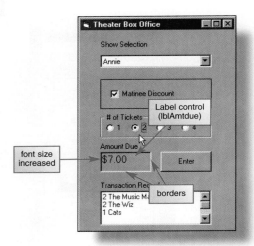

FIGURE 2-68

BorderStyle and FontSize Properties

In the Theater Box Office application, a Label control (lblAmtdue) is used to display the total purchase price (Figure 2-68). A Label control is used instead of a TextBox control so the user of the application cannot change the value displayed during run time. Two features of the Label control (lblAmtdue) shown in Figure 2-68 make it different from the other Label controls in the Theater Box Office application.

First, you may have thought it was a TextBox control because it has a border around it. **Borders** are added to a Label control by setting the **BorderStyle property**. Second, the size of the characters inside the lblAmtdue control is larger than the size of the characters in the other labels on the Theater Box Office form (Figure 2-68). The size of the characters is set by using the **FontSize property** of the control. Perform the following steps to set the BorderStyle property and FontSize property of the labels.

Steps To Set BorderStyle and FontSize Properties

1 **Select the Label control (it displays only as a solid gray rectangle on the form) by clicking it or by selecting its name, lblAmtdue, in the Object list box in the Properties window.**

Sizing handles display around the control, and the control's properties display in the Properties window (Figure 2-69).

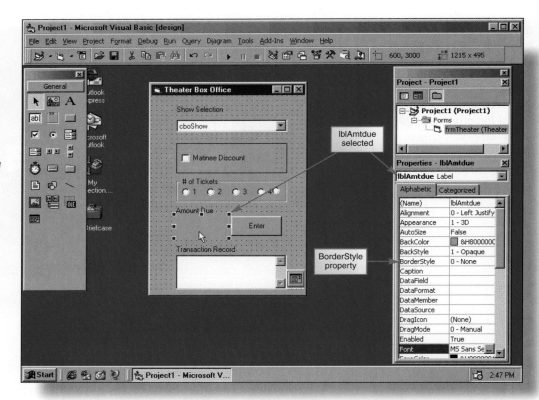

FIGURE 2-69

2 **Double-click the BorderStyle property in the Properties list.**

The value of the BorderStyle property changes from the default value of 0 - None to the new value, 1 - Fixed Single and a border displays around the control (Figure 2-70).

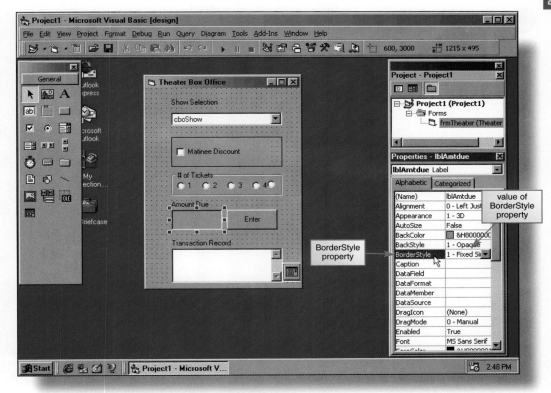

FIGURE 2-70

3 **Scroll the Properties list until the Font property is visible. Click the Font property. Click the Font properties button.**

The Font dialog box displays (Figure 2-71).

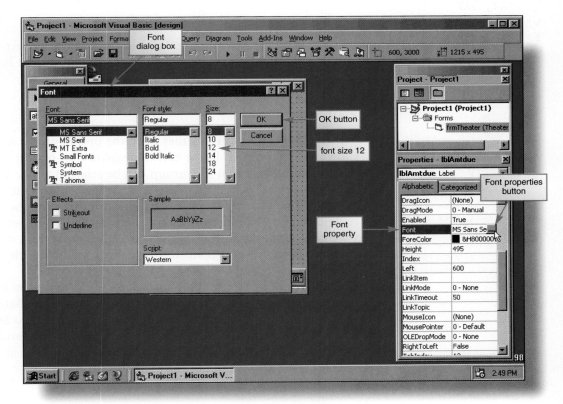

FIGURE 2-71

4 **Click 12 in the Size list. Click the OK button.**

The Font dialog box closes (Figure 2-72).

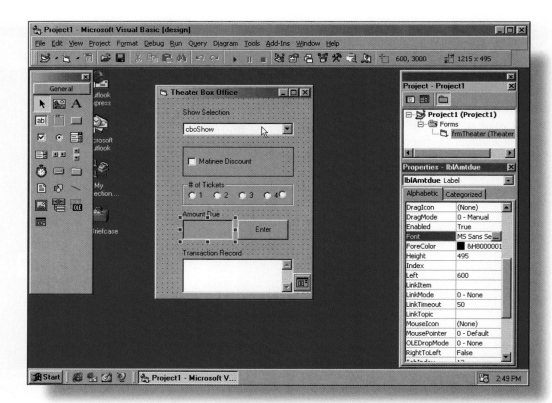

FIGURE 2-72

All controls that contain text or have Caption properties have the FontSize property. Additional Font properties also are available in the Font dialog box. You will work with these other Font properties in later projects.

Visible Property

The five option buttons that form the option group within the Frame control are shown in Figure 2-73. In the earlier discussion of option buttons, you learned that only one option button in a group can be selected at one time. Selecting a second option button automatically deselects the first option button.

When the Theater Box Office application starts, none of the four option buttons representing the number of tickets purchased are to be selected. In addition, when you click the Enter button on the form, all four of these option buttons are to be deselected. These actions are accomplished using the fifth option button added earlier.

Later, you will write code that selects the fifth option button when the Enter button is clicked. Clicking the fifth option button automatically deselects any one of the other four option buttons previously selected. You are making it *seem* that no button is selected, however, by making the fifth button invisible. The **Visible property** of a control determines whether the control can be seen at run time. Perform the following steps to make the Option5 control invisible.

More About

The Visible Property

To hide an object at startup, set the Visible property to False at design time. Setting this property in code enables you to hide and later redisplay a control at run time in response to a particular event.

Steps **To Set the Visible Property**

① **Select the option button named Option5 by clicking it or by selecting its name from the Object list box in the Properties window.**

Sizing handles display around the control, and the control's properties display in the Properties window (Figure 2-73).

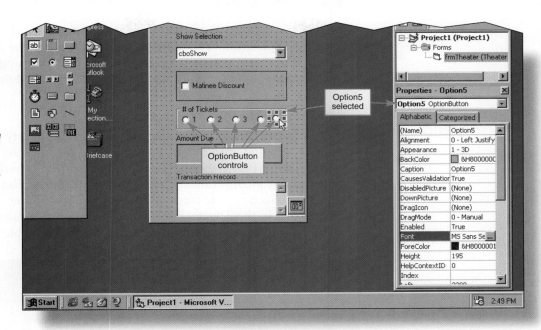

FIGURE 2-73

② **Scroll the Properties list and then double-click the Visible property.**

The value of the Visible property changes from the default value of True to the new value, False (Figure 2-74).

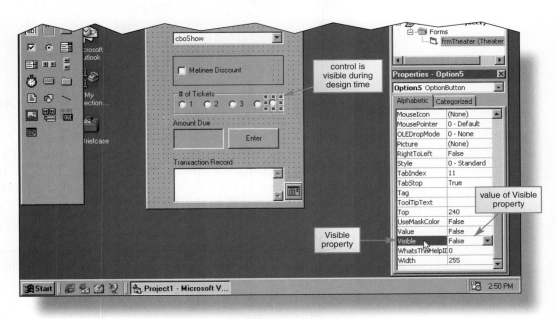

FIGURE 2-74

The Option5 control still is visible on the form during design time. At run time, however, the control will not display on the form.

Writing Code

You have created the interface and set the properties of the controls in the Theater Box Office application. The remaining step is to write the code for the application. Project 1 introduced you to writing Visual Basic code using statements that change the properties of controls during run time. These statements take the following general form:

```
controlname.property = value
```

The name of the control and the name of the property to be changed are separated with a period, and the value of the property to be set follows an equal sign.

The Theater Box Office application requires you to write more complex code statements that incorporate variables and the **If...Then...Else statement**. You also will cut and paste (copy) code from one subroutine to another.

Six events in the Theater Box Office application require Event procedures (subroutines). These events and their actions are listed in Table 2-5.

Table 2-5		
CONTROL	*EVENT*	*ACTIONS*
General	Declarations	Creates a variable that will be used in multiple procedures
Option1	Click	Calculates the cost of one ticket and displays the amount due
Option2	Click	Calculates the cost of two tickets and displays the amount due
Option3	Click	Calculates the cost of three tickets and displays the amount due
Option4	Click	Calculates the cost of four tickets and displays the amount due
cmdEnter	Click	Adds the number of tickets and the name of the show to the transaction list; clears option buttons, selection box, and amount due box
frmTheater	Double-click	Displays the Color dialog box for developer to allow demonstration of different colors

The code for the Theater Box Office application will be written one event at a time using the Code window. Before proceeding with the code writing, you should save the project. In the following steps, the form and project files are saved to a formatted floppy disk in the 3½ Floppy (A:) drive.

TO SAVE THE FORM

1 Click the Save Project button on the Standard toolbar.

2 Type Theater in the File name box in the Save File As dialog box.

3 Click 3½ Floppy (A:) in the Save in list box.

4 Click the Save button in the Save File As dialog box.

5 Type Theater in the File name box in the Save Project As dialog box.

6 Click the Save button in the Save Project As dialog box.

The form and project files are saved. The file names are shown in the Project window (Figure 2-75).

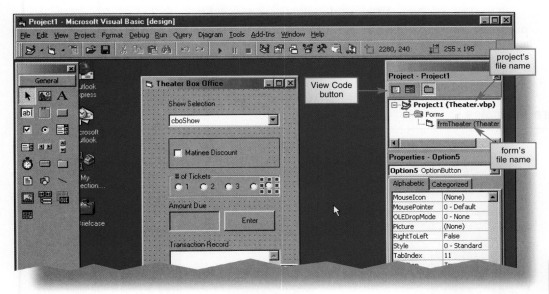

FIGURE 2-75

Variables

Variables are used in code statements to store the temporary values used by other code statements. Visual Basic **variables** have a name you create and a data type. The **data type** determines what kind of data the variable can store (numeric or character). You must follow a few rules when choosing names for variables.

1. The name must begin with a letter.
2. The name cannot be more than 255 characters.
3. The name cannot contain punctuation or blank spaces.

The easiest way to create a variable is to assign a value to the variable's name in a code statement, such as rate = 3.5 or name = "John". Variables created in this way can hold either numbers (numeric data) or characters (string data). Character data, called a **string**, is placed within quotation marks. In addition, variables can be assigned the value of another variable or the value of a mathematical expression. Table 2-6 lists several examples of code statements that create a variable and assign a value to it.

When variables are created simply by using them, they are said to be **implicitly declared**. Variables also can be **explicitly declared** in a separate code statement. The declaration statement has the following form:

Dim *variablename* As *datatype*

Data types of the variable may be Byte, Boolean, Integer, Long, Currency, Single, Double, Date, String, Object, Variant, a user-defined type, or an object type. Data types are discussed in greater detail in a later project. The **scope** of a variable refers to whether or not a variable is available for use by different subroutines. Variables declared within a subroutine can be used only within the subroutine in which they were created and lose their value between calls unless they are declared **static**. For code statements in different subroutines to use the value stored in a variable, the variable must be declared in the form's **General declarations** section.

Table 2-6	
EXAMPLE TYPE	**STATEMENT**
Numeric data	Price = 5
Numeric data	Discount = 1.15
String data	show = "Hamlet"
Value of another variable	Cost = price
Value of an expression	Cost = price * discount
Value of an expression	Amtdue = price * 1.05

The Theater Box Office application uses a variable named num that stores the number of tickets to be purchased. The variable is used in more than one event subroutine, and therefore it must be declared in the General declarations section. Perform the following steps to write a declaration for this variable.

 Steps To Explicitly Declare Variables

1 **Click the View Code button in the Project window. If necessary, click (General) in the Object list box.**

The Code window opens (Figure 2-76). The insertion point is located at the top-left corner of the Code window.

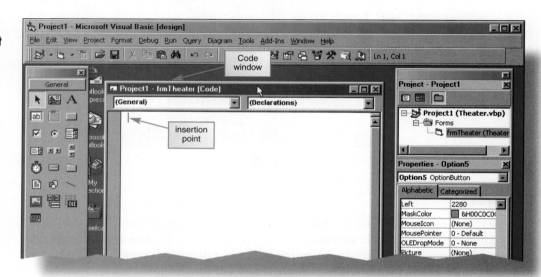

FIGURE 2-76

2 **Type** Dim num As Integer **in the Code window and then press the ENTER key.**

When you press the ENTER key, the insertion point moves to the beginning of the next line (Figure 2-77).

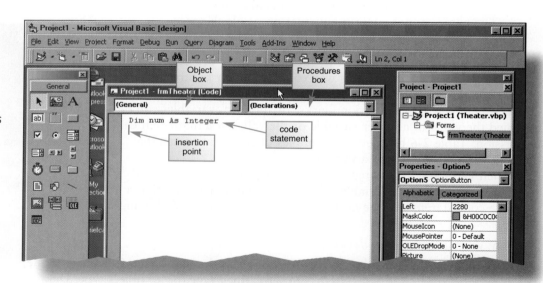

FIGURE 2-77

 **Other Ways**

1. On View menu click Code

When you press the ENTER key at the end of a code statement, Visual Basic inspects the code for many common errors. If it finds an error, the Microsoft Visual Basic dialog box opens. Some of the characters' case and color are changed automatically for ease in reading the code.

In Project 1, you learned how to open the Code window and select a control from the Object list box by double-clicking the control in the Form window. If you are going to write procedures for several controls, it can be awkward, however, to move between the Form window and the Code window just to select different controls in the Code window. A more general way to enter, edit, or view a subroutine in the Code window involves these steps (refer to Figure 2-77).

1. Select the control to which you will assign code from the Object list box.
2. Select the desired event from the Procedures list box.
3. Enter the code statements.

Arithmetic Expressions and the If...Then...Else Structure

The last two rows in Table 2-6 on page VB 2.43 contain code statements that perform mathematical operations on variables. These **arithmetic expressions** can involve certain Control properties as well as variables. For example, in Project 1, you wrote a code statement that made the Caption property of a label equal to the product of the value of a text box's Text property times a number. Table 2-7 lists the arithmetic operators available in Visual Basic. As is the case in Algebra, a set of parentheses can be used to change the normal **order of precedence**, which is exponentiation, multiplication and division, integer division, modulus arithmetic, addition, and subtraction.

The next step is to write the code for the four visible option buttons (Option1 through Option4) located inside the Frame control labeled # of Tickets (Figure 2-75 on page VB 2.43). The code for each option button is nearly identical. The following paragraphs describe the code for the Click event of the first option button (Option1_Click subroutine). Later, the code will be copied for the Click events of the other three option buttons.

The Click subroutine for each option button must do the following:

1. Assign the number of tickets purchased to the num variable.
2. Determine the ticket price.
3. Calculate the amount due as num * price and display it as dollars and cents in the Amount Due box.

More *About*

Editor Options

Visual Basic has several optional code writing and editing features such as automatically verifying correct syntax after you enter a line of code. You can enable or disable these features on the Editor tab sheet in the Options dialog box, accessed on the Visual Basic Tools menu.

Table 2-7

ARITHMETIC OPERATOR	MEANING
^	Used to raise a number to the power of an exponent
*	Used to multiply two numbers
/	Used to divide two numbers and return a floating-point result
\	Used to divide two numbers and return an integer result
MOD	Used to divide two numbers and return only the remainder
+	Used to sum two numbers
-	Used to find the difference between two numbers or to indicate the negative value of a numeric expression

The first code statement must set the variable (num) equal to the number of tickets corresponding to that option button (selecting Option1 represents 1 ticket). The values assigned to num for the other three option buttons are 2, 3, and 4, respectively. Thus, for the first option button, the following statement sets the variable num equal to 1:

```
num = 1
```

The second code statement will use a single-line If...Then...Else statement to determine the price of the tickets purchased (based on whether the matinee discount is being given). In the Theater Box Office application, the regular price for all shows is $5, and the matinee price for all shows is $3.50.

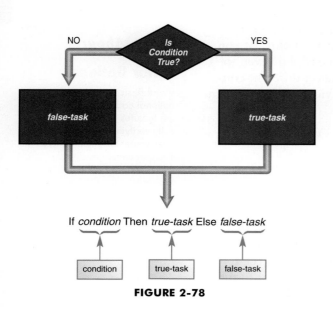

FIGURE 2-78

Single-line If...Then...Else statements are used to execute one statement or another conditionally. A partial flowchart and the form of the single-line If...Then...Else statement is shown in Figure 2-78. The condition follows the keyword **If**. A condition is made up of two expressions and a **comparison operator**. Table 2-8 lists the comparison operators and their meanings.

Table 2-8	
COMPARISON OPERATOR	MEANING
=	Is equal to
<	Is less than
>	Is greater than
<=	Is less than or equal to
>=	Is greater than or equal to
<>	Is not equal to

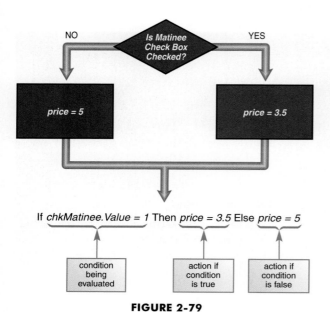

FIGURE 2-79

The statement to be executed when the condition is true follows the keyword **Then**. The statement to be executed when the condition is false follows the keyword **Else**. Figure 2-79 shows the logic and single-line If...Then...Else statement to determine the price of the ticket(s) purchased.

Recall that the Value property of a CheckBox control is 1 when the box is checked and 0 when it is not checked. The chkMatinee.Value is equal to 1 or 0 depending on whether the user of the application has selected the Matinee Discount option. If the Matinee Discount option is selected, then the price of a ticket is $3.50, or else the price of a ticket is $5.

In the Box Office application, the amount due is equal to the number of tickets purchased times the price. Thus, the formula num * price determines the amount due. The application displays amount due as the caption of the lblAmtdue control, using dollars and cents. The following statement determines the amount due and formats the amount due as dollars and cents:

```
lblAmtdue.Caption = Format$(num * price, "currency")
```

lblAmtdue is the name of the Amount Due box. **Format$** is a function that takes the first item in parentheses, num * price, and formats it to the second item in the parentheses, "currency". Currency is a predefined format name, which means Visual Basic will display the value num * price in a more readable fashion in the Amount Due box. The **$ character** appended to Format instructs Visual Basic to change the numeric result of num * price to a string before it is assigned as the caption of the Label control lblAmtdue. Table 2-9 summarizes the more frequently used predefined formats in Visual Basic.

Table 2-9

FORMAT	DESCRIPTION
General Number	Displays the number as is
Currency	Displays the number with a dollar sign, thousands separator with two digits to the right of the decimal; negative numbers display in parentheses
Fixed	Displays at least one digit to the left and two digits to the right of the decimal separator
Standard	Displays the number with thousands separator; if appropriate, displays two digits to the right of the decimal
Percent	Displays the number multiplied by 100 with a % sign
Yes/No	Displays No if the number is 0; otherwise displays Yes

Perform the following steps to write the If...Then...Else statement, mathematical expression, and other code for the Option1_Click subroutine.

To Write an If...Then...Else Statement and Mathematical Expression

1 **Click the Object box arrow in the Code window.**

The Object list box displays (Figure 2-80).

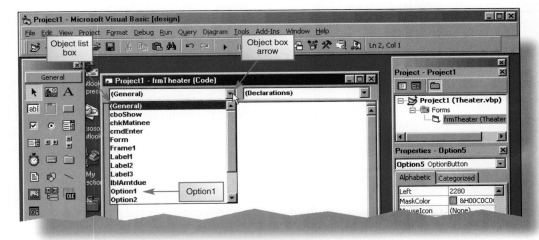

FIGURE 2-80

2 **Click Option1 in the Object list box.**

The Option1_Click subroutine displays in the Code window (Figure 2-81).

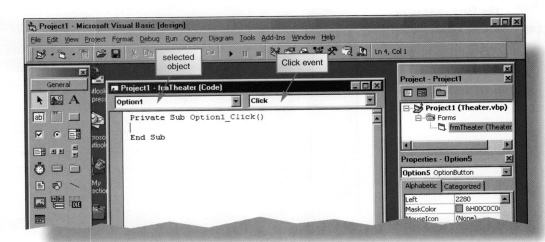

FIGURE 2-81

3 **Drag the Code window's right border to extend the Code window's width. Enter the following four statements in the Code window as shown in Figure 2-82.**

```
'calculate and
   display amount due
num = 1
If chkMatinee.Value
   = 1
Then price = 3.5
Else price = 5
lblAmtdue.Caption =
   Format$(num *
   price, "currency")
```

The Code window displays as shown in Figure 2-82.

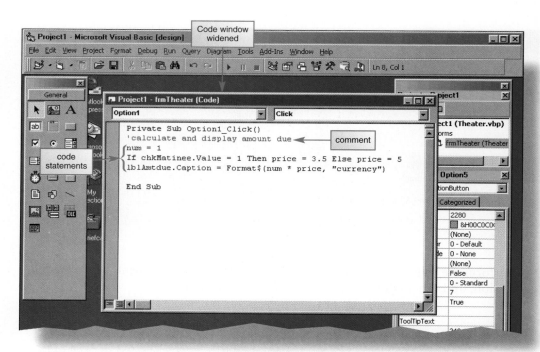

FIGURE 2-82

Copying Code Between Procedures

As previously mentioned, the subroutines for the other three option button Click events are very similar to this first one. Instead of typing all of the code statements in all of the subroutines, you can copy the code from the first subroutine to the other three and then make the necessary minor changes within the copied subroutines. Perform the following steps to copy code between the Option1 and other OptionButton Click event procedures.

 ## To Copy Code Between Procedures

1 **Point to the left of the first character (apostrophe) in the second line of code.**

The mouse pointer is an I-beam (Figure 2-83).

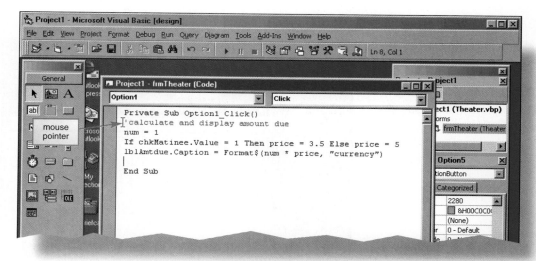

FIGURE 2-83

2 **Drag downward through the next to the last line of code. Click Edit on the menu bar and then point to Copy.**

The code statements are highlighted and the Edit menu displays (Figure 2-84).

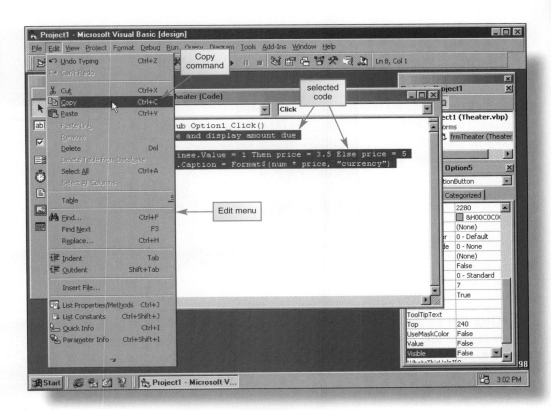

FIGURE 2-84

3 **Click Copy and then click the Object box arrow in the Code window.**

The highlighted text is copied to the Clipboard, and the Object list box displays (Figure 2-85).

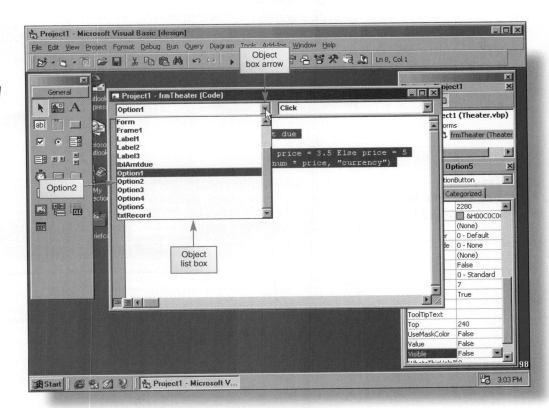

FIGURE 2-85

4 **Click Option2 in the Object list box.**

The Option2_Click subroutine displays with the insertion point at the beginning of the second line (Figure 2-86). If necessary, position the insertion point on the second line.

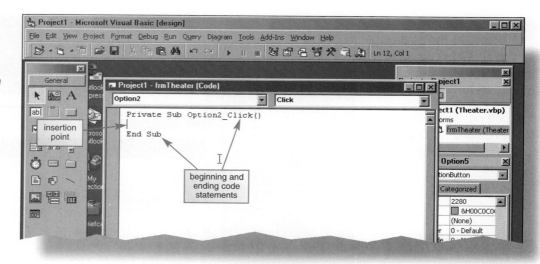

FIGURE 2-86

5 **Click Edit on the menu bar and then click Paste.**

The code is copied from the Clipboard to the procedure in the Code window (Figure 2-87).

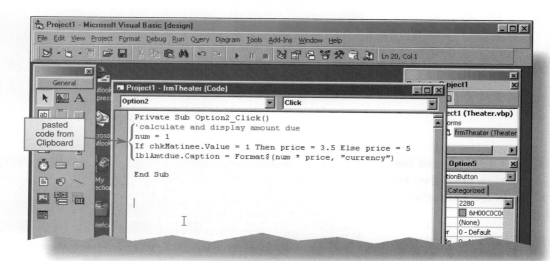

FIGURE 2-87

6 **Type** num = 2 **to edit the code by changing the second line.**

This change affects only what is different when 2 tickets are purchased (Figure 2-88).

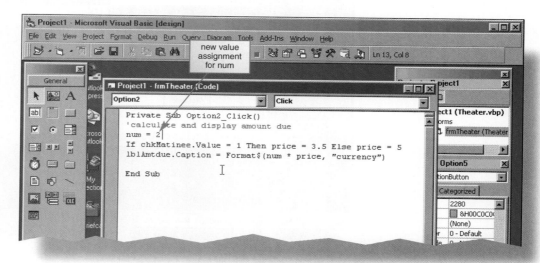

FIGURE 2-88

7 **Repeat Step 4 through Step 6 to copy the code and edit it for the Option3_Click event and the Option4_Click event, changing the value of num to 3 and 4, respectively.**

The completed Option4_Click event procedure is shown in Figure 2-98.

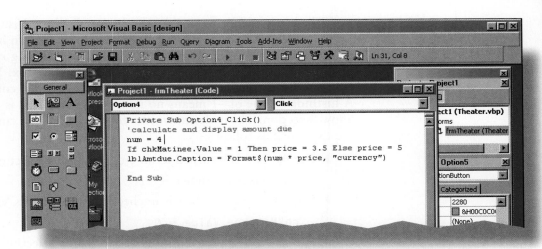

FIGURE 2-89

Once code has been copied to the Clipboard, it is not necessary to copy it each time you want to paste it in a procedure. You can continue to paste it as many times as is needed. Each time you copy code to the Clipboard, the previous contents of the Clipboard are erased.

Using Constants and Concatenating Text

The **cmdEnter_Click event** occurs when you click the Enter button (cmdEnter) on the form. This event adds the number of tickets and the show's name to the top of a scrollable list in the transaction record (txtRecord) and clears the show name, number of tickets, and amount due. To accomplish this task, several functions involving the manipulation of string data are used.

The value of a text box's Text property is a single string (group of characters). To have the transaction record behave the way it does, it is necessary to add special **control code characters** to the string that cause a new line to be started each time the cmdEnter event occurs. These characters are chr$(13) and chr$(10). The characters **chr$(13)** instruct Visual Basic to return the insertion point to the beginning of the line. The characters **chr$(10)** instruct Visual Basic to move the insertion point down one line.

A **constant** is similar to a variable in that it is a reserved space in memory. As its name implies, however, it retains a *constant* value throughout the execution of a program. Constants can be defined with the **Const statement** in the General declarations section. Visual Basic has a large set of predefined constants. The **vbNewLine constant** is equivalent to the characters chr$(10) & chr$(13). You can use constants anywhere in your code in place of actual values.

Because the Theater Box Office record must contain all of the previous sales information, it is necessary to add the new data to the old rather than replace it with the new data. This process of adding strings together is called **concatenation** and is performed with the ampersand (&) character. The code statement to accomplish this is as follows:

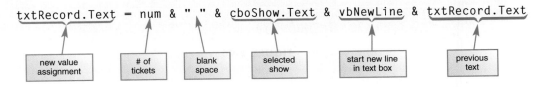

More About

CommandButton Click Events

You can enable the user to press the ENTER key during run time as a substitute method for clicking a command button by changing that CommandButton control's Default property. Only one command button on a form can be the default command button. When Default is set to True for one command button, it automatically is set to False for all other command buttons on the form.

When you add items to a combo box or list box, Visual Basic assigns each item (in this case show name) a consecutive number called an **index**. The first item is given an index of 0. When an item is selected by a user during run time, the **ListIndex property** of the control is given the value of that item's index. You can select an item from the list through a code statement by changing the control's ListIndex property. A ListIndex value of –1 means no item is selected. This is how you will clear the Show Selection. The code statements for the rest of the cmdEnter_Click subroutine are explained as follows:

▶ The list box is returned to an empty state by selecting a blank list item:

```
cboShow.ListIndex = -1
```

▶ The matinee check box is unchecked by setting its Value property:

```
chkMatinee.Value = 0
```

▶ The selected option button is deselected by selecting the Option5 (invisible) option button:

```
Option5.Value = True
```

▶ The amount due is cleared by setting the value of its Caption property equal to the **null string** (two consecutive quotation marks):

```
lblAmtdue.Caption = ""
```

Perform the following steps to write the cmdEnter_Click subroutine, which includes the use of a constant and text concatenation.

 To Use Constants and Concatenate Text

1 Select the cmdEnter control in the Object list box in the Code window.

The cmdEnter_Click subroutine displays in the Code window (Figure 2-90).

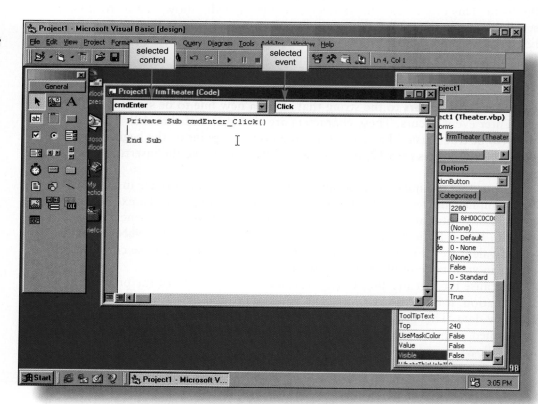

FIGURE 2-90

2 **Enter the following two statements in the Code window:**

```
'update transaction
  list and clear
  settings
txtRecord.Text =
  num & " " &
  cboShow.Text &
  vbNewLine &
  txtRecord.Text
```

As you type the code, the Code window scrolls. Pressing the ENTER key advances the insertion point to the beginning of the next line (Figure 2-91).

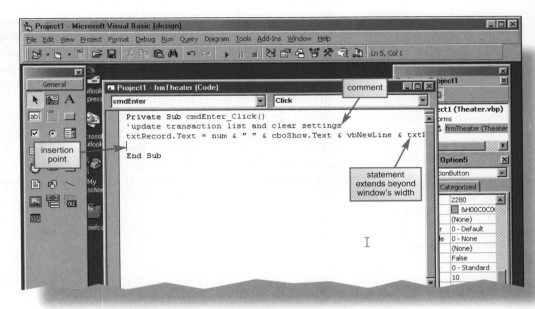

FIGURE 2-91

3 **Enter the following four statements in the Code window:**

```
cboShow.ListIndex =
  -1
chkMatinee.Value = 0
Option5.Value = True
lblAmtdue.Caption =
  ""
```

The Code window displays as shown in Figure 2-92.

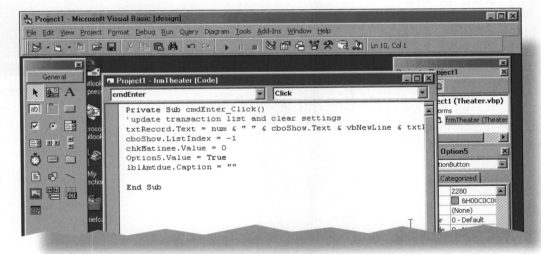

FIGURE 2-92

A code statement that sets a CheckBox control's Value property to 1 checks a check box. Setting the Value property to 0 removes the check mark. An option button is selected and deselected with code by setting its Value property to True or False, respectively. **True** is a Visual Basic constant for the value –1 and **False** is a constant for the value 0. Therefore, the code statement Check1.Value = False is acceptable, but the code statement Check1.Value = True will cause a run-time error.

Writing Code for the CommonDialog Control

When you demonstrate the Theater Box Office prototype, you want to show different color possibilities. You do not want to offer this feature to the user, however. For this reason, you have chosen a *hidden* way to access the Color dialog box by double-clicking the form itself.

More About

CommonDialog Controls

The CommonDialog control provides an interface between Visual Basic and the routines in the Microsoft Windows dynamic-link library Commdlg.dll. As such, a common dialog within your application automatically has Windows context-sensitive help. In order for your application to create a dialog box using this control during run time, Commdlg.dll must be in your Microsoft Windows SYSTEM directory.

A common dialog is displayed during run time by applying one of the **Show methods** to the CommonDialog control using code. To display the Color dialog box, you will apply the **ShowColor method**. For each of the dialog boxes available through the CommonDialog control, you can further define the dialog box's properties and behavior with different values of the **Flags property**. In this application you will use the default value of the Flags property.

When the user selects a color and clicks the OK button, the selected color is recorded as the Color property of the CommonDialog control. You must write code that then assigns that color as the **BackColor property** of the form and all controls, which do not have a BackStyle property equal to Transparent. Perform the following steps to write code for the CommonDialog control to display the Color dialog box.

 ### To Write CommonDialog Control Code

1 Select the Form control from the Object list box in the Code window, and then select the DblClick event from the Procedures list box.

The frmTheater_DblClick subroutine displays in the Code window (Figure 2-93).

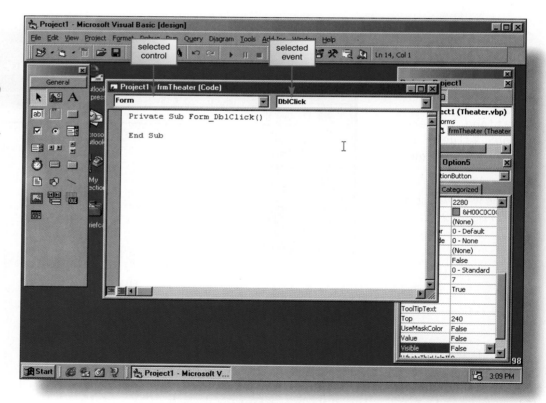

FIGURE 2-93

2 **Enter the following statements in the Code window:**

```
'display color dialog
   and set background
   color
CommonDialog1.ShowColor
frmTheater.BackColor =
   CommonDialog1.Color
cboShow.BackColor =
   CommonDialog1.Color
chkMatinee.BackColor =
   CommonDialog1.Color
Frame1.BackColor =
   CommonDialog1.Color
Option1.BackColor =
   CommonDialog1.Color
Option2.BackColor =
   CommonDialog1.Color
Option3.BackColor =
   CommonDialog1.Color
Option4.BackColor =
   CommonDialog1.Color
lblAmtdue.BackColor =
   CommonDialog1.Color
txtRecord.BackColor =
   CommonDialog1.Color
```

The Code window displays as shown in Figure 2-94.

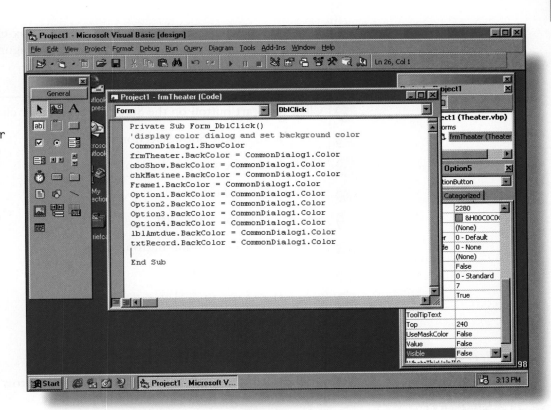

FIGURE 2-94

In the previous steps you wrote code to change the BackColor property of several of the controls on the Theater form. Unlike the Label control, these controls do not have a BackStyle property and, therefore, code must be written.

Saving and Running the Application

The Theater Box Office application now is complete. Before running the application, save the form and the project again.

TO SAVE THE PROJECT

1 Click the Save button on the Standard toolbar.

2 Click the Code window's Close button.

The previous versions of the .frm and .vbp files are replaced. If you wanted to save the form and project with different names, you would have to click Save As on the File menu.

Perform the following steps to run your Theater Box Office application. After Step 14, your application should display as shown in Figure 2-95.

TO RUN THE APPLICATION

1 Click the Start button on the Standard toolbar, or click Start on the Run menu.

2 Select Annie in the ShowSelection list.

3 Click the 2 tickets option button.

4 Click the Enter button.

5 Select Cats in the shows list.

6 Click the 3 tickets option button.

7 Click the Enter button.

8 Select The Music Man in the shows list.

9 Click the 3 tickets option button.

10 Click the Enter button.

11 Double-click the form. Click the pale blue color (row 1, column 5) and then click the OK button.

12 Select The Wiz in the shows list.

13 Click the Matinee Discount check box.

14 Click the 2 tickets option button.

15 To close (end) the application, click the End button on the Standard toolbar, or click the Theater Box Office form's Close button.

16 To close Visual Basic, click File on the menu bar and then click Exit or click the Close button on the Visual Basic menu bar and toolbar window.

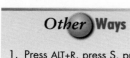

Other Ways

1. Press ALT+R, press S, press F10, press ALT+R, then press E

The application displays as shown in Figure 2-95.

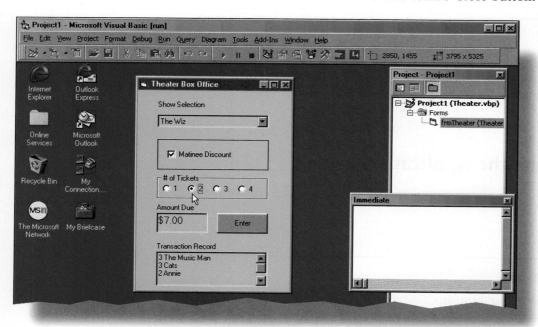

FIGURE 2-95

Project Summary

In this project, you used additional properties of the controls you learned about in Project 1, as well as several additional controls. You added an ActiveX control to the Toolbox and used it in an application. You learned more about writing code by writing six event subroutines and a declaration procedure. You learned how to copy controls and copy code between subroutines. You used variables and constants in code statements and used code statements to concatenate string data. You used an If...Then...Else structure within a procedure.

No single, correct interface exists for a given application, nor is one single method the correct way to write code. In building this application, you may have thought of different ways to design the interface. You may have realized the events and code could have been written in a number of ways. Experiment with other ways to design the interface and to create the events. Building applications in a graphical environment is an exciting, creative enterprise.

What You Should Know

Having completed this project, you now should be able to perform the following tasks:

▶ Add a CheckBox Control *(VB 2.16)*

▶ Add a ComboBox Control *(VB 2.13)*

▶ Add a CommonDialog Control *(VB 2.22)*

▶ Add a Frame Control *(VB 2.18)*

▶ Add a Label Control and Set its AutoSize and BackStyle Properties *(VB 2.8)*

▶ Add Label, CommandButton, and TextBox Controls *(VB 2.21)*

▶ Add a Shape Control *(VB 2.15)*

▶ Align Controls *(VB 2.24)*

▶ Build an OptionButton Group *(VB 2.19)*

▶ Copy Code Between Procedures *(VB 2.48)*

▶ Copy Controls *(VB 2.10)*

▶ Explicitly Declare Variables *(VB 2.44)*

▶ Name Controls *(VB 2.27)*

▶ Run the Application *(VB 2.56)*

▶ Save the Form *(VB 2.42)*

▶ Save the Project *(VB 2.55)*

▶ Set BorderStyle and FontSize Properties *(VB 2.38)*

▶ Set Caption and Text Properties *(VB 2.30)*

▶ Set the ComboBox Control's Style and List Properties *(VB 2.32)*

▶ Set the Locked, MultiLine, and ScrollBars Properties *(VB 2.36)*

▶ Set the Size and Location of a Form *(VB 2.7)*

▶ Set the Visible Property *(VB 2.41)*

▶ Use Constants and Concatenate Text *(VB 2.52)*

▶ Write an If...Then...Else Statement and Mathematical Expression *(VB 2.47)*

▶ Write CommonDialog Control Code *(VB 2.54)*

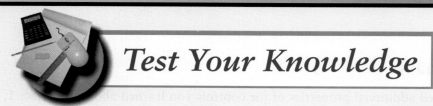

Test Your Knowledge

1 True/False

Instructions: Circle T if the statement is true or F is the statement is false.

T F 1. Projects generally are built using a three-step process of creating the interface, setting properties, and writing code.

T F 2. It is not possible to copy an existing control and paste the copy somewhere else on the form.

T F 3. The Shape control can be used only to add ovals or circles to a form.

T F 4. Frame controls are not the same as Shape controls.

T F 5. Within the same grouping, more than one option button can be selected at the same time.

T F 6. Within the same grouping, more than one check box can be checked at the same time.

T F 7. The Name property of a control must have the same value as the Caption property of that control.

T F 8. The type of ComboBox control that displays is determined by its Style property.

T F 9. To make a variable global, it must be declared as Public in the General declarations procedure of a module.

T F 10. When the MultiLine property of the TextBox control is set to True, a ScrollBars control is added automatically to the TextBox control.

2 Multiple Choice

Instructions: Circle the correct response.

1. The _____ property set to True will make a label the size of its caption automatically.
   a. Stretch/Shrink
   b. AutoSize
   c. Min/Max
   d. AutoFit

2. When creating several similar controls, it would not be advantageous to set the _____ property before copying and pasting the controls.
   a. AutoSize
   b. Caption
   c. Appearance
   d. BorderStyle

3. Use a _____ control when the application should have a drop-down list that items must be selected from.
   a. ComboBox (Style = 2)
   b. ListBox
   c. ComboBox (Style = 1)
   d. ComboBox (Style = 0)

Test Your Knowledge

4. The _____ control is used to indicate selection or deselection of one or more individual items at the same time.
   a. CheckBox
   b. ListBox
   c. TextBox
   d. ComboBox

5. A Frame control is used as a _____ for other controls.
   a. container
   b. decoration
   c. shape
   d. border

6. The suggested three-letter prefix for a control name designates the _____ of a control.
   a. order
   b. property
   c. caption
   d. type

7. The _____ property of a TextBox control allows for more than one line of text to be placed in the box.
   a. WordWrap
   b. MoreLines
   c. MultiLine
   d. TextWrap

8. With the Default property of a CommandButton control set to True, the _____ key can be pressed to execute the CommandButton control's code statements.
   a. ENTER
   b. ALT
   c. END
   d. CTRL

9. The syntax of a code statement that changes the properties of a control at run time is in the form of
   _____.
   a. property.value = controlname
   b. value.controlname = property
   c. controlname.property = value
   d. value.property = controlname

10. Code statements to be carried out at run time when the form is moved into memory should be placed in the
    _____.
    a. Option Click subroutine
    b. General object declarations procedure
    c. Command Click subroutine
    d. Form_Load event

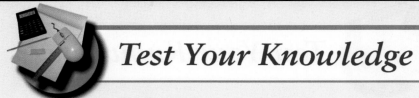

Test Your Knowledge

3 Understanding Code Statements

Instructions: Carefully read each of the following descriptions. Write code statements to accomplish specific tasks. Record your answers on a separate sheet of paper. Number your answers to correspond to the code descriptions.

1. Write a code statement that will display the characters Salutations in a Label control with a name of lblGreeting.
2. Write a code statement that will clear a TextBox control with the name of txtBlank.
3. Write a code statement that will create a variable called total to be used in multiple subroutines. The variable should have a data type of Short.
4. Write a code statement that will add Saturday to a drop-down list box with a name of cboDays.
5. Write a code statement that concatenates the contents of two TextBox controls named txtWord1 and txtWord2 to be displayed in a Label control with a name of lblFinal.
6. If a CheckBox control with a name of chkGreeting is checked, write a code statement that displays Salutations in a Label control with a name of lblGreeting otherwise it displays Farewell in the same Label control.

4 Understanding Mathematical Operators in Visual Basic

Instructions: The following variables, controls, and their values are to be used to determine the answers for the code statements. Each code statement is separate from the others. Write your responses on a separate sheet of paper in the same order as the questions display.

txtRate.Text = 30
hours = 40
deduction = 100
chkDeduction.Value = 1
cmdCalculate
lblPay

1. If chkDeduction.Value = 1 Then lblPay.Caption = hours * txtRate.Text
   lblPay.Caption: _____
2. If hours > 40 Then txtRate.Text = txtRate.Text * 1.5
   txtRate.Text: _____
3. deduction = txtRate.Text * hours / 24
   deduction: _____
4. cmdCalculate.Default = True
   txtRate.Caption: _____
5. If chkDeduction.Value = 1 Then deduction = txtRate.Text * hours / 6 Else deduction = txtRate.Text * hours / 20
   deduction: _____

Use Help

1 Reviewing Project Activities

Instructions: Perform the following tasks using a computer.

1. Start Visual Basic.
2. Click Help on the menu bar and then click Index. The MSDN Library Viewer for Visual Studio 6.0 will display with the Index tab selected. If necessary, select Visual Basic Documentation as the Active Subset on the drop-down list box.
3. Click the text box for entering keywords to find and type `default property`. Double-click Default property highlighted in the list box. Read and print the information.
4. Click the Applies To link and then double-click the topic CommandButton Control. Read and print the information that displays. Hand in the printouts to your instructor.
5. Highlight the contents of the text box and type `math operators`. Click the Display button. Double-click operator precedence in the Topics Found dialog box. Read and print the information. Click each of the underlined links and print each definition that displays by right-clicking the screen and clicking Print on the shortcut menu. Return to the previous page by clicking the Back button on the toolbar. Click the See Also link and then double-click operator summary in the Topics Found dialog box. Click Arithmetic Operators and, one by one, click each operator. As you click each operator, read and print the information. Hand in the printouts to your instructor.

2 Expanding on the Basics

Instructions: Use the MSDN Library to understand the topics and answer the questions listed below. Answer the questions on your own paper to hand in to your instructor.

1. Click Help on the menu bar and then click Contents. The MSDN Library Viewer for Visual Studio 6.0 will display with the Contents tab selected. If necessary, select Visual Basic Documentation as the Active Subset on the drop-down list box.
2. In the Navigation area under this tab, double-click MSDN Library Visual Studio 6.0 to open the books. Double-click the Visual Basic Documentation book. Click the Visual Basic Start Page. Click the Programmer's Guide underlined link. Click the Visual Basic Basics underlined link. Click the Locate button. Double-click the Visual Basic Specifications, Limitations, and File Formats book in the navigation area. Read the information in the topic area.
3. Double-click the Project Limitations book in the navigation area. Read the information in the topic area and answer the following questions.
   a. What are at least three project identifiers?
   b. How long can a variable name be?
   c. How long can a form, control, module, or class name be?
4. One by one, click Control Limitations, Code Limitations, Data Limitations, and System Resource Limitations in the navigation area. As you click each one, read the information that displays in the topic area and answer the following questions.
   a. What can be done to reduce consumption of system resources?
   b. How many control names can be used per form?

(continued)

Use Help

Expanding on the Basics *(continued)*

c. What are at least three other controls, their properties, and their limitations?
d. How long can control property names be?
e. What is the code line limit?
f. What is the limit to the number of bytes per line of code?
g. What is the limit to the number of blank spaces acceptable before text on a line of code?
h. What is the limit to the number of continuation characters per logical line of code?

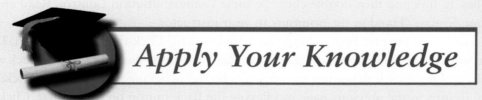

Apply Your Knowledge

1 Selecting Options Using Multiple OptionButton Control Groups

Instructions: Start Visual Basic. Open the project, Shape Change Properties, from the Student Data Disk. This application incorporates multiple OptionButton control groups. One OptionButton control group is used to set the Shape property of the Shape control. The OptionButton group you will add is used to set the BorderStyle property of the Shape control. Perform the following tasks to complete this application as shown in Figure 2-96.

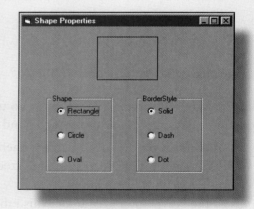

FIGURE 2-96

1. Size and position the form as shown.
2. Add a second Frame control to the right of the existing Frame control. Within the new Frame control, add 3 OptionButton controls. Remember that an OptionButton control is only part of a group if individually placed within a Frame control.
3. Set appropriate Name and Caption properties for each of the new controls. The Frame you have just added contains the option buttons to make the Shape control border style solid, dashed, or dotted.
4. Open the Code window by double-clicking the first new OptionButton control. Type code similar to `shpNewShape.BorderStyle = 1` where a border style of 1 is solid. Add a comment to explain what the code is accomplishing.
5. One by one, select the second and third new OptionButton controls from the Object list box in the Code window. Type code similar to `shpNewShape.BorderStyle = 1` replacing the 1 with a 2 for a dashed border style for the second new OptionButton control and then a 3 for a dotted border style for the third new OptionButton control. Add comments to explain the code statements.
6. Save the form and the project using the file name, Shape Properties.
7. If necessary, run the application and correct any errors. If changes have been made, save the form and project again using the same file names.
8. Print the Form Image, Code, and Form As Text for the Current Module.

In the Lab

1 Changing Properties at Run Time with CheckBox Controls

Problem: You have decided to build an application to assist the math students whom you tutor. The application should provide the capability of allowing the students to enter two numbers. They also should be able to select whether to add, subtract, multiply, or divide the two numbers or any combination of these operations. The results of each operation should display after they have been calculated. The application should look similar to the one shown in Figure 2-97.

Instructions: Perform the following tasks.

1. Open a new project in Visual Basic.
2. Add to the form two TextBox controls for typing in numbers, four CheckBox controls to select whether to add, subtract, multiply, or divide, four Label controls to display the results of the math operations, and one CommandButton control to perform the calculations.
3. Name the form and each of the controls appropriately.
4. Set the Caption property of each of the controls that require it.
5. Write the CommandButton control code to execute each of the choices indicated by the four CheckBox controls according to the following sample:

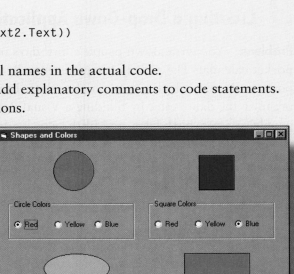

FIGURE 2-97

```
If chkCheckBox1.Value = 1 Then
lblLabel1.Caption = (Val(txtText1.Text) + Val(txtText2.Text))
End If
```

Replace the default control names by the appropriate control names in the actual code.
Add comments to explain what the code is accomplishing. Add explanatory comments to code statements.

6. Save the form and project using the file name, Math Operations.
7. Run the application and correct any errors. If any changes have been made, save the form and project again using the same file names.
8. Print the Form Image, Code, and Form As Text for the Current Module.

2 Changing Properties at Run Time with OptionButton Controls

Problem: As a daycare assistant, you have been asked to develop an application to help children learn both shapes and colors. The finished application is shown in Figure 2-98.

Instructions: Perform the following tasks.

1. Open a new project in Visual Basic.
2. Add one of each circle, square, oval, and rectangle Shape controls to the form.

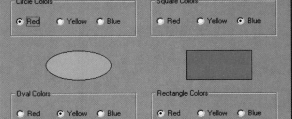

FIGURE 2-98

(continued)

In the Lab

Changing Properties at Run Time with OptionButton Controls *(continued)*

3. Add one Frame control to correspond to each one of the Shape controls. The Frame controls should be large enough to contain three OptionButton controls each.
4. Add three OptionButton controls to each of the Frame controls.
5. Give the form and all of the controls appropriate names. As you name the controls, keep in mind that each one of the Frame controls contains the OptionButton controls to change the color of one of the Shape controls.
6. Set the Caption property of each of the controls that require it. Set the FillStyle property of each of the Shape controls to 0 - Solid.
7. Write the code for the first OptionButton control in the first Frame control. Sample code is shpShape1. FillColor = VBRed where shpShape1 will be replaced with the actual name given to each of the Shape controls. Constant color values to use for the three OptionButton controls are VBRed, VBYellow, and VBBlue. The code will be similar for each of the three OptionButton controls in each Frame control. Add comments to explain what the code is accomplishing.
8. Save the form and the project using the file name, Shapes and Colors.
9. Run the application and correct any errors. Remember to resave the form and the project if any changes have been made.
10. Print the Form Image, Code, and Form As Text for the Current Module.

3 Creating a Drop-Down Application

Problem: You write down people's birthdays on various scraps of paper, on various notepads, and in your pocket calendar. The pieces of paper eventually tend to get lost or misplaced and you do not always carry your pocket calendar, which has incomplete data. Because of this, you miss everyone's birthdays and have decided to organize the data better by building a Visual Basic application. The new application will permit you to view people's names, birthdates, and birth signs by dropping down a list. You further determine that the application should have the capability of adding new data to the existing list.

Instructions: Perform the following tasks to build the application as displayed in Figure 2-99.

1. Start a new project in Visual Basic.
2. Add a ComboBox control (as a drop-down list box), a TextBox control, and a CommandButton control to the form.
3. Name the form and each of the controls appropriately.
4. Write the code to add names, birth dates, and birth signs to the drop-down list. Add a comment to explain what the code is accomplishing. (*Hint*: Review the AddItem method in Help.)
5. Save the form and the project using the file name, Birthday List.
6. Run the application and add the data for several people to the drop-down list.
7. If any errors are encountered, correct them, resave the form and project using the same file names.
8. Print the Form Image, Code, and Form As Text for the Current Module.

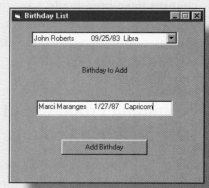

FIGURE 2-99

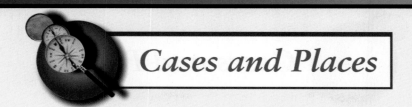

Cases and Places

The difficulty of these case studies varies:
▶ are the least difficult; ▶▶ are more difficult; and ▶▶▶ are the most difficult.

1 ▶ Lions, Tigers, and Bears is a progressive pet clinic with personal computers in each examination room. You have been hired to develop an application for the veterinary assistants to record patient temperatures. The assistants want an easy to use application that will display the temperature for the veterinarian. After some discussion, it is determined that they would like to record the patient's temperature by selecting option buttons. The temperature will be represented by a rectangular Shape control that will increase in width and change color. A far below normal temperature will be a short, VBCyan rectangle. A slightly below normal temperature will be the original rectangle width * 2.5 and VBBlue. A normal temperature will be the original rectangle width * 3.5 and VBMagenta. A slightly above normal temperature will be the original rectangle width * 4.5 and VBYellow. A far above normal temperature will be the original rectangle width * 5.5 and VBRed. As a button is selected, the corresponding visual representation of the selection will display. The code for each OptionButton control must set the width of the shape and the color of the shape. The colors used are Visual Basic color constants. Use the concepts and techniques presented in this project to create the application.

2 ▶ Lions, Tigers, and Bears pet clinic is impressed with your previous work for them and have hired you for another small project. The veterinary assistants would like an application that displays basic services. The application should be designed with check boxes to select the various services such as office calls, vaccinations, grooming, hospitalization, heartworm preventive, boarding, dentistry, x-rays, laboratory work, and prescriptions. As each service is selected the charge for the service should display. After all selections have been made, the charges should be added together to arrive at a total amount due and displayed when a CommandButton control is clicked. If the patient's owner thinks the total is too high, a way to clear the CheckBox controls, the corresponding service charges, and the total amount to begin selecting again should be available. Use the concepts and techniques presented in this project to create the application.

3 ▶▶ During tax season, you work for Tax Prep, Inc. Each tax season, several clients pay for their tax preparation with invalid checks. During the past few tax seasons, you have observed that these invalid checks are received from the same clients each tax season. Currently, a handwritten list of these clients is distributed to the tax preparers. These lists frequently are misplaced or accidentally destroyed. You have shared your observation with the manager who has decided you should build a Visual Basic application for the tax preparers. The application should have a drop-down list of these clients including their Social Security numbers as further identification. A text box and an associated command button should be included so additions can be made to the list when new clients pay with invalid checks. Add at least seven clients to the list. Use the concepts and techniques presented in this project to create the application.

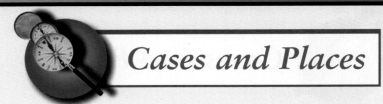

Cases and Places

4 ▶▶ The county government computing center where you work has given you a new assignment. The file clerks in the recorder's office frequently encounter problems filing records alphabetically. They would like an application that will allow them to enter two different names and compare them to each other. You have decided command buttons with corresponding code can be used to determine if the two names are equal to each other, one name is less than the other, or one name is greater than the other. Appropriate messages also should display on the form to indicate the result of the comparison and whether it is True or False. *Hint:* This application would be comparing two strings to each other. Visual Basic has a string compare (StrComp) that can be researched using the Index tab in Help.

5 ▶▶▶ Your city library has hired you on a consulting basis to provide them with an application for overdue charges. The charges apply to overdue books, records, tapes, CDs, and video tapes. The books can be one of two types; either hardbound or paperback. The librarians want an easy way to select the overdue items keeping in mind that a borrower could be returning multiple overdue items of the same type or of different types. Some method of selecting the number of overdue items up to a maximum of five for each item selected should be included. The charges for each category then should be multiplied by the number of overdue items and the amount due should be displayed for each category. The total amount due should be displayed on the form as well. *Hint:* The total amount due is a running total that will require a looping construct. Look in Help for assistance with looping.

6 ▶▶▶ As an intern for Klassic Kar Insurance, you have received a request to develop an application. The application you will build is to assist the insurance agents in quickly calculating the cost of auto coverage. The application should have a drop-down list to select various coverage types. The coverage types can be obtained from insurance companies along with sample costs. Include a check box to indicate if the insurance client is deserving of a multi-vehicle discount. The costs of coverage also will depend on what category of vehicle is to be covered. It is suggested that the vehicle categories be represented with option buttons. The categories can be obtained from an insurance company. Selections are made from the drop-down list, the check box, and option buttons. After all selections have been made, a total amount due should be calculated and displayed. If the client should change his or her mind, there should be a provision for clearing the selections and amount due to start over.

7 ▶▶▶ You received a generous sum of money in U.S. dollars from the Caribou Club to attend school in Europe. You have decided to develop an application to keep track of what you have spent. This application should be built to accept U.S. dollars, convert them to various currencies, and add each amount spent to a drop-down list. The U.S. dollars spent should be added to a running total and displayed on the form as each foreign currency amount is added to the drop-down list. Current currency conversion rates can be obtained from financial newspapers or via the Internet.

Microsoft **Visual Basic 6**

PROJECT

3

Microsoft Visual Basic 6

Multiple Forms, Dialogs, Debugging, and EXEs

OBJECTIVES

You will have mastered the material in this project when you can:

- Add additional forms to a project
- Specify a Startup form
- Specify a form's Startup location
- Set a form's BorderStyle property
- Specify an icon for an application
- Use an Image control in an application
- Use ScrollBar controls in an application
- Use Line controls in an application
- Build an About... dialog box
- Create application dialog boxes with the MsgBox function
- Work with multiple form Code windows
- Use the IsNumeric function in code
- Use the If...Then...Else block code structure
- Use the Show, Unload, and SetFocus methods in code
- Write code using financial functions
- Write procedures for the Change, Scroll, and Load events
- Use line continuations in code
- Use Visual Basic's Debug features
- Make an application executable

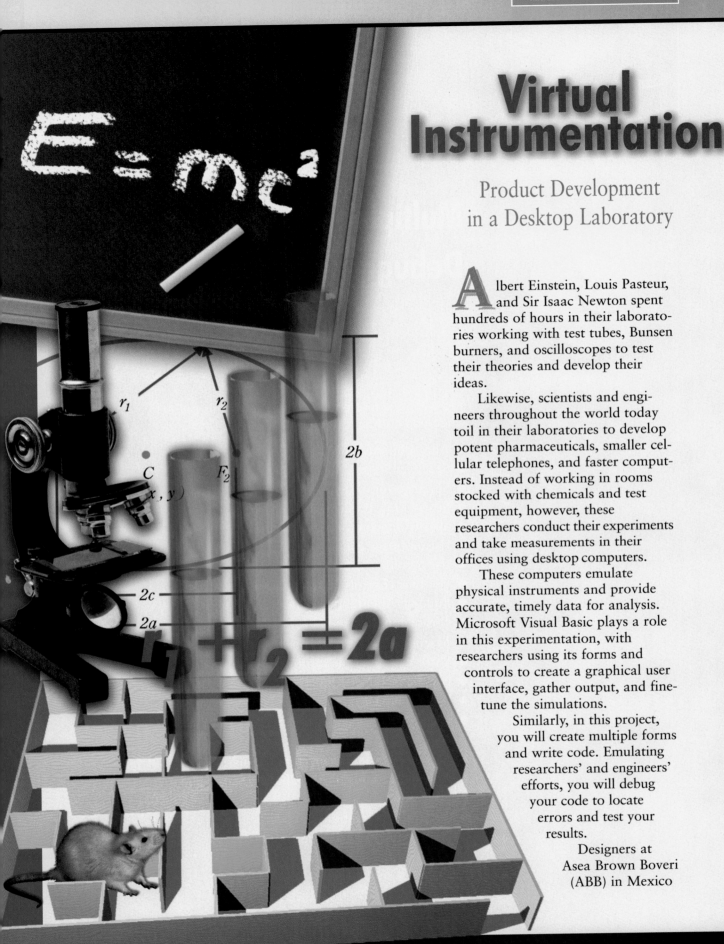

Virtual Instrumentation

Product Development in a Desktop Laboratory

Albert Einstein, Louis Pasteur, and Sir Isaac Newton spent hundreds of hours in their laboratories working with test tubes, Bunsen burners, and oscilloscopes to test their theories and develop their ideas.

Likewise, scientists and engineers throughout the world today toil in their laboratories to develop potent pharmaceuticals, smaller cellular telephones, and faster computers. Instead of working in rooms stocked with chemicals and test equipment, however, these researchers conduct their experiments and take measurements in their offices using desktop computers.

These computers emulate physical instruments and provide accurate, timely data for analysis. Microsoft Visual Basic plays a role in this experimentation, with researchers using its forms and controls to create a graphical user interface, gather output, and fine-tune the simulations.

Similarly, in this project, you will create multiple forms and write code. Emulating researchers' and engineers' efforts, you will debug your code to locate errors and test your results.

Designers at Asea Brown Boveri (ABB) in Mexico

```
Private Sub Form_Load()
'create captions for labels
Label1.Caption =
        U Natio      Loan A        & vbNewLine &
        ating            " & v
        igh          Nat        orp."
        tion
        eloped        Nation     & vbNewLine &
      "By Sarah Carter"
Label3.Caption = _
      "Warning: This computer program is protected by" & vbNewLine &
      "copyright law and international treaties."
End Sub
```

use a Visual Basic application to provide quotes for clients in less than 30 minutes, a process that formerly took several days to complete without the program. ABB, a $35 billion engineering corporation with offices throughout the world, specializes in environmental applications related to clean, reliable electric-power generation, transmission, and distribution. Its Mexico City campus develops and manufactures industrial electrical panels.

When potential customers contact ABB, the designers ask a series of questions regarding electrical specifications and budget constraints. Then, they execute the Visual Basic program and work with controls prompting for parameters such as the number of circuit breakers, electrical configurations, and type of electrical panel. This data is used in several algorithms to generate a graphical representation of the proposed panel, a list of materials, and a cash-flow analysis.

Five programmers developed this Visual Basic application in eight weeks, but three of the weeks were spent debugging one piece of code in an algorithm that distributes circuit breakers.

You have used Visual Basic's Toolbox to add a variety of controls to your forms. Researchers using this software, however, often need additional tools to meet their specialized requirements in their desktop laboratories. For example, they may use digital knobs to turn equipment on and off, analog knobs to set a precise value, and thermometers to indicate temperature variations.

National Instruments, a third-party vendor who supplies supplementary controls for scientific and engineering applications, is predominant in computer and instrumentation technology, promoting international technological standards. One of its products, ComponentWorks, adds tools to the Visual Basic Toolbox. With this virtual instrumentation, users can reduce the time needed to manufacture their end products and can improve quality. Augmenting Visual Basic with ComponentWorks, they can create a user interface that mimics the front panel of test equipment and gathers test data. This output can be loaded into spreadsheets or databases and used to generate statistics and monitor production-line tolerances.

Visual Basic applications abound in a variety of locations today — from the business office to the virtual laboratory. But no matter where the venue, the software helps create useful, powerful products in record time.

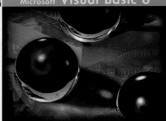

Microsoft Visual Basic 6

Multiple Forms, Dialogs, Debugging, and EXEs

PROJECT

3

C A S E   P E R S P E C T I V E

Often when considering a large purchase, the first question many people ask is, "How much will the monthly payment be?" This is because many purchases, such as a home or a car, are paid by obtaining a loan for the purchase amount. The loan then is repaid by making regular monthly payments over a period of time. The sum of payments is typically more than the loan amount because of the amount of interest paid for the loan. The monthly payment is a function of the loan amount, called the principal; the interest rate, usually expressed as an annual percentage rate (APR); and the number of payments to be made (such as 60 payments for a five-year loan).

SavU National Bank wants a small utility application to calculate quickly a payment amount and sum of payments for potential loan applicants. This would allow bank personnel to respond quickly to customer inquiries regarding loans for various periods in years and at varying interest rates. You have been assigned to build a prototype of a Loan Analyzer for the bank.

Introduction

The applications built in Project 1 and Project 2 consisted of several controls and one form. In this project, you will build an application with additional controls and multiple forms. You also will use Visual Basic's library of built-in financial functions and create dialog boxes within the application. **Dialog boxes** are common in Windows applications and are used during run time to give information about the application to the user or to prompt the user to supply information to the application.

No matter how carefully you build a project, applications often do not work as planned and give erroneous results because of errors in the code. In this project, you will work with the Debug window and some of its features for finding errors in code. The applications you built in Project 1 and Project 2 could not be run outside of the Visual Basic system. In this project, you will make an EXE file that allows your application to run without the Visual Basic development system.

Project Three – SavU Loan Analyzer

The completed SavU Loan Analyzer application is shown in Figure 3-1. The loan amount is entered into a TextBox control from the keyboard. The number of years and the APR are entered by using ScrollBar controls. As you click the scroll arrows, the value supplied to the loan calculation changes and displays on the form. You can change the value more quickly by dragging the scroll box or by pointing to one of the scroll arrows and then pressing and holding the mouse button.

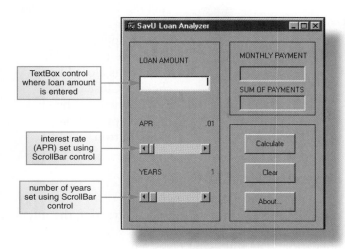

FIGURE 3-1

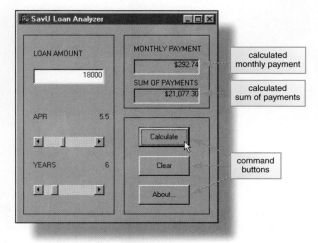

FIGURE 3-2

The SavU Loan Analyzer window contains three command buttons labeled Calculate, Clear, and About... . When you click the **Calculate button** or press the ENTER key, the function is computed, and the monthly payment and the total amount to be repaid are displayed on the form (Figure 3-2). If the amount of the loan entered from the keyboard is not a valid numerical amount, the dialog box shown in Figure 3-3 displays to alert you to this input error. Clicking the OK button closes the dialog box and clears the text box so a new loan amount can be entered.

Clicking the **Clear button** in the SavU Loan Analyzer window erases the loan amount, monthly payment, and sum of payments and returns the scroll bars to their lowest values. Clicking the **About... button** in the SavU Loan Analyzer window displays the dialog box shown in Figure 3-4. Clicking the OK button in the About... dialog box closes the dialog box.

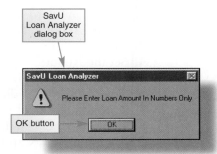

FIGURE 3-3

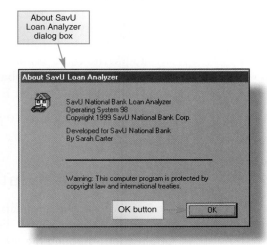

FIGURE 3-4

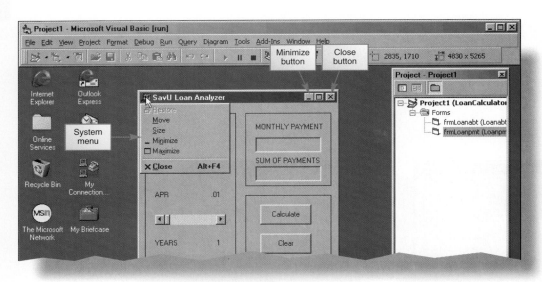

The SavU Loan Analyzer window has a System menu (Figure 3-5) that is opened by clicking the System menu (Control-box) icon. The application can be minimized on the desktop by clicking Minimize on the System menu or by clicking the application's Minimize button. The window is closed by clicking Close on the System menu or by clicking the application's Close button.

FIGURE 3-5

Project Steps

Applications are built with Visual Basic in a three-step process: creating the interface, setting properties, and writing code. You will follow this three-step process to build the SavU Loan Analyzer application. The following tasks will be completed in this project.

1. Start a Standard EXE project in Visual Basic.
2. Set the About… dialog box form's size and position.
3. Add Label, Image, Line, and CommandButton controls.
4. Set the About… dialog box form's border style.
5. Set control's Name, Caption, Font, and Picture properties.
6. Save the About… dialog box form.
7. Add an additional form to the project.
8. Add Shape, Label, TextBox, CommandButton, and ScrollBar controls.
9. Set Alignment, Caption, Text, and Name properties.
10. Set the properties of a ScrollBar control.
11. Set a form's Icon property.
12. Save the second form.
13. Specify a Startup form.
14. Write the ScrollBar Change and Scroll event procedures.
15. Write the CommandButton Click event procedures.
16. Save, run, and debug the project.
17. Make and run an EXE file for the application.

The following pages contain a detailed explanation of each of these steps.

Creating the Interface

You will create the application's interface (adding controls and setting properties) one form at a time. After the interface is completed, you will write the code for the application. **Creating the interface** consists of sizing and locating the form and then adding each of the controls to the form and adjusting their sizes and positions. Before you begin creating the interface, however, you need to start Visual Basic and arrange the Visual Basic windows on the desktop.

The Visual Basic Desktop

Begin this project by starting Visual Basic as described on page VB 1.7 in Project 1 or by opening a new Standard EXE project if you already are running Visual Basic. If necessary, you should complete the steps on page VB 1.10 in Project 1 to arrange your desktop to resemble Figure 3-6.

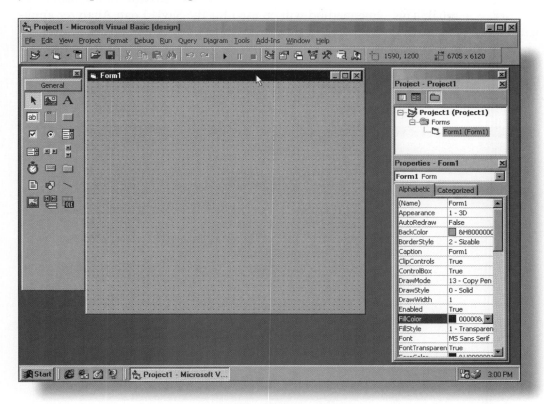

FIGURE 3-6

More About

Dialog Boxes

Dialog boxes are used in Windows-based applications to prompt the user for data needed by the application or to display information to the user. Standard dialog boxes, such as Print and File Open, can be created using the CommonDialog control. Predefined dialog boxes can be created using the MsgBox or InputBox functions. Customized dialog boxes can be created using a standard form.

The About... Dialog Box Form and Its Controls

The About... dialog box shown in Figure 3-4 is created as a form within the project. The **About... dialog box** is common in Windows applications and is used to provide information about the application such as its version number, copyright date, and authors' names. To build the About... dialog box, you will perform the following tasks.

1. Set the size of the form.
2. Add the controls.
3. Set the properties of the form and its controls.
4. Save the form as a file on a floppy disk.

Setting the Size and Position of the Form

In Project 1 and Project 2, the form's size was set by dragging the form's borders. The values of the form's Height property and Width property changed as the borders were dragged to new locations. In the steps on the next page, the size of the About... dialog box form will be changed by directly changing the values of the Height and Width properties in the Properties window. You can change a form's size during run time by writing code statements that, when executed, change the values of the form's Height and Width properties.

More About

StartUpPosition

You can set the StartUpPosition property in the Properties window or in code statements. The StartUpPosition property is an integer that specifies the position of the object as: 0 - Manual: no initial setting specified; 1 - CenterOwner: center on the item to which the form belongs; 2 - Center-Screen: center on the whole screen; or 3 - Windows Default: position in the upper-left corner of the screen.

The form's Top and Left properties determine the position of the upper-left corner of the form on the desktop. The form's location can be changed at run time by using code statements that change the values of the form's Top and Left properties. The form's **StartUpPosition** property determines where a form first displays on the desktop at run time. In Project 1 and Project 2, the form's first position at run time was the same as its position during design time because its StartUpPosition property was set to manual. This same method will be used for the SavU Loan Analyzer application. Perform the following steps to set the size of the About... dialog box form.

 To Set the Size of a Form Using the Properties Window

1 **Click the Properties window.**

The Properties window becomes the active window (Figure 3-7).

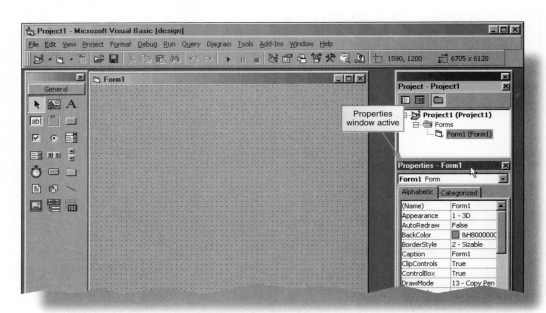

FIGURE 3-7

2 **Scroll through the Properties list and then double-click the Height property. Type** 3960 **and then press the ENTER key.**

The form's bottom border moves to match the value entered in the properties value box (Figure 3-8).

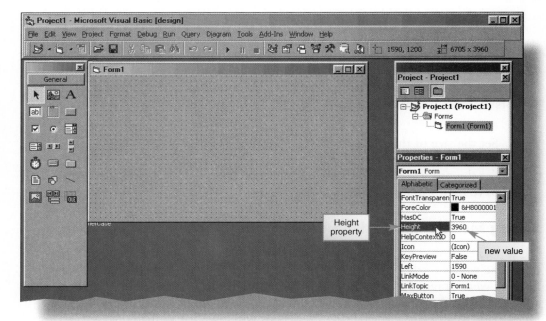

FIGURE 3-8

3 **Scroll through the Properties list and then double-click the Width property. Type** 5550 **and then press the ENTER key.**

The form's right border moves to match the value entered in the properties value box (Figure 3-9).

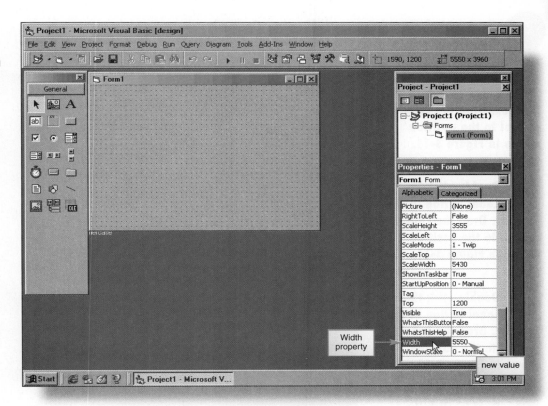

FIGURE 3-9

Because the Top and Left properties were not changed, setting values of the form's Height and Width properties caused only the form's bottom and right borders to move. The form's current location is acceptable for both design time and run time.

Adding the CommandButton and Label Controls

The About... dialog box form contains three Label controls and one Command-Button control, as shown in Figure 3-10. Perform the steps on the next page to add the labels and command button to the About... dialog box form.

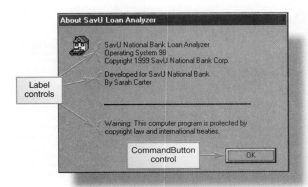

FIGURE 3-10

To Add Label and CommandButton Controls

1 Double-click the Label button in the Toolbox. Drag the Label1 control to the position shown in Figure 3-11.

2 Double-click the Label button in the Toolbox. Drag the Label2 control to the position shown in Figure 3-11.

3 Double-click the Label button in the Toolbox. Drag the Label3 control to the position shown in Figure 3-11.

4 Double-click the CommandButton button in the Toolbox. Drag the Command1 control to the position shown in Figure 3-11.

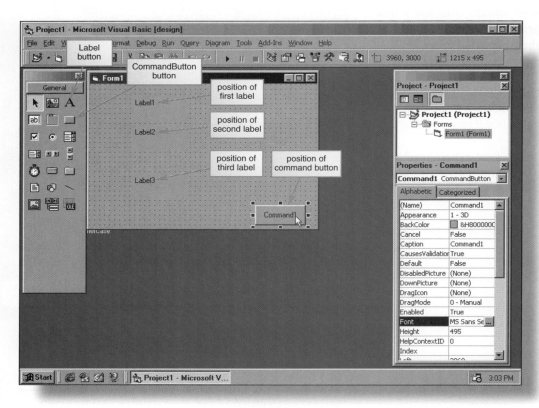

FIGURE 3-11

5 Drag the command button bottom border up one grid mark to reduce its height.

The command button displays on the form with its new height (Figure 3-12).

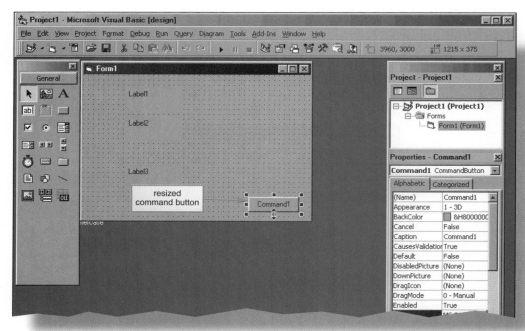

FIGURE 3-12

The Image Control

An **Image control** can be used as a container for graphical images, such as icons or bitmapped graphics files. The Image control acts like a command button, so it often is used to create custom buttons such as those found in Standard toolbars. An Image control is used to add the SavU Loan Analyzer application's icon to the About... dialog box form (Figure 3-13). Perform the following steps to add an Image control to the About... dialog box form.

FIGURE 3-13

 To Add an Image Control

1 **Double-click the Image button in the Toolbox.**

An Image control, Image1, is added to the center of the form (Figure 3-14).

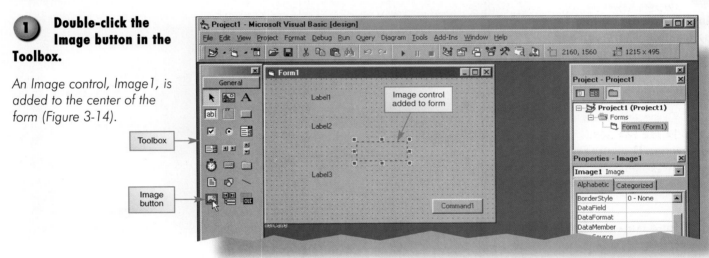

FIGURE 3-14

2 **Drag the Image control to the location shown in Figure 3-15.**

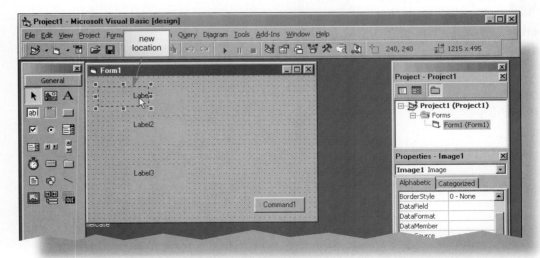

FIGURE 3-15

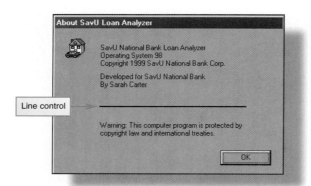

FIGURE 3-16

The Line Control

The **Line control** is used to add straight lines between pairs of points on a form. The About... dialog box form contains a Line control to separate the information on the form visually into two areas (Figure 3-16). Perform the following steps to add a Line control to the About... dialog box form.

 Steps **To Add a Line Control**

1 **Click the Line button in the Toolbox.** **Move the mouse pointer to the location where one end of the line is to display.**

The mouse pointer changes to a cross hair (Figure 3-17).

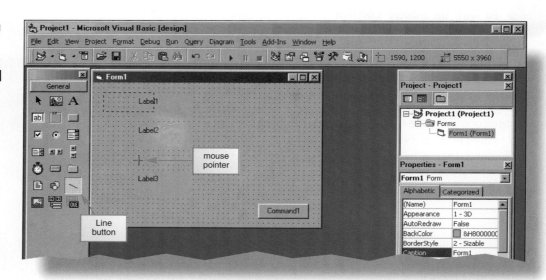

FIGURE 3-17

2 **Drag to the location where you want the other end of the line to display.**

A gray outline of the line displays as you drag the mouse pointer (Figure 3-18).

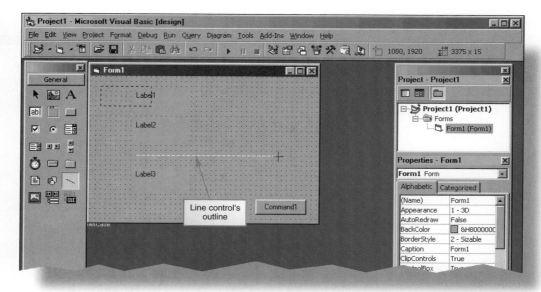

FIGURE 3-18

Release the mouse button.

A solid line replaces the gray outline (Figure 3-19).

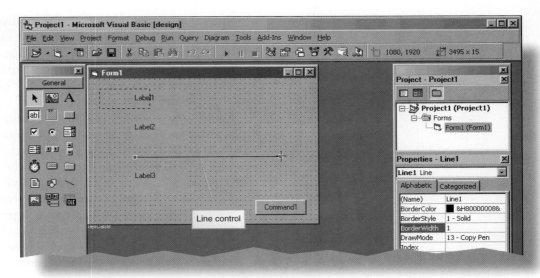

FIGURE 3-19

You can lengthen, shorten, or reposition Line controls by dragging one end at a time to the new position desired.

Setting Properties for the About... Dialog Box Form and Its Controls

The next step is to **set the properties** for the About... dialog box form and its controls. In addition to setting the Name and Caption properties presented in previous projects, the following properties will be set.

- WindowState property of forms
- BorderStyle property of forms
- Font properties of controls
- Picture property of Image controls
- BorderWidth property of Line controls

The WindowState Property of Forms

The **WindowState property** is a property of a form that corresponds with the window's size on the desktop during run time. The WindowState property takes one of three values, as listed in Table 3-1.

Form Location and Size

The Left, Top, Height, and Width properties cannot be changed on a minimized or maximized form.

Table 3-1	
VALUE	WINDOW'S SIZE
0 - Normal	Window is open on the desktop
1 - Minimized	Window is reduced to a button on the taskbar
2 - Maximized	Window is enlarged to its maximum size

Microsoft **Visual Basic 6**

no System
menu icon

no Minimize,
Maximize, or
Close buttons

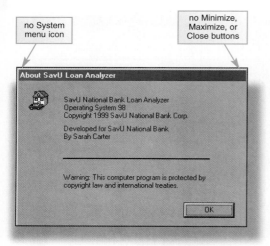

About SavU Loan Analyzer

SavU National Bank Loan Analyzer
Operating System 98
Copyright 1999 SavU National Bank Corp.

Developed for SavU National Bank
By Sarah Carter

Warning: This computer program is protected by
copyright law and international treaties.

OK

FIGURE 3-20

When the About... dialog box form displays on the desktop at run time, it has a WindowState property value of 0 - Normal (Figure 3-20). If you look closely, you will see that its WindowState property cannot be changed because it does not have a Minimize, Maximize, or Close button in the upper-right corner of the window. Also, the System menu icon is not present.

You can control the capability of making run-time changes to the WindowState property by including or removing Minimize and Maximize buttons from the form. You set the values of the **MinButton property** and the **MaxButton property** of the form to True if you want to include the button or to False to exclude the button. Setting the value to False also removes the corresponding command on the System menu. Setting the form's **ControlBox property** to False removes the System menu icon and the Minimize, Maximize, and Close buttons. Perform the following steps to prevent the About... form from having its WindowState property changed during run time.

TO SET THE CONTROLBOX PROPERTY

1 Click the Form object name, Form1, in the Object list box in the Properties window.

2 Scroll through the Properties list until the ControlBox property is visible. Double-click the ControlBox property in the Properties list.

controls
still visible at
design time

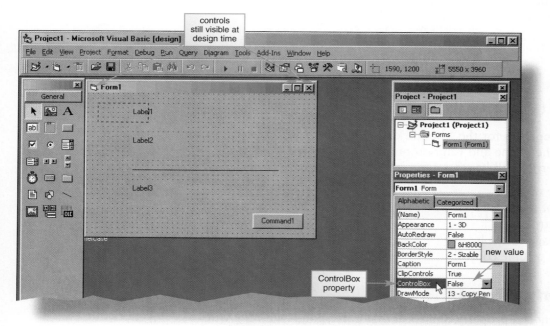

ControlBox
property

FIGURE 3-21

The new value of False displays in the Properties list (Figure 3-21).

When the ControlBox property is set to False, the form still contains a System menu icon and Minimize, Maximize, and Close buttons at design time (Figure 3-21). At run time, however, the buttons will not display on the form (Figure 3-20).

The BorderStyle Property of Forms

The capability of changing the size of a window at run time by dragging its borders is determined by the value of the form's BorderStyle property. The **BorderStyle property** of a form affects the form's appearance and controls. A sizable form has borders that can be dragged to new positions. A form's BorderStyle property can take one of six values and affects whether certain controls display on the form, as listed in Table 3-2.

Table 3-2

CONTROL	BORDERSTYLE					
	0 - NONE	1 - FIXED SINGLE	2 - SIZABLE	3 - FIXED DIALOG	4 - FIXED TOOLWINDOW	5 - SIZABLE TOOLWINDOW
Minimize button	No	Optional	Optional	No	No	No
Maximize button	No	Optional	Optional	No	No	No
Control-menu box	No	Optional	Optional	Optional	Optional	Optional
Title bar	No	Optional	Optional	Optional	Optional	Optional
Sizable form	No	No	Yes	No	No	Yes

The **ShowInTaskbar property** determines whether a Form object displays on the Windows 98 taskbar. Changing the setting of the BorderStyle property of a Form object may change the settings of the MinButton, MaxButton, and ShowInTaskbar properties. When the BorderStyle property is set to 1 - Fixed Single or 2 - Sizable, the MinButton, MaxButton, and ShowInTaskbar properties are set automatically to True. When the BorderStyle property is set to 0 - None, 3 - Fixed Dialog, 4 - Fixed ToolWindow, or 5 - Sizable ToolWindow, the MinButton, MaxButton, and ShowInTaskbar properties are set automatically to False.

The About SavU Loan Analyzer dialog box is typical of most dialog boxes. Generally, a dialog box's WindowState property cannot be changed, and it is not sizable. Perform the following steps to prevent the About... dialog box form from being resized during run time.

TO SET THE BORDERSTYLE PROPERTY

1 Check to be certain the Form1 form object is selected. If it is not, click its name, Form1, in the Object list box in the Properties window.

2 Scroll through the Properties list until the BorderStyle property is visible. Click the BorderStyle property to select it.

3 Click the BorderStyle property value box arrow.

4 Click 3 - Fixed Dialog in the property values list.

The new value displays in the Properties window (Figure 3-22).

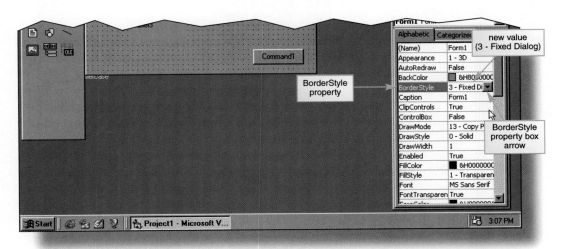

FIGURE 3-22

Microsoft **Visual Basic 6**

The form remains sizable at design time, no matter what the value of its Border-Style property. At run time, however, the form displays with the selected value of the BorderStyle property.

Control Names and Captions

In Project 2, you learned that naming controls makes it easier for you to write code and makes your code easier for other people to understand. Not all of the controls in Project 2, however, were given names different from their default names. It is important to name forms, especially in projects that contain more than one form. If only one instance of a type of control is on a form, or if a control is not referred to by an event or procedure, it is not as important to have a name other than the default name Visual Basic assigns.

Perform the following steps to name the form and to assign captions to the controls on the About... dialog box form. To ensure the captions fit inside the controls, you also will set the labels ' AutoSize property to True.

TO SET THE NAME, CAPTION, AND AUTOSIZE PROPERTIES

1 Check to be certain the Form1 form object is selected. If not, click its name in the Object list box in the Properties window. Double-click the Name property in the Properties list.

2 Type frmLoanabt and then press the ENTER key.

3 Double-click the Caption property in the Properties list.

4 Type About SavU Loan Analyzer and then press the ENTER key.

5 Click the Label1 control in the Object list box in the Properties window. Double-click the AutoSize property in the Properties list.

6 Repeat Step 5 for the Label2 control and then repeat Step 5 for the Label3 control.

7 Click the Command1 control in the Object list box in the Properties window. Double-click the Caption property in the Properties list.

8 Type OK and then press the ENTER key.

The frmLoanabt form displays as shown in Figure 3-23.

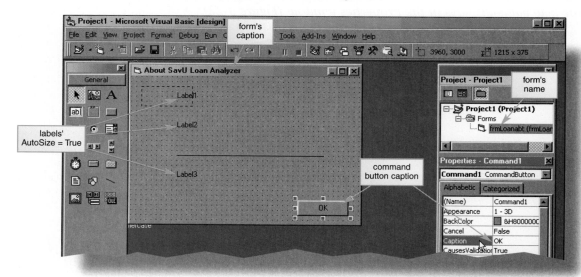

FIGURE 3-23

Font Properties

In Project 2, you changed the size of text characters on a Label control by changing the value of Size in the Font dialog box. During design time, you use the **Font dialog box** to change the fonts, the font size, and/or the font style you use for text and data fields. These font characteristics also can be changed at run time through code statements. The property names you use in code statements do not match the Font dialog box directly, as shown in Table 3-3.

You may have questioned why you did not enter the captions for the labels in the previous steps. The reason is that instead of using one label for each line of text that displays in the dialog box, the dialog box uses only three labels, each with multiple lines (Figure 3-24). You will create these multiline captions with code statements later in the project.

The Font, Font Style, and Size settings all have an effect on the size of the text that displays on a control. Although you set a label's AutoSize property value to True, the form does not have a similar property. The selection of a large font size for the Label controls would cause characters to extend beyond the right border of the form where they would not display. Perform the following steps to set the Font properties for the labels in the About... dialog box.

TO SET THE FONT PROPERTIES

1 Click the Label1 control in the Object list box in the Properties window.

2 Double-click Font in the Properties list to open the Font dialog box (Figure 3-25).

3 Click MS Sans Serif in the Font list box.

4 Click Regular in the Font style list box.

5 Click 8 in the Size list box.

6 Click the OK button in the Font dialog box.

7 Click the Label2 control and repeat Step 2 through Step 6.

8 Click the Label3 control and repeat Step 2 through Step 6.

The Font dialog box for the Label controls displays as shown in Figure 3-25.

Table 3-3	
FONT DIALOG	*PROPERTY*
Font	FontName
Font Style: Italic	FontItalic
Font Style: Bold	FontBold
Font Style: Bold Italic	(FontBold = True and FontItalic = True)
Font Style: Regular	(FontBold = False and FontItalic = False)
Size	FontSize
Effects: Strikeout	FontStrikethru
Effects: Underline	FontUnderline

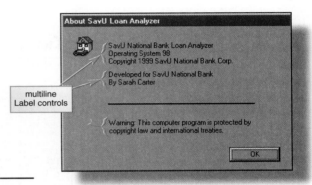

multiline Label controls

FIGURE 3-24

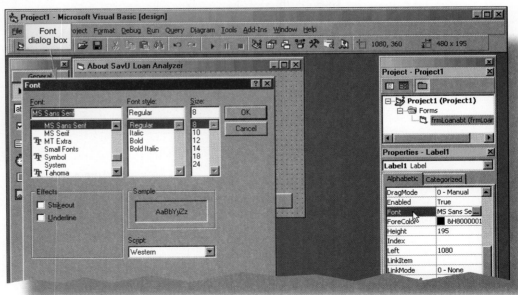

FIGURE 3-25

The list of available fonts (Step 3) depends on which fonts have been installed in your copy of Windows. Style and Effects properties can be used alone or in combination. For example, setting the value of the Font style to Bold and clicking Underline in the Effects area will display the selected font in bold and underlined.

The Picture Property of Image Controls

You can add graphics to forms and certain controls at design time by setting the control's **Picture property** in the Properties window. The graphic image used on the frmLoanabt form comes from the set of icon files with the **.ico extension** supplied as part of the Visual Basic system. It also is available on the Data Disk that accompanies this book. When a form containing graphical data (such as an icon or picture) is saved, Visual Basic automatically creates an additional file with the same file name as the form but with an **.frx extension**.

Perform the following steps to add an icon to the Image1 control.

To Add a Graphic to an Image Control

1 **Click the Image1 control in the Object list box in the Properties window. Double-click the Picture property in the Properties list.**

The Load Picture dialog box displays (Figure 3-26). The Load Picture dialog box is similar to other common dialog boxes used in Windows applications.

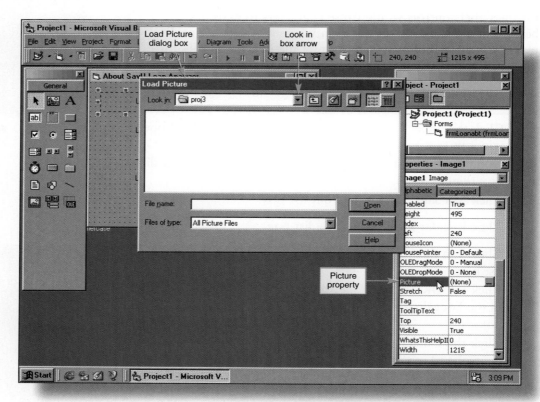

FIGURE 3-26

2 If necessary, insert the Student Data Disk in drive A. Click the Look in box arrow. If necessary, scroll through the list, and then point to 3½ Floppy (A:) (Figure 3-27).

See the inside back cover for instructions on how to obtain a copy of the Student Data Disk.

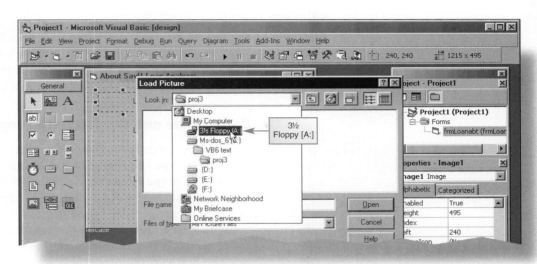

FIGURE 3-27

3 Click 3½ Floppy (A:) and then point to the House.ico file name.

All files in the selected folder with any of the eight picture file types that Visual Basic supports display in the list (Figure 3-28).

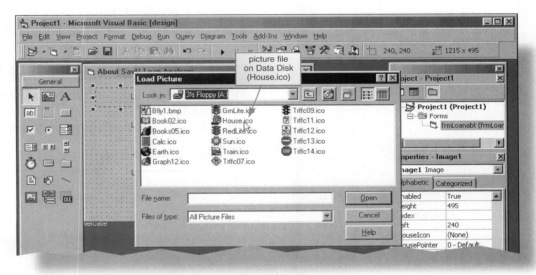

FIGURE 3-28

4 Double-click House.ico.

Visual Basic loads the house icon into the Image control located in the upper-left corner of the About... dialog box form (Figure 3-29).

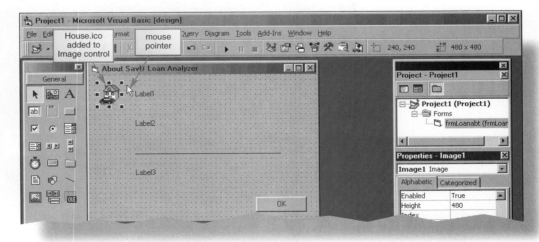

FIGURE 3-29

When Visual Basic loaded the icon, the size of the Image control was adjusted automatically to the size of its contents (the house icon). This automatic sizing occurred because the default value of the Image control's Stretch property is False. If you set the Stretch property of the Image control to True, Visual Basic does not adjust the Image control's size automatically.

BorderStyle and BorderWidth Properties of Line Controls

The next step is to change the appearance of the horizontal line that runs across the center of the About... dialog box form. The **BorderStyle property** of the Line control determines the appearance of the line, such as solid or dashed. The seven possible values of the BorderStyle property for the Line control are listed in Table 3-4.

The BorderStyle property of the line on the frmLoanabt form is Solid, which is the default value (Figure 3-30).

The **BorderWidth property** is used to set the width of the line. The values of the BorderWidth property are integers from 1 to 8,192. The line on the frmLoanabt form is wider than the default width of 1 (Figure 3-30). Perform the following steps to change the width of the Line control located on the frmLoanabt form.

Table 3-4	
VALUE	**DESCRIPTION**
0	Transparent
1	(Default) Solid - border is centered on the edge of the shape
2	Dash
3	Dot
4	Dash-Dot
5	Dash-Dot-Dot
6	Inside Solid - outer edge of the border is the outer edge of the shape

TO SET THE BORDERWIDTH PROPERTY OF THE LINE CONTROL

1 Click the Line1 control in the Object list box in the Properties window.

2 Double-click the BorderWidth property in the Properties list.

3 Type 2 and then press the ENTER key.

The Line control displays as shown in Figure 3-31.

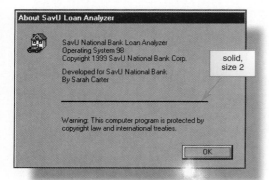

FIGURE 3-30

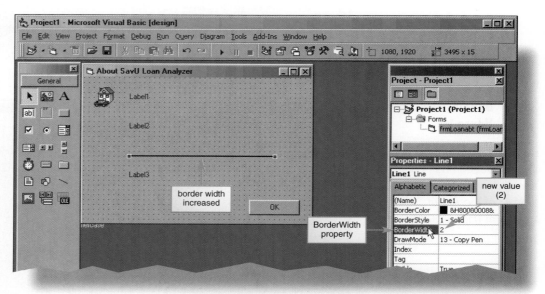

FIGURE 3-31

If the BorderWidth property is set to a value greater than 1, the only effective settings of the BorderStyle property are 1 - Solid and 6 - Inside Solid.

Saving the Form

The frmLoanabt form now is complete. Before proceeding with building the second form in the project, save the form. Perform the following steps to save the form on the Data Disk in drive A.

 To Save a Form File

1 **Click File on the menu bar and then point to Save frmLoanabt As.**

The form's name is listed on the File menu (Figure 3-32).

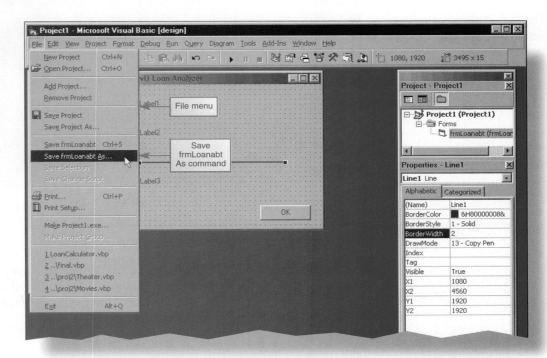

FIGURE 3-32

2 **Click Save frmLoanabt As.**

The Save File As dialog box displays, and the form's name displays in the File name text box (Figure 3-33).

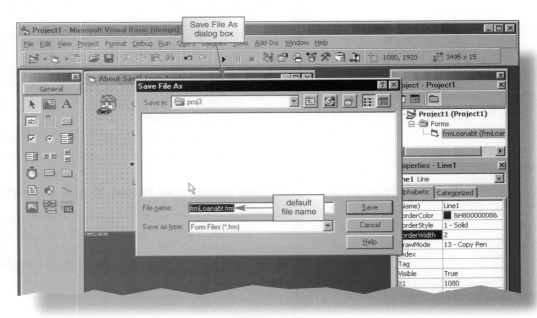

FIGURE 3-33

③ **Type** Loanabt **as the file name. Click the Save in box arrow. If necessary, scroll through the list and then click 3½ Floppy (A:). Click the Save button in the Save File As dialog box.**

The form is saved as a file on the floppy disk, and the dialog box closes. The form's file name is shown following the form's name in the Project window (Figure 3-34).

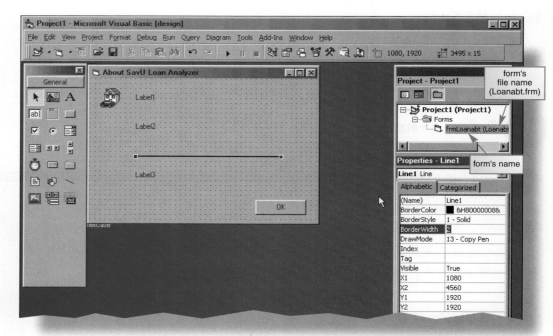

FIGURE 3-34

Because form files automatically have the .frm extension added when you save them, the frm prefix in the form's name was not included in the file name. You can save a file with any name, and the file name can be different from Visual Basic's value of the Name property of the form.

The SavU Loan Analyzer Form and Its Controls

The second form in this project is the SavU Loan Analyzer form shown in Figure 3-35. Because this form is the second one in the project, you must add a new form. You will build the SavU Loan Analyzer form following this sequence of activities.

1. Add a new form to the project.
2. Set the size of the form.
3. Add the controls.
4. Set the properties of the form and its controls.
5. Save the form as a file on a floppy disk.

Adding Additional Forms to the Project

You can have multiple Form windows open on the desktop at the same time. It reduces confusion, however, if you minimize the windows of forms you currently are not using. Perform the following steps to minimize the About... dialog box form (frmLoanabt) and to add a new form to the project.

FIGURE 3-35

TO ADD A NEW FORM

1 Click the About... dialog box form's (frmLoanabt's) Minimize button.

2 Click the Add Form button on the Standard toolbar.

3 Double-click the Form icon on the New tab sheet in the Add Form dialog box.

The About... dialog box form's (frmLoanabt's) window is reduced to a button on the lower-left corner of the desktop. A new form with the default name, Form1, is added to the project, and its window opens on the desktop (Figure 3-36).

Setting the Form Size and Position

Perform the following steps to change the size of the SavU Loan Analyzer form by directly changing the values of the Height and Width properties in the Properties window, using the same procedure you used for the About... dialog box form. The form's position will be changed by dragging the resized form.

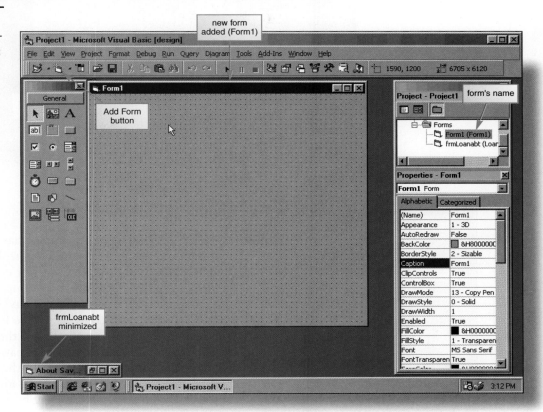

FIGURE 3-36

TO SET THE SIZE OF THE FORM USING THE PROPERTIES WINDOW

1 Click the Properties window to make it the active window.

2 Scroll through the Properties list and then double-click the Height property. Type 5265 and then press the ENTER key.

3 Scroll through the Properties list and double-click the Width property. Type 4845 and then press the ENTER key.

4 Drag the form to approximately the location shown in Figure 3-37 on the next page.

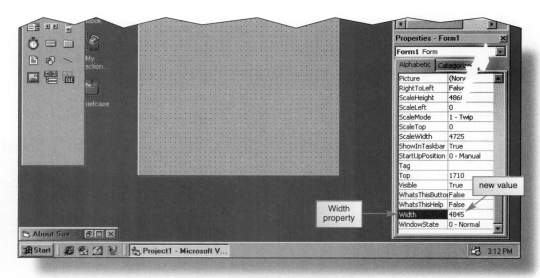

FIGURE 3-37

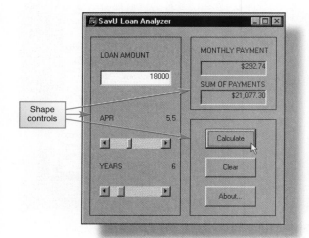

FIGURE 3-38

Adding Shape Controls

The SavU Loan Analyzer form has three Shape controls, as shown in Figure 3-38. These controls are not functional within the application because no events or code statements are associated with them. They do serve an important purpose, however.

Shape controls are used in the SavU Loan Analyzer application to group related controls on the form visually. All the controls within the shape on the left of the form are related to the **inputs**, or data, needed by the application to carry out its function. The shape on the top right of the form groups all of the controls related to the results of the application's function, called **outputs**. The shape located on the bottom right contains controls used to initiate different actions within the application. Perform the following steps to add three Shape controls to the form.

 To Add Shape Controls

1 **Click the Shape button in the Toolbox, and then move the mouse to the location where the top-left corner of the shape will display.**

The Shape button is recessed in the Toolbox. The mouse pointer changes to a cross hair (Figure 3-39).

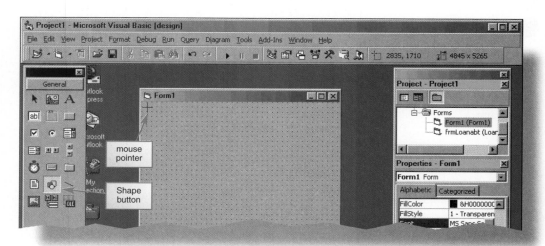

FIGURE 3-39

2 **Drag down and to the right as shown in Figure 3-40. Release the mouse button.**

As you drag the mouse, a gray outline of the control displays on the form. When you release the mouse button, the Shape control is drawn in the position of the outline (Figure 3-40).

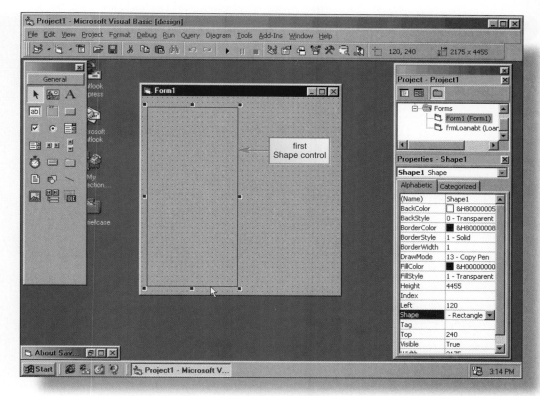

FIGURE 3-40

3 **Repeat Step 1 and Step 2 to draw a second Shape control (Figure 3-41).**

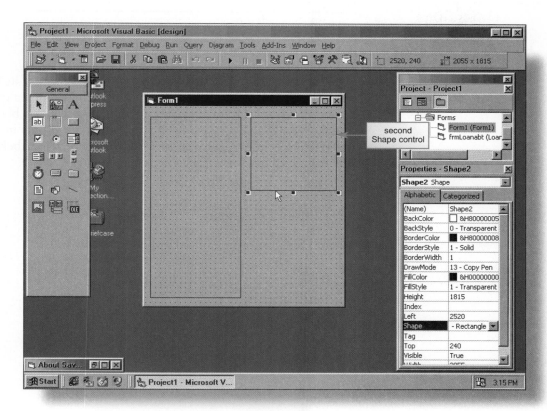

FIGURE 3-41

④ **Repeat Step 1 and Step 2 to draw a third Shape control (Figure 3-42).**

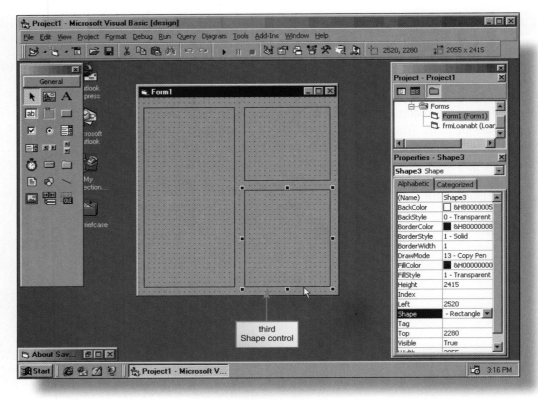

FIGURE 3-42

Adding and Copying Label Controls

The SavU Loan Analyzer form contains nine labels, as identified in Figure 3-43. The two labels used to display the outputs of the loan calculation have borders around them. At run time, their contents (captions) are blank until you click the Calculate button. The reason for displaying the outputs in this way is that an empty box visually communicates *something goes here*. The labels above the boxes communicate what that *something* is.

In Project 2, you learned how to copy controls using the mouse and the Edit menu. In the following example, controls are copied using the keyboard. Perform the following steps to add the seven borderless labels and then to add the two labels with borders.

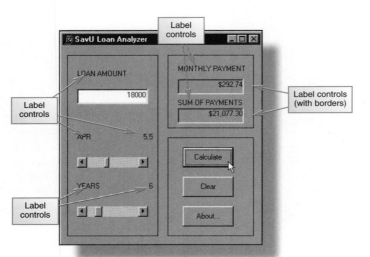

FIGURE 3-43

Steps **To Add Borderless Label Controls**

1 **Add a default-sized Label control to** the center of the form by double-clicking the Label button in the Toolbox. Drag the control to the position shown in Figure 3-44.

2 **Set the label's AutoSize property** value to True by double-clicking the AutoSize property in the Properties window.

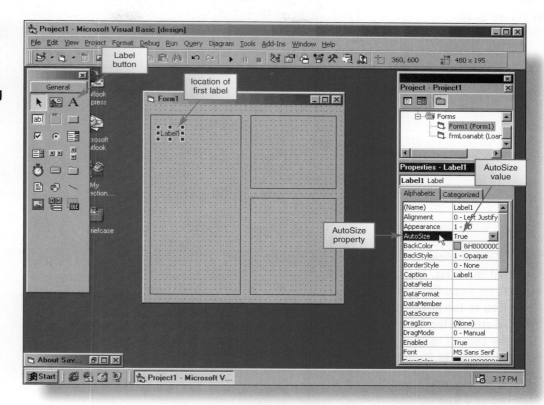

FIGURE 3-44

3 **Click the Label control. Press the** CTRL+C keys. Press the CTRL+V keys. Click the No button in the Microsoft Visual Basic dialog box.

An additional Label control with its AutoSize property value set to True displays on the form. When you copy a control, all of its property values also are copied. Thus, the second Label control has the caption Label1 (Figure 3-45).

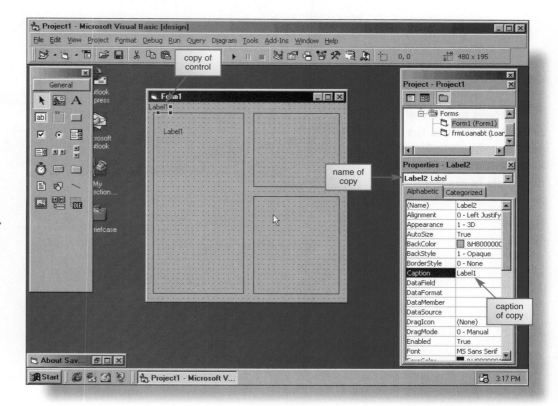

FIGURE 3-45

4 Drag the label to the position shown in Figure 3-46.

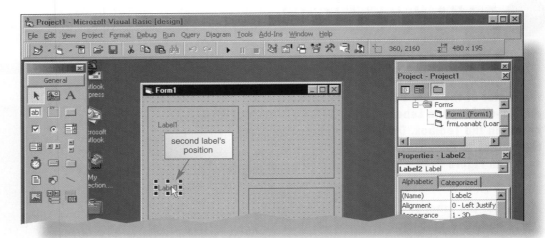

FIGURE 3-46

5 Click a blank area of the form. Press the CTRL+V keys. Click the No button in the Microsoft Visual Basic dialog box. Drag the control to the position shown in Figure 3-47.

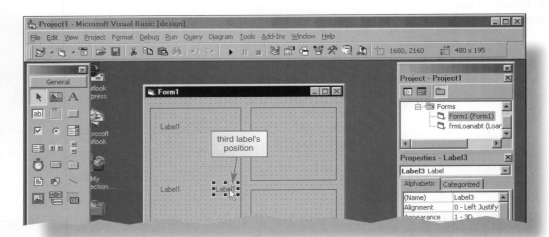

FIGURE 3-47

6 Repeat Step 5 four times to add the remaining labels in the positions shown in Figure 3-48. Be careful to position the labels in the order shown.

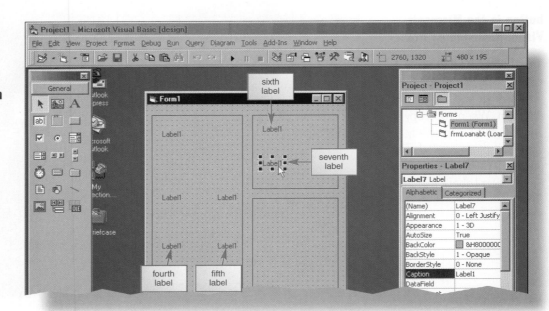

FIGURE 3-48

Pressing the CTRL+C keys copies the selected control to the Clipboard. Pressing the CTRL+V keys pastes the control from the Clipboard to the form. Seven similar labels have been added to the form. Perform the following steps to add the remaining two labels used to contain the application's outputs.

 To Add Additional Label Controls

1 **Double-click the Label button in the Toolbox and then drag the control to the position shown in Figure 3-49. Double-click the BorderStyle property in the Properties window.**

The label is positioned as shown in Figure 3-49 and the label's BorderStyle property value changes from 0 - No Border to 1 - Fixed Single.

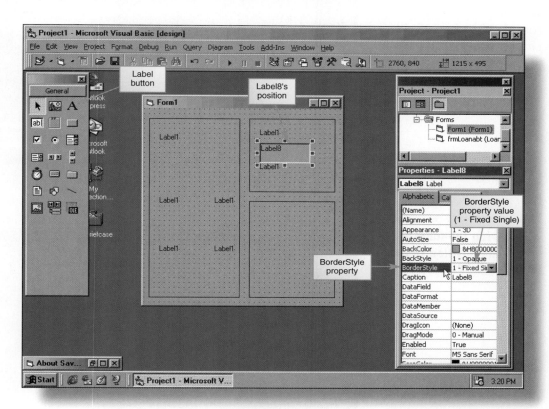

FIGURE 3-49

2 **Drag the Label8 control's lower-right sizing handle up and to the right, as shown in Figure 3-50.**

The new size is shown in a gray shaded line (Figure 3-50).

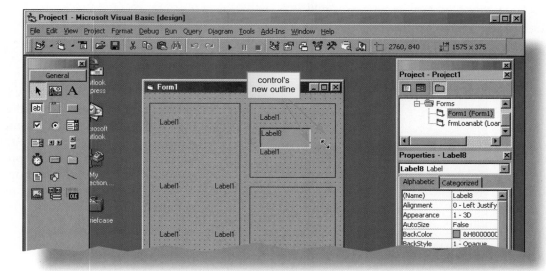

FIGURE 3-50

③ **Release the mouse button. Click the Label8 control. Press the CTRL+C keys. Press the CTRL+V keys. Click the No button in the Microsoft Visual Basic dialog box.**

An identically sized Label control with its BorderStyle property value set to 1 displays on the form (Figure 3-51).

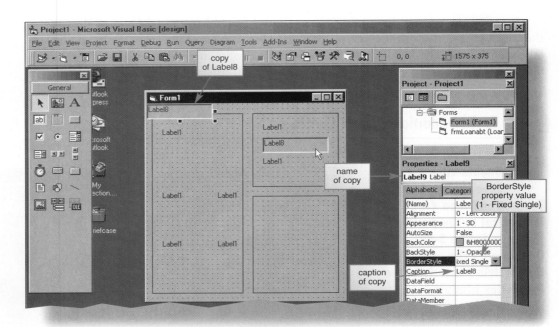

FIGURE 3-51

④ **Drag the label to the position shown in Figure 3-52.**

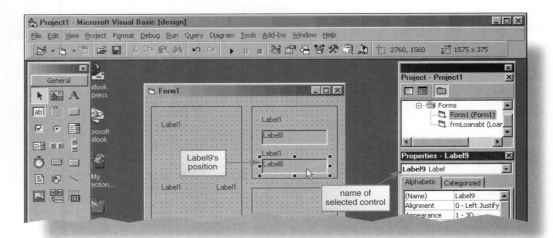

FIGURE 3-52

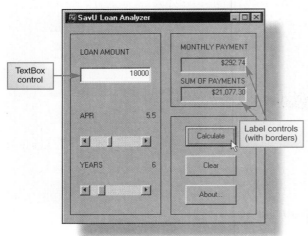

FIGURE 3-53

All of the Label controls now have been added to the form. Compare the positions and appearance of the Label controls in Figure 3-52 to the completed form shown in Figure 3-53. Generally, all of the form's controls are added before setting properties. In the preceding example, you set the AutoSize and BorderStyle properties immediately so you could take advantage of copying property values when copying a control.

Copying the labels with the property values already set will save you time because you will not have to set each label's AutoSize or BorderStyle property when you set the rest of the properties later. By copying the first output label (Label8), you did not have to draw or resize the second output label (Label9) to match the size of the first.

Adding the TextBox Control

The SavU Loan Analyzer form contains one TextBox control, which is used at run time to accept the loan amount (Figure 3-53). You use a **TextBox control** to enter the loan amount instead of a label because a label's contents can be changed during run time only with a code statement.

Perform the following steps to add the TextBox control to the form.

 To Add a TextBox Control

1 **Double-click the TextBox button in the Toolbox and then drag the control to the position shown in Figure 3-54.**

A default-sized text box is added to the form.

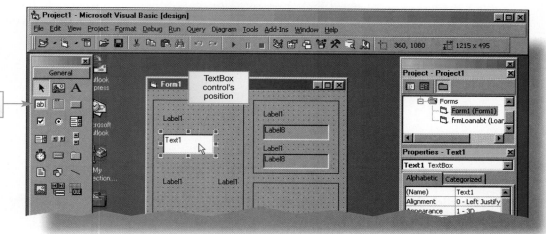

FIGURE 3-54

2 **Drag the control's lower-right sizing handle up and to the right to resize the control as shown in Figure 3-55.**

Dragging the lower-right sizing handle up and to the right decreases the control's height and increases its width (Figure 3-55).

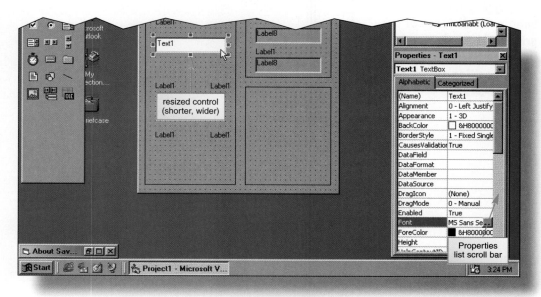

FIGURE 3-55

ScrollBar Controls

When you use a scroll bar as an indicator of quantity or as an input device, you use the Max and Min properties to set the appropriate range for the control. This range can be any integer values between -32,768 and 32,767.

Adding ScrollBar Controls

Scroll bars commonly are used to view the contents of a control when the contents cannot fit within the control's borders. An example is the Properties list scroll bar in the Properties window. Visual Basic has two different ScrollBar controls; the horizontal ScrollBar (HScrollBar) control and the vertical ScrollBar (VScrollBar) control. Their names reflect the orientation of the control on the form, not its use. You control its use. For example, you can use a vertical scroll bar to control the horizontal scrolling of a control on a form.

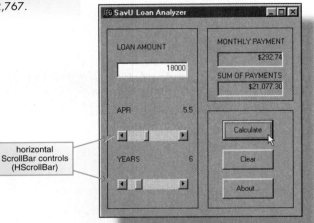

FIGURE 3-56

Another use of the ScrollBar control is to give a value to an input. One benefit of using a ScrollBar control for input is that it prevents you from entering an improper value by mistake, such as a letter instead of a number. The two horizontal ScrollBar controls shown in Figure 3-56 are used as input controls for the annual interest rate and for the number of years of the loan.

Perform the following steps to add the two ScrollBar controls.

To Add ScrollBar Controls

1 **Double-click the HScrollBar button in the Toolbox. Extend the HScrollBar control's width by dragging its sizing handle the distance of two grid marks on the form. Drag the HScrollBar control to the position shown in Figure 3-57.**

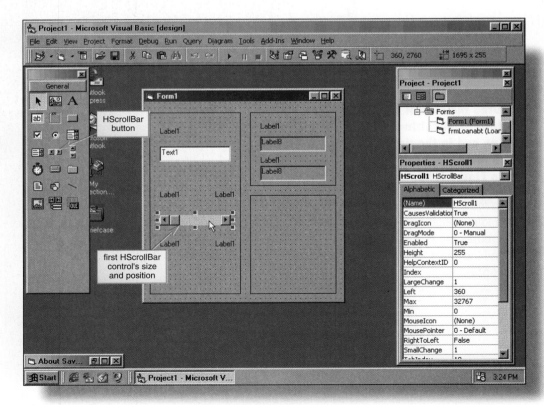

FIGURE 3-57

2 **Double-click the HScrollBar button in the Toolbox. Extend the new HScrollBar control's width by dragging its sizing handle the distance of two grid marks on the form. Drag the HScrollBar control to the position shown in Figure 3-58.**

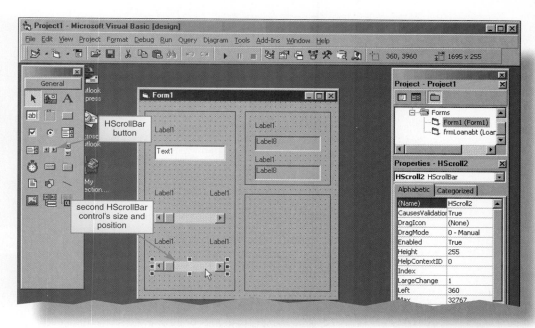

FIGURE 3-58

In the SavU Loan Analyzer application, the caption of the label located above the right end of the scroll bar is used to display the current value of the input controlled by that scroll bar. When you click a scroll arrow or drag the scroll box, the scroll bar's **Change event** is triggered. A code statement will be written later in this project that will link the caption of the label to the Change event.

Adding CommandButton Controls

The last three controls to be added to the SavU Loan Analyzer form are the three command buttons identified in Figure 3-59.

The command buttons used in this application are the default size, so you can add them to the form by using the double-click method instead of drawing them.

TO ADD COMMANDBUTTON CONTROLS

1 Double-click the CommandButton button in the Toolbox. Drag the Command1 command button inside and to the top of the Shape control in the lower right of the Form window.

2 Double-click the CommandButton button in the Toolbox. Drag the Command2 command button inside and to the center of the Shape control in the lower right of the Form window.

3 Double-click the CommandButton button in the Toolbox. Drag the Command3 command button inside and to the bottom of the Shape control in the lower right of the Form window.

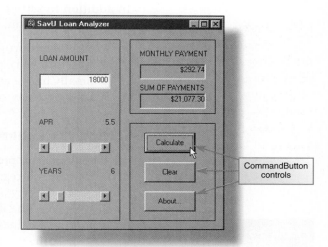

FIGURE 3-59

The command buttons display as shown in Figure 3-60 on the next page.

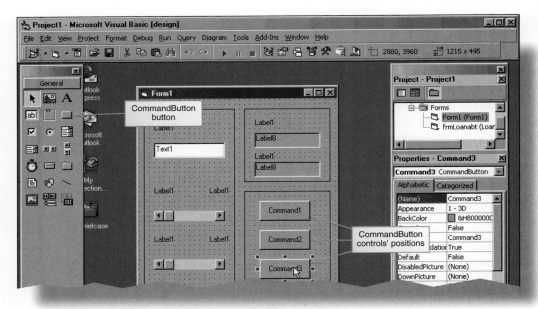

FIGURE 3-60

You now have completed the design of the SavU Loan Analyzer form. The next step in the development process is to set the properties for the form and its controls.

Setting Properties of the SavU Loan Analyzer Form and Its Controls

In addition to setting the Caption and Name properties of the controls on the SavU Loan Analyzer form, you will set the following properties.

▶ Alignment property of text boxes and labels
▶ Min and Max properties of ScrollBar controls
▶ SmallChange and LargeChange properties of ScrollBar controls
▶ Icon property of forms

Setting the Alignment Property of TextBox and Label Controls

The **Alignment property** specifies where the caption will display within the borders of a control, regardless of whether the borders are visible. The values of the Alignment property are listed in Table 3-5.

The default value of the Alignment property is left-justified. Because the values display in the Properties list in the same order as in Table 3-5, you can change from left-justify to right-justify by double-clicking the Alignment property in the Properties list instead of selecting the property values list and then clicking 1 - Right Justify. The five controls with right-justified alignment are identified in Figure 3-61.

The TextBox control is among the five right-justified controls. To change a text box's alignment, the value of its MultiLine property must be equal to True. Perform the following steps to set the Alignment property.

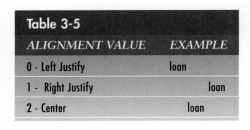

Table 3-5	
ALIGNMENT VALUE	*EXAMPLE*
0 - Left Justify	loan
1 - Right Justify	loan
2 - Center	loan

TO SET THE ALIGNMENT PROPERTY

1 Click the Text1 control on the form or in the Object list box in the Properties window. Double-click the Alignment property.

2 Scroll down the Properties list and then double-click the MultiLine property in the Properties list.

3 Click the Label3 control in the Object list box in the Properties window. Double-click the Alignment property.

4 Click the Label5 control in the Object list box in the Properties window. Double-click the Alignment property.

5 Click the Label8 control on the form or in the Object list box in the Properties window. Double-click the Alignment property.

6 Click the Label9 control on the form or in the Object list box in the Properties window. Double-click the Alignment property.

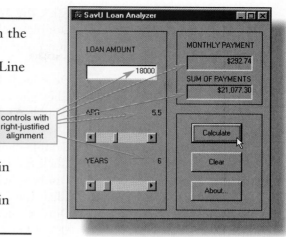

controls with right-justified alignment

FIGURE 3-61

The form displays as shown in Figure 3-62a.

Setting the Caption and Text Properties

Figure 3-62a shows the SavU Loan Analyzer form as it displays in the current stage of development and Figure 3-62b shows how it will display when completed. The differences between these two figures relate to the Caption property of the Form, Label, and CommandButton controls and to the Text property of the one TextBox control. At run time, the text box should start out empty. This text box is made empty by setting the initial value of its Text property to be blank. Perform the following steps to set the Caption property and Text property.

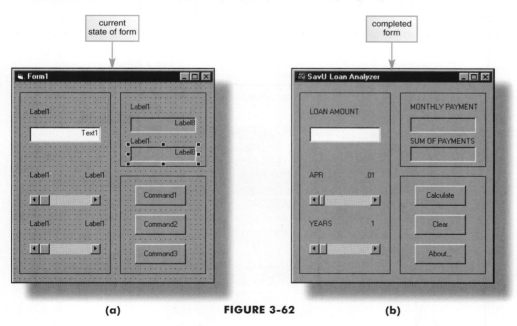

current state of form

completed form

(a)   **FIGURE 3-62**   (b)

TO SET THE CONTROLS' CAPTION AND TEXT PROPERTIES

1 Click the Form1 form control in the Object list box in the Properties window. Double-click the Caption property in the Properties list. Type SavU Loan Analyzer and then press the ENTER key.

2 Click the Label1 control in the Object list box in the Properties window. Double-click the Caption property. Type LOAN AMOUNT and then press the ENTER key.

(continued)

(3) Click the Text1 control in the Object list box in the Properties window. Double-click the Text property. A drop-down text box opens. Drag the insertion point over the text in the text box to highlight it. Press the DELETE key.

(4) Click the Label2 control in the Object list box in the Properties window. Double-click the Caption property. Type APR and then press the ENTER key.

(5) Click the Label3 control in the Object list box in the Properties window. Double-click the Caption property. Type .01 and then press the ENTER key.

(6) Click the Label4 control in the Object list box in the Properties window. Double-click the Caption property. Type YEARS and then press the ENTER key.

(7) Click the Label5 control in the Object list box in the Properties window. Double-click the Caption property. Type 1 and then press the ENTER key.

(8) Click the Label6 control in the Object list box in the Properties window. Double-click the Caption property. Type MONTHLY PAYMENT and then press the ENTER key.

(9) Click the Label7 control in the Object list box in the Properties window. Double-click the Caption property. Type SUM OF PAYMENTS and then press the ENTER key.

(10) Click the Label8 control in the Object list box in the Properties window. Double-click the Caption property. Press the DELETE key.

(11) Click the Label9 control in the Object list box in the Properties window. Double-click the Caption property. Press the DELETE key.

(12) Click the Command1 control in the Object list box in the Properties window. Double-click the Caption property. Type Calculate and then press the ENTER key.

(13) Click the Command2 control in the Object list box in the Properties window. Double-click the Caption property. Type Clear and then press the ENTER key.

(14) Click the Command3 control in the Object list box in the Properties window. Double-click the Caption property. Type About... and then press the ENTER key.

More *About*

Command Button Captions

You can use the Caption property to assign an access key to a CommandButton control. In the caption, include an ampersand (&) immediately preceding the character you want to designate as an access key. The character is underlined. During run time, you can press the ALT key plus the underlined character to execute the command button's Click event.

The SavU Loan Analyzer form displays as shown in Figure 3-63.

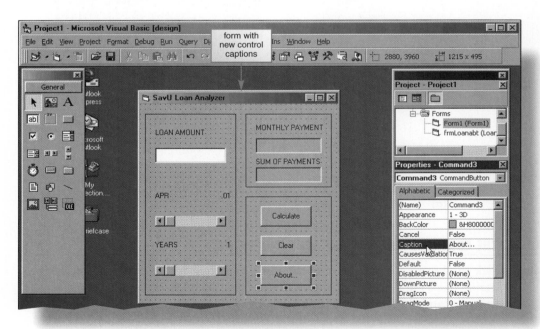

FIGURE 3-63

Naming the Controls

In addition to the form control itself, four labels, two scroll bars, three command buttons, and one text box on the SavU Loan Analyzer form will be referred to in the events and code statements that you will write later. These controls, with their current (default) names, are shown in Figure 3-64. It would be confusing to write events and code statements using the default names of these controls. Perform the following steps to rename the controls that will be referred to in code statements.

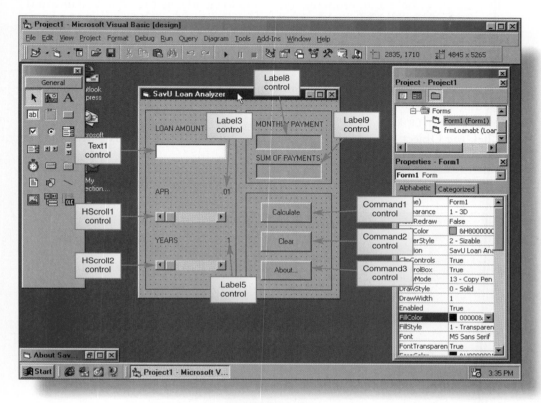

FIGURE 3-64

TO NAME CONTROLS

1 Click the Form1 control in the Object list box in the Properties window. Double-click the Name property. Type the control name frmLoanpmt and then press the ENTER key.

2 Click the Text1 control in the Object list box in the Properties window. Double-click the Name property. Type txtAmount as the control name and then press the ENTER key.

3 Click the Label3 control in the Object list box in the Properties window. Double-click the Name property in the Properties list. Type lblRate as the control name and then press the ENTER key.

4 Click the HScroll1 control in the Object list box in the Properties window. Double-click the Name property in the Properties list. Type hsbRate as the control name and then press the ENTER key.

5 Click the Label5 control in the Object list box in the Properties window. Double-click the Name property in the Properties list. Type lblYears as the control name and then press the ENTER key.

6 Click the HScroll2 control in the Object list box in the Properties window. Double-click the Name property. Type hsbYears and then press the ENTER key.

(continued)

7 Click the Label8 control in the Object list box in the Properties window. Double-click the Name property. Type `lblPayment` as the control name and then press the ENTER key.

8 Click the Label9 control in the Object list box in the Properties window. Double-click the Name property. Type `lblSumpmts` as the control name and then press the ENTER key.

9 Click the Command1 control in the Object list box in the Properties window. Double-click the Name property. Type `cmdCalculate` as the control name and then press the ENTER key.

10 Click the Command2 control in the Object list box in the Properties window. Double-click the Name property. Type `cmdClear` as the control name and then press the ENTER key.

11 Click the Command3 control in the Object list box in the Properties window. Double-click the Name property. Type `cmdAbout` as the control name and then press the ENTER key.

12 Click the Object box arrow to display the Object list of controls with their new names.

The controls are identified by their new names as shown in Figure 3-65.

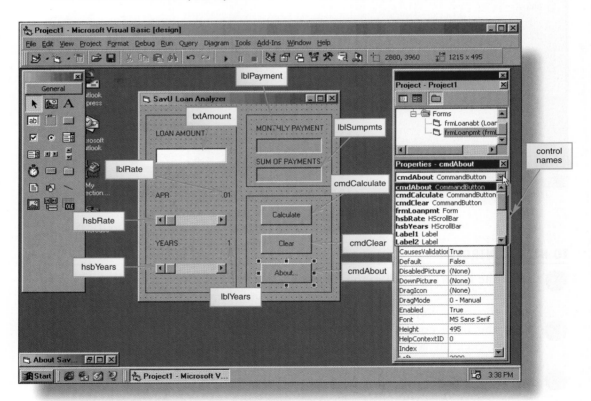

FIGURE 3-65

Setting the Scroll Bar Properties

The **Value property** of a scroll bar is an integer number that changes in relation to the position of the scroll box within the scroll bar. The lowest and highest numbers that the Value property can take are set with the **Min property** and **Max property** of the scroll bar. In a horizontal ScrollBar control, these values correspond to the farthest left and farthest right positions of the scroll box.

The amount that the value changes each time you click one of the scroll arrows is set by the **SmallChange property** of the scroll bar. The amount that the value changes by clicking the area between the scroll box and one of the two scroll arrows is set with the **LargeChange property** of the scroll bar. Perform the following steps to set the properties of the ScrollBar controls.

TO SET THE SCROLL BARS PROPERTIES

1 Click the YEARS scroll bar on the form or its name, hsbYears, in the Object list box in the Properties window.

2 Double-click the Max property in the Properties list. Type 30 and then press the ENTER key.

3 Double-click the Min property in the Properties list. Type 1 and then press the ENTER key.

4 Double-click the LargeChange property in the Properties list. Type 5 and then press the ENTER key.

5 Click the APR scroll bar on the form or its name, hsbRate, in the Object list box in the Properties window.

6 Double-click the Max property in the Properties list. Type 1500 and then press the ENTER key.

7 Double-click the Min property in the Properties list. Type 1 and then press the ENTER key.

8 Double-click the LargeChange property in the Properties list. Type 10 and then press the ENTER key.

The new values of these properties are visible by scrolling through the Properties list.

The preceding steps set properties of the scroll bars so the value of the scroll bar used to set years (hsbYears) will range from 1 to 30 and the value of the scroll bar used to set the APR (hsbRate) will range from 1 to 1500. It was not necessary to set the SmallChange property because its default value is 1. The caption of the label (lblYears), located above the scroll bar at the right end, will be the value of the scroll bar hsbYears, representing the number of years to repay the loan (from 1 to 30).

The annual interest rate displayed as the caption of the label (lblRate), located above the upper scroll bar (hsbRate), will work differently. Percentage rates on loans usually are expressed as a one- or two-digit number followed by a decimal point and a two-digit decimal fraction, such as 12.25 percent or 6.30 percent. Because the value of a scroll bar cannot include a fraction, you will multiply the value of the scroll bar hsbRate by .01 to get the value of the caption of the label (lblRate), located above the scroll bar.

For example, a scroll bar value of 678 will represent an APR of 6.78 percent, and a scroll bar value of 1250 will represent an APR of 12.50 percent. Multiplying a scroll bar value by a decimal is a common way to make scroll bars capable of representing numbers with fractional parts. You set the range of the APR scroll bar (hsbRate) values from 1 to 1500 so it can be used as described above to represent .01 to 15.00 percent.

The Icon Property of Forms

When a window is minimized, it displays on the taskbar as a button with a small graphical image called an **icon**. You can specify the graphical image used to represent the form by setting the form's **Icon property**. Perform the steps on the next page to select an icon for the Loanpmt form.

More About

Form Icons

You can see a form's icon in Windows 98 in the upper-left corner of the form when the form's WindowState property either is normal or maximized. If the form is minimized, the BorderStyle property must be set either to 1 - Fixed Single or 2 - Sizable, and the MinButton property must be set to True for the icon to be visible.

To Set a Form's Icon Property

1 **Click an empty area of the Loanpmt form. Scroll through the Properties list and point to the Icon property (Figure 3-66).**

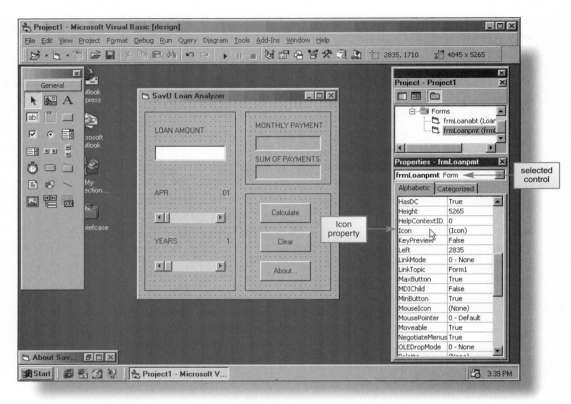

FIGURE 3-66

2 **Double-click the Icon property in the Properties list.**

The Load Icon dialog box displays (Figure 3-67). The icon file (House.ico) for this project is included on the Student Data Disk.

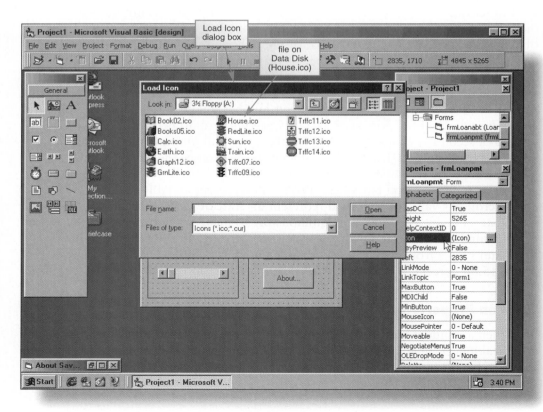

FIGURE 3-67

3 **Double-click House.ico in the File list box.**

The Load Icon dialog box closes, and the icon is added to the form (Figure 3-68).

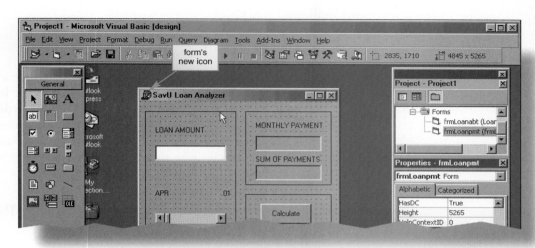

FIGURE 3-68

Saving the Form

The frmLoanpmt form now is complete. Before proceeding, you should save the form. Complete the following steps to save the Loanpmt form on the Data Disk in drive A.

TO SAVE THE FORM

1 Click File on the menu bar and then click Save frmLoanpmt As.

2 Type Loanpmt in the File name text box. If necessary, click 3½ Floppy (A:) in the Save in list box, and then click the Save button in the Save File As dialog box.

3 Minimize the frmLoanpmt window by clicking the Form window's Minimize button.

The frmLoanpmt's name displays in the Project window, followed by its file name (Figure 3-69).

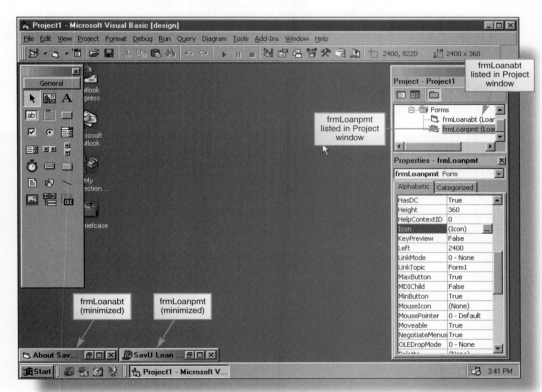

FIGURE 3-69

Writing Code

Event procedures (subroutines) must be written for nine events in the SavU Loan Analyzer application. These events and their actions are listed in Table 3-6.

The code for the SavU Loan Analyzer application will be written one event at a time using the Visual Basic Code window in the same manner as in Project 1 and Project 2. In a project that has more than one form, however, each form has its own Code window. Before writing the subroutines, a Startup form for the project will be specified.

The Startup Form

At run time, the **Startup form** is the first form in a project loaded into the computer's memory and added to the desktop. By default, the Startup form is the first form you create in a project. The SavU Loan Analyzer application should begin by displaying the frmLoanpmt form on the desktop. Because frmLoanpmt was not the first form created, it must be specified as the Startup form. Perform the following steps to make frmLoanpmt the Startup form.

Table 3-6

FORM	CONTROL	EVENT	ACTIONS
frmLoanpmt	hsbYears	Change	Update caption of lblYears
frmLoanpmt	hsbYears	Scroll	Update caption of lblYears
frmLoanpmt	hsbRate	Change	Update caption of lblRate
frmLoanpmt	hsbRate	Scroll	Update caption of lblRate
frmLoanpmt	cmdCalculate	Click	Perform monthly payment and sum of payment calculations, and display results in lblPayment and lblSumpmts
frmLoanpmt	cmdClear	Click	Clear the contents of txtAmount, lblPayment, and lblSumpmts; reset hsbYears and hsbRate to lowest values
frmLoanpmt	cmdAbout	Click	Add About... dialog box to desktop
frmLoanabt	Form	Load	Set captions of labels
frmLoanabt	Command1	Click	Remove About... dialog box from desktop

 To Set a Startup Form

① Click Project on the menu bar and then point to Project 1 Properties.

The Project menu displays (Figure 3-70).

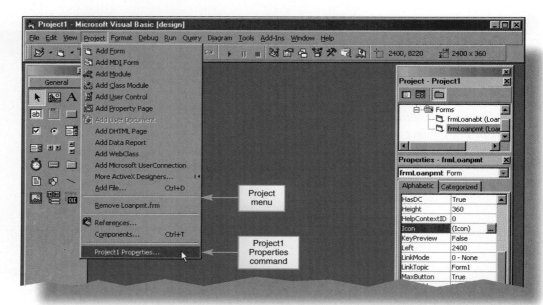

FIGURE 3-70

2 **Click Project1 Properties. If necessary, click the General tab in the Project1 - Project Properties dialog box.**

The Project1 - Project Properties dialog box displays (Figure 3-71).

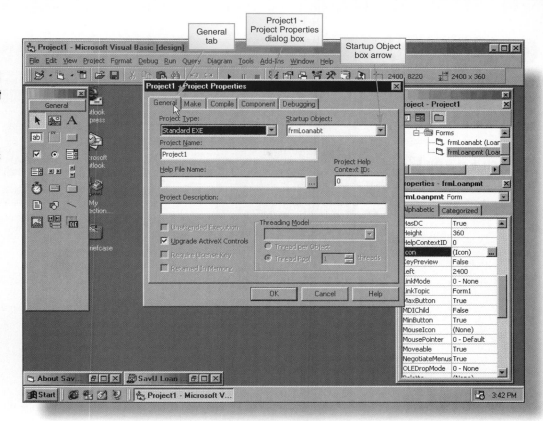

FIGURE 3-71

3 **Click the Startup Object box arrow and then point to frmLoanpmt.**

The Startup Object list box displays with possible values (Figure 3-72).

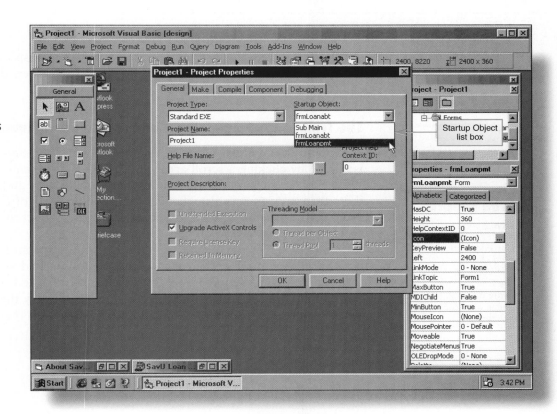

FIGURE 3-72

**Click frmLoanpmt in
the list and then
point to the OK button.**

*frmLoanpmt is now the
Startup form (Figure 3-73).*

5 **Click the OK button.**

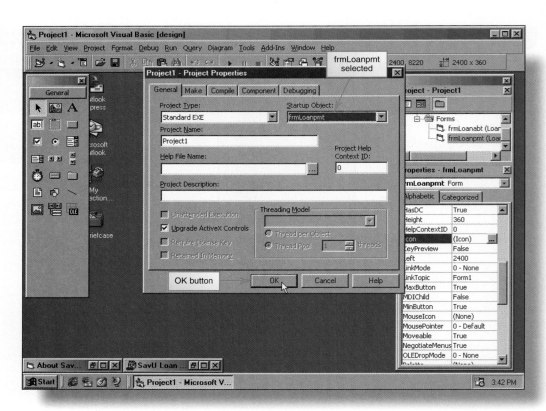

FIGURE 3-73

In Project 1 and Project 2, a Startup form was not specified explicitly because
when a project consists of a single form (as those projects did), the form automatically is set as the Startup form.

The frmLoanpmt hsbYears_Change and Scroll Events

A ScrollBar control's **Change event** is triggered any time the control's scroll box
is moved by clicking a scroll arrow, releasing the mouse button after dragging the
scroll box, or clicking the space between the scroll box and scroll arrow. Each of
these three movements also changes the **Value property** of the scroll bar. The **Scroll
event** occurs whenever the scroll box is dragged. The scroll event also changes the
Value property of the scroll bar.

In the SavU Loan Analyzer application, a movement of the scroll box must be
linked to a new number displayed in the caption located above the scroll bar. Perform the following steps to establish this link within the Change event procedure by
setting the Caption property of the label used to display the years (lblYears) to equal
the Value property of the scroll bar located below it on the form (hsbYears).

TO WRITE THE SCROLLBAR CHANGE EVENT PROCEDURE

1 Click the View Code button in the Project window.

2 Click the hsbYears control in the Object list box in the frmLoanpmt (Code) window. If necessary, click the Change procedure in the Procedure list box.

3 Type the following statements in the Code window, pressing the ENTER key at the end of each line.
```
'update lblYears caption when scrollbox is moved
lblYears.Caption = hsbYears.Value
```

The Code window displays as shown in Figure 3-74.

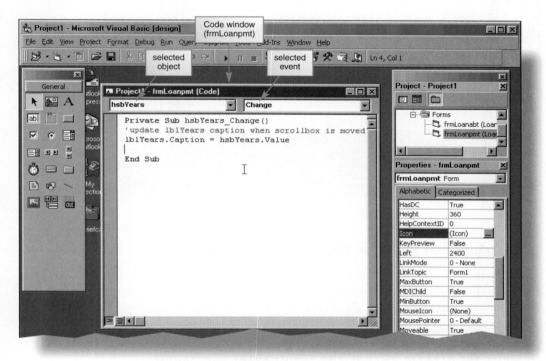

FIGURE 3-74

The lblYears control now will be updated whenever the Change event occurs. To update the lblYears control while dragging the scroll box requires the same code to be written for the Scroll event procedure. Perform the following steps to copy the code to the Scroll event procedure.

TO WRITE THE SCROLLBAR SCROLL EVENT PROCEDURE

1 Highlight the two lines of code you wrote for the hsbYears_Change event.

2 Right-click the selected code and then click Copy on the shortcut menu that displays.

3 Click Scroll in the Procedure list box in the Code window.

4 Right-click the beginning of the second (blank) line in the Code window and then click Paste on the shortcut menu that displays.

The code is copied for the hsbYears_Scroll event (Figure 3-75 on the next page).

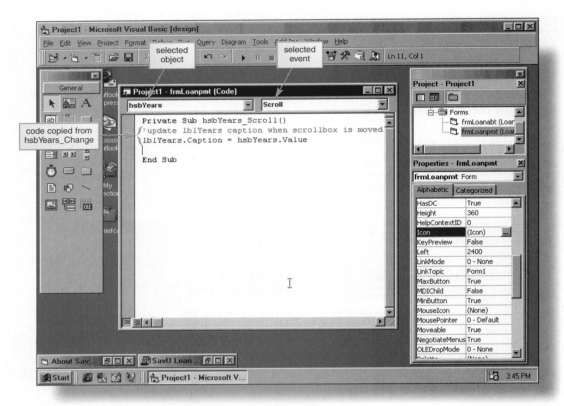

FIGURE 3-75

The frmLoanpmt hsbRate_Change and Scroll Events

This event is similar to the Change event for hsbYears. The only difference is the interest rate displayed as the caption of lblRate must be converted from the value of hsbRate by multiplying it by .01. Perform the following steps to write the hsbRate_Change event and then copy it to the hsbRate_Scroll event.

TO WRITE THE HSBRATE_CHANGE AND SCROLL EVENT PROCEDURES

1. Click the hsbRate control in the Object list box in the frmLoanpmt (Code) window. If necessary, click the Change procedure in the Procedure list box.

2. Enter the following statements in the Code window:
```
'update lblRate caption when scrollbox is moved
lblRate.Caption = hsbRate.Value * 0.01
```

3. Highlight the two lines of code you wrote for the hsb Rate_Change event. Right-click the selected code and then click Copy on the shortcut menu that displays.

4. Click Scroll in the Procedure list box in the Code window. Right-click the beginning of the second (blank) line in the Code window and then click Paste on the shortcut menu that displays.

The code is copied for the hsbRate_Scroll event (Figure 3-76).

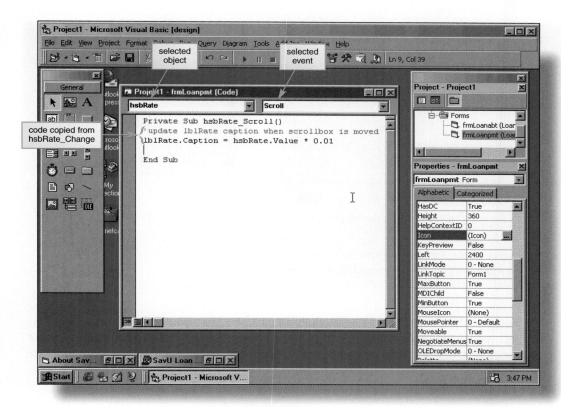

FIGURE 3-76

The frmLoanpmt cmdCalculate_Click Event

The **cmdCalculate_Click event** is used to perform the loan payment calculation and display the results. The actual computation is performed by one of Visual Basic's financial functions, the Pmt function. For a complete list and descriptions of all the Visual Basic financial functions, use online Help to search on the words, financial functions. The **Pmt function** returns the payment for a loan based on periodic, constant payments and a constant interest rate. The function is used in a code statement in the following manner:

Pmt(rate, nper, pv, fv, due)

The entries within parentheses that are supplied to a function are called **arguments**. Arguments within the Pmt function are described in Table 3-7 on the next page.

In the cmdCalculate_Click event, the inputs of the SavU Loan Analyzer application are substituted for the arguments of the Pmt function described in Table 3-7. Remember that the value of hsbRate runs from 1 to 1500 and that the decimal interest rate is .0001 times that value. The Pmt function arguments and values assigned in this project are listed in Table 3-8 on the next page.

When you use the Pmt function, all of the arguments must be numbers (or variables whose value is a number). What if you typed, Hello, as the amount of the loan in the txtAmount text box at run time and then clicked the Calculate button? The function would be unable to calculate a value, and the program would end abruptly. It is possible for you to make an error when typing the loan amount, so you want some way to trap this error and to correct it without the program ending abruptly.

Table 3-7

ARGUMENT	DESCRIPTION
rate	Interest rate per period. For example, if you get a car loan at an annual percentage rate of 9 percent and make monthly payments, the rate per period is 0.09/12 or .0075.
nper	Total number of payment periods in the loan. For example, if you make monthly payments on a five year car loan, your loan has a total of 5 * 12 (or 60) payment periods.
pv	Present value that a series of payments to be made in the future is worth now (to the lender). For example, if you borrow $10,000 to buy a car, its pv is -10,000.
fv	Future value or cash balance you want after you have made the final payment. The future value of a loan is 0.
due	Number indicating when payments are due. Use 0 if payments are due at the end of the period, and use 1 if the payments are due at the beginning of the period.

Table 3-8

ARGUMENT	VALUE
rate	.0001 * hsbRate.Value / 12
nper	hsbYears.Value * 12
pv	-1 * txtAmount.Text
fv	0
due	1

Because the Text property of a text box can be either numbers (numeric) or text (string), you need to write some additional code that checks to see if the contents are numeric. This checking is done with the Visual Basic **IsNumeric function**. The function is used within code statements as follows:

IsNumeric(txtAmount.Text)

The function will return a True value if the contents are a number and a False value if the contents are not a valid number. The logical flow of actions within the cmdCalculate_Click event is shown in Figure 3-77.

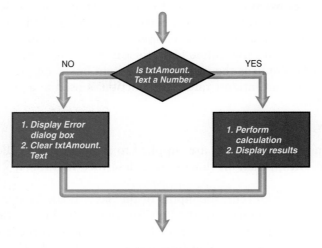

FIGURE 3-77

In Project 2, this type of logical structure was represented in code by using an If...Then...Else statement. This project uses an extension to the If...Then...Else statement called an If...Then...Else block. The **If...Then...Else block** evaluates a condition similarly to the If...Then...Else statement. The block allows you to have multiple code statements executed, however, as illustrated in Figure 3-78.

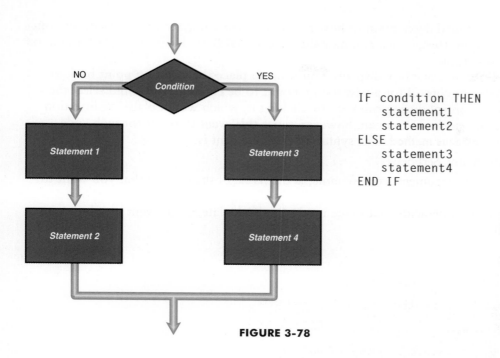

```
IF condition THEN
    statement1
    statement2
ELSE
    statement3
    statement4
END IF
```

FIGURE 3-78

If the value is not a number, you first want to display a dialog box that alerts you to the error, and then erase the contents of txtAmount. Creating customized forms is one way you can add dialog boxes to your applications (as you did with the About... dialog box). Another way is to use the Visual Basic **MsgBox statement** to display message dialog boxes.

The dialog box shown in Figure 3-79 is used to alert the user when an error has been made in entering a value for the loan amount. The dialog box is created with a MsgBox statement in the application's code. The generalized form of the MsgBox code statement consists of three parts: MsgBox text, type, and title, which are described in Table 3-9.

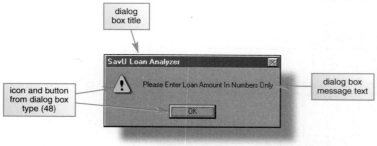

FIGURE 3-79

Table 3-9	
ARGUMENT	**DESCRIPTION**
Text	The text that displays in the body of the dialog box. It is enclosed in quotes in the code statement.
Type	A number that represents the type of button(s) displayed, the icon displayed, and whether or not the dialog box is modal.
Title	The text that displays in the title bar of the dialog box. It is enclosed in quotes in the code statement.

For a detailed description of how to use different values of type for various combinations of buttons, icons, and modality, use Visual Basic Help to search for help on the MsgBox topic.

After the message box displays, you want to place the insertion point back in the txtAmount control for a new loan amount to be entered. You could select the txtAmount control during run time by clicking it, which would place the insertion point in the text box. You can, however, cause this event to occur through code using the **SetFocus method**. The syntax of the statement is:

controlname.SetFocus

The single argument, controlname, is the name of the control that you want to select.

The code statements that make up the cmdCalculate_Click event are shown in Figure 3-80.

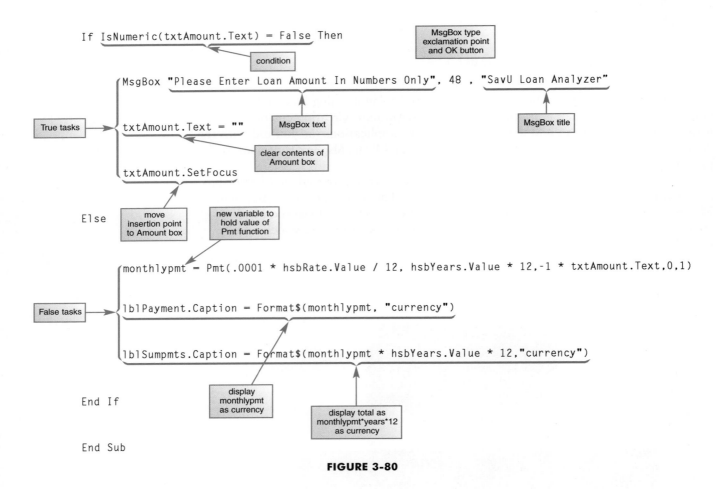

FIGURE 3-80

Perform the following steps to write the cmdCalculate_Click event using IsNumeric, Pmt, and Format$ functions, the If...Then...Else structure, and the MsgBox statement.

TO USE THE ISNUMERIC AND PMT FUNCTIONS AND IF...THEN...ELSE BLOCK IN CODE

(1) Drag the borders of the Code window to extend its width (Figure 3-81).

(2) Click cmdCalculate in the Object list box in the Code window.

(3) Enter the following statements in the Code window. Use the TAB key to indent lines as shown in Figure 3-81.

```
'if amount is not a number, then message else perform calculations
If IsNumeric(txtAmount.Text) = False Then
    MsgBox "Please Enter Loan Amount In Numbers Only",
     48, "SavU Loan Analyzer"
    txtAmount.Text = ""
    txtAmount.SetFocus
Else
    monthlypmt = Pmt(0.0001 * hsbRate.Value / 12, hsbYears.Value
     * 12, -1 * txtAmount.Text,0,1)
    lblPayment.Caption = Format$(monthlypmt,"currency")
    lblSumpmts.Caption = Format$(monthlypmt * hsbYears.Value * 12,
     "currency")
End If
```

The Code window should display as shown in Figure 3-81. Indents have no effect on the execution of the code, but make it easier to read.

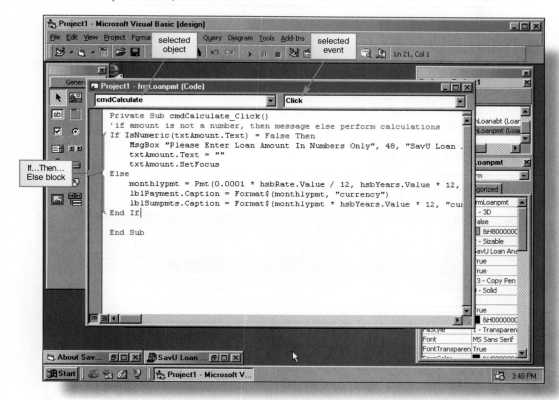

FIGURE 3-81

Line 8 in Figure 3-81 creates a variable named monthlypmt to hold the value returned by the Pmt function. This step makes the statement in Line 9 easier to read, where that value (monthlypmt), formatted as currency, is assigned to the Caption property of the lblPayment control.

In Line 10, the sum of payments is calculated as the monthly payment times the number of years times 12 months in a year, and it also is formatted as currency.

The frmLoanpmt cmdClear_Click Event

During run time, you click the Clear button (cmdClear) to remove any currently displayed inputs or outputs from the form. These include the loan amount (txtAmount.Text), length of loan period (lblYears.Caption), APR (lblRate.Caption), monthly payment (lblPayment.Caption), and sum of payments (lblSumpmts. Caption). You also want the ScrollBars (hsbYears and hsbRate) controls to return to their farthest left positions. Each of these actions will be accomplished by a statement that changes the value of the appropriate property of each control.

You do not need to change the number of years (the caption of lblYears) or the APR (the caption of lblRate) directly. A code statement that changes the Value property of the ScrollBar controls activates their Change event, which sets the captions of those labels.

After these actions are completed, you want the insertion point to move back to the Loan Amount box (txtAmount control) for a new amount to be entered. This procedure will be accomplished using the SetFocus method described on page VB 3.50. Perform the following steps to write the code for the Clear event.

TO WRITE THE CMDCLEAR_CLICK EVENT

1 Click cmdClear in the Object list box in the Code window.

2 Enter the following statements in the Code window:

```
'clear input amount and outputs;  reset scrollbars to minimums
txtAmount.Text = ""
hsbYears.Value = 1
hsbRate.Value = 1
lblPayment.Caption = ""
lblSumpmts.Caption = ""
txtAmount.SetFocus
```

The Code window displays as shown in Figure 3-82.

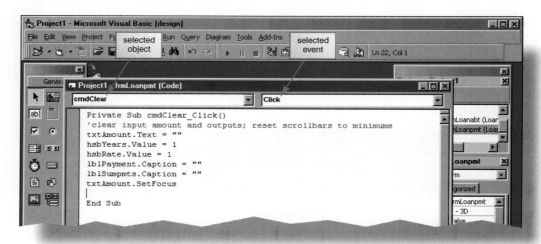

FIGURE 3-82

The frmLoanpmt cmdAbout_Click Event

The **cmdAbout_Click event** is triggered at run time when you click the About... command button. This event is used to display the frmLoanabt form. In Windows applications, a dialog box usually displays on top of all other open windows on the desktop, and you cannot work with any other window until you close the dialog box. A form or window with these characteristics is called a **modal** form. Forms without these properties are called **modeless**.

You make forms visible on the desktop and control their modality at run time with the **Show method** in a code statement. The statement has these parts (as described in Table 3-10):

form.Show *style*

Table 3-10	
ARGUMENT	DESCRIPTION
form	Name of the form to display.
style	Integer value that determines if the form is modal or modeless. If the style is 0, the form is modeless. If the style is 1, the form is modal. If a value for the style is not included, the form is modeless.

Perform the following steps to write the cmdAbout_Click event using the Show method.

TO USE THE SHOW METHOD IN CODE

1 Click the cmdAbout control in the Object list box in the frmLoanpmt Code window.

2 Enter the following statements in the Code window:
```
'display modal about dialog form
frmLoanabt.Show 1
```

The Code window displays as shown in Figure 3-83.

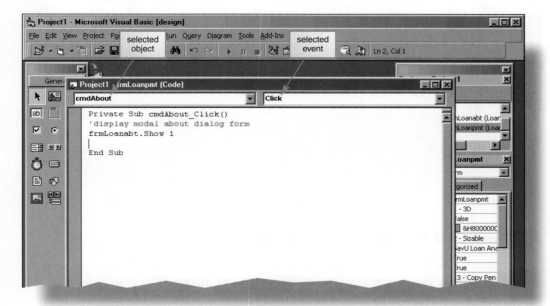

FIGURE 3-83

The frmLoanabt Command1_Click Event

The **Command1_Click event** is triggered when you click the command button labeled OK on the About... form. The action of this event removes the About... dialog box from the desktop. You remove forms from the desktop during run time by using the **Unload method** code statement. Perform the following steps to close the frmLoanpmt Code window, open the frmLoanabt Code window, and write the Command1_Click event using the Unload method.

TO USE THE UNLOAD METHOD IN CODE

1 Click the Close button in the frmLoanpmt Code window.

2 Click the frmLoanabt form in the Project window. Click the View Code button.

3 Click the Command1 control in the Object list box in the Code window. If necessary, click the Click event in the Procedure list box.

4 Enter the following statements in the Code window:
```
'remove about dialog form
Unload frmLoanabt
```

The Code window displays as shown in Figure 3-84.

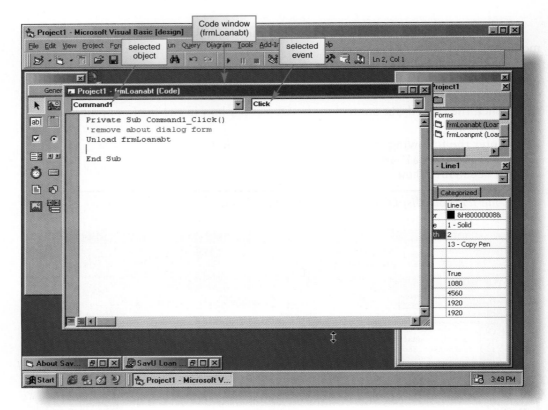

FIGURE 3-84

The Form_Load Event and Line Continuation

A form's **Load event** causes a subroutine of code statements to be carried out when the form is loaded into the computer's memory at run time. You will use the frmLoanabt's Load event to assign the captions of the labels in the About... dialog box.

A **line-continuation character** is the combination of a space followed by an underscore (_) used in the development environment to extend a single logical line of code to two or more physical lines. This has no effect on the execution of code, but can make it much easier to read and understand. You cannot use a line-continuation character to continue a line of code within a string expression and you cannot continue one statement into more than ten lines.

Perform the following steps to write a form Load event that assigns captions to labels and uses line-continuation characters and indents for easier reading.

TO USE LINE CONTINUATIONS IN CODE

1 Be certain the frmLoanabt (Code) window is open and resized as shown. If not, click its name, frmLoanabt, in the Project window and then click the View Code button.

2 Click the Form object in the Object list box in the Code window. If necessary, click the Load event in the Procedure list box.

3 Enter the following statements in the Code window with indents as shown. Be sure that you enter the statements with a space before each underscore (_) character and before and after each ampersand (&).

```
'create captions for labels
Label1.Caption = _
    "SavU National Bank Loan Analyzer" & vbNewLine & _
    "Operating System 98" & vbNewLine & _
    "Copyright 1999 SavU National Bank Corp."
Label2.Caption = _
    "Developed for SavU National Bank" & vbNewLine & _
    "By Sarah Carter"
Label3.Caption = _
    "Warning: This computer program is protected by" & vbNewLine & _
    "copyright law and international treaties."
```

The Code window displays as shown in Figure 3-85.

FIGURE 3-85

Saving the Project

The SavU Loan Analyzer project is complete. When you save a form, the events you wrote for that form are saved as part of that form's .frm file. The forms were saved earlier, before the code had been written. Before running the project, the form files should be saved again and the project should be saved as a .vbp file.

Perform the following steps to save the forms with their changes and save the project on the Data Disk in drive A.

TO SAVE A PROJECT

1 Close the frmLoanabt Code window.

2 Click the Save Project button on the Standard toolbar.

3 Type `LoanAnalyzer` in the File name text box and then click the Save button in the Save Project As dialog box.

4 Click the Start button on the Standard toolbar.

5 Run the application by entering a loan amount, selecting an APR and YEARS value, and then clicking calculate.

6 Click the End button on the Standard toolbar.

When you saved the project, the .frm files were updated and a .vbp file was created. If any errors occurred in the test, you should retrace your steps in creating the project.

Debugging Applications

No matter how carefully you build a project, applications often do not work as planned and give erroneous results because of errors in the code, called **bugs**. The process of isolating and correcting these errors is called **debugging**. When you run an application, Visual Basic opens a special window, called the **Immediate window**, that can be used to help debug your application.

You can temporarily halt the execution of your application by clicking the **Break button** on the Standard toolbar, and then resume execution by clicking the **Continue button**. During the period of time when execution is stopped, the application is said to be in break mode.

Debugging features available through Visual Basic include:

1. Viewing the values of variables and properties (setting and viewing watch expressions).
2. Halting execution at a particular point (setting a breakpoint).
3. Executing your code one line at a time (stepping through the code).
4. Executing code immediately (the Immediate window).

Setting and Viewing Watch Expressions

In **break mode**, you can isolate and view the values of particular variables and properties as a way of checking for errors. You specify which variables and properties you want to monitor by setting **watch expressions**. You can set a watch expression in advance of running the application and then cause the application to break when that expression's value changes. You also can check the value of any variable

More *About*

Break Mode

You can specify that any error encountered during run time causes the project to enter break mode. To select this feature, click the Break On All Errors option button in the Error Trapping frame on the General tab sheet in the Options dialog box.

or property in break mode by setting an **immediate watch**. You can specify a particular point at which you want to break execution by setting a **breakpoint**. Perform the following steps to set a breakpoint and then perform an immediate watch during break mode.

 To Set a Breakpoint and Immediate Watch

① Click frmLoanpmt in the Project window. Click the View Code button in the Project window. Click cmdCalculate in the Object list box in the Code window. Click at the beginning of the ninth line of code.

The insertion point displays at the beginning of the selected code line in the cmdCalculate_Click event procedure in the frmLoanpmt Code window (Figure 3-86).

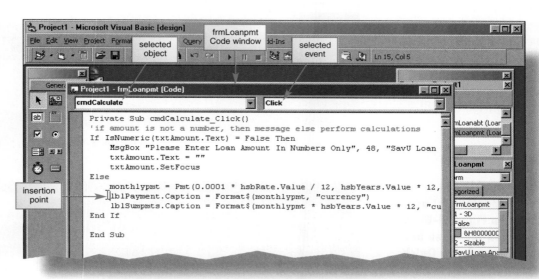

FIGURE 3-86

② Click Debug on the menu bar and then click Toggle Breakpoint.

The code statement is highlighted in red (Figure 3-87).

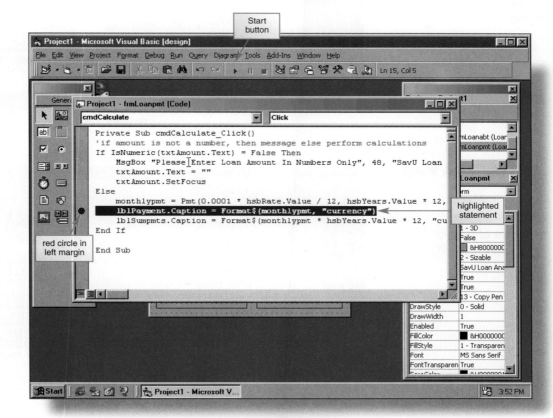

FIGURE 3-87

3 Click the Start button on the Standard toolbar. Enter 18000 for the loan amount, 6 for the number of years, and 5.5 as the APR. Click the Calculate button.

The program executes up to the highlighted code statement and then enters break mode. The Code window displays and the next code line to be executed has a yellow highlight (Figure 3-88).

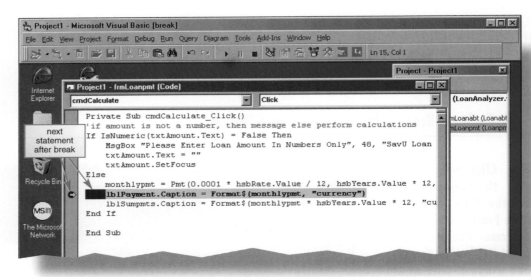

FIGURE 3-88

4 Highlight monthlypmt as shown in Figure 3-89. Click Debug on the menu bar and then point to Quick Watch.

The Debug menu displays (Figure 3-89).

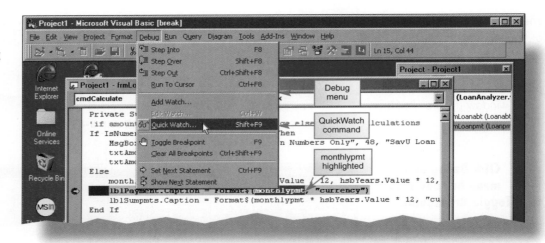

FIGURE 3-89

5 Click Quick Watch.

The Quick Watch dialog box displays the context and current value of the monthlypmt variable (Figure 3-90).

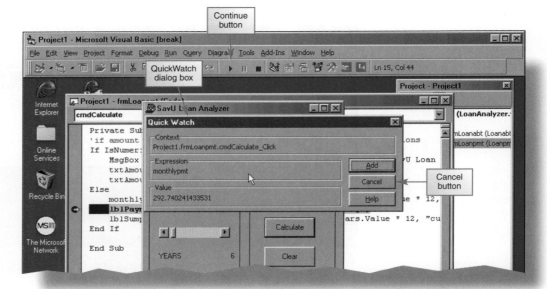

FIGURE 3-90

6 Click the Cancel button in the Quick Watch dialog box. Click the Continue button on the Standard toolbar.

The application resumes execution and displays as shown in Figure 3-91.

7 Click the End button to stop the application.

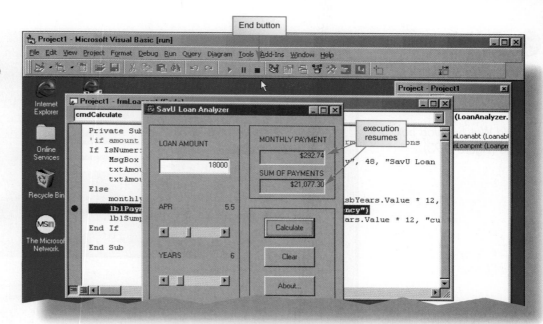

FIGURE 3-91

Other Ways

1. Click beginning of code line, then press SHIFT+F9

In the preceding steps, you used debug commands on the Debug menu. Many of these commands also can be accessed on the Debug toolbar. The Debug toolbar is opened by clicking Debug on the Toolbars submenu of the View menu.

Setting a Watch Expression and Stepping Through Code

You also can set watch expressions in advance of running the application, and also can step through code statements one at a time as additional ways to help isolate errors. Perform the following steps to set a watch expression for the IsNumeric function and then step through the cmdCalculate_Click event procedure.

Steps To Set a Watch Expression and Step Through Code

1 Click the red circle in the left margin of the Code window next to the highlighted code statement. Click in the left margin beside the IF statement.

The breakpoint is changed to the If statement now highlighted in red (Figure 3-92).

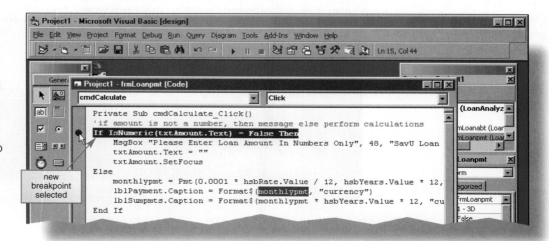

FIGURE 3-92

2 **Highlight IsNumeric (txtAmount.Text). Click Debug on the menu bar and then click Add Watch.**

The Add Watch dialog box displays (Figure 3-93).

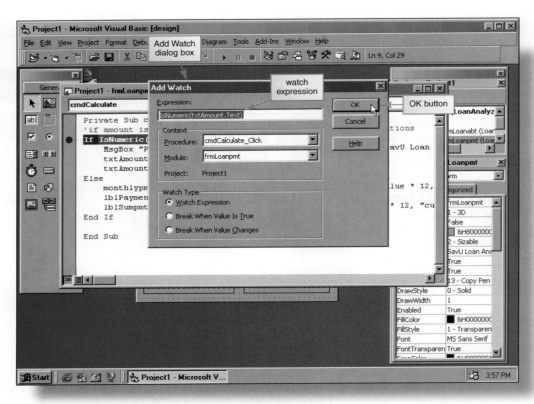

FIGURE 3-93

3 **Click the OK button. If a Watches or Immediate window opens, click the Close button. Click the Start button on the Standard toolbar. Enter** 18000 **for the loan amount,** 6 **for the number of years, and** 5.5 **as the APR. Click the Calculate button.**

Execution halts at the new breakpoint (Figure 3-94).

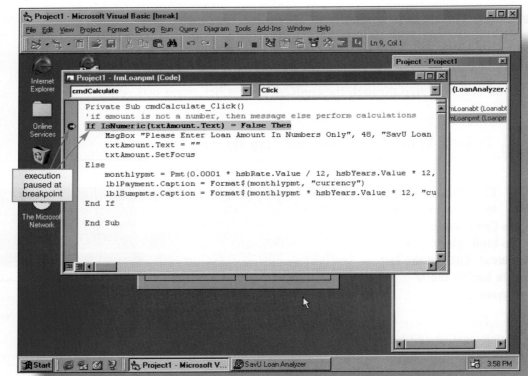

FIGURE 3-94

④ **Click View on the menu bar and then click the Watch Window command.**

The current value of the IsNumeric function displays (Figure 3-95).

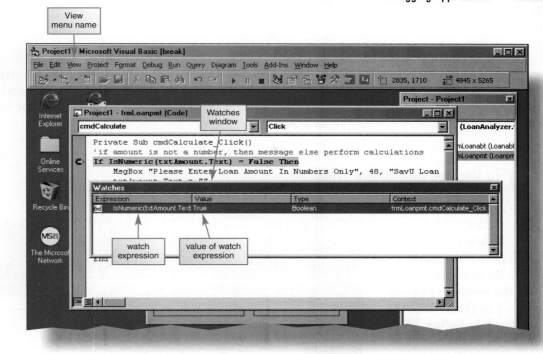

FIGURE 3-95

⑤ **Click the Code window. Click Debug on the menu bar and then click Step Into.**

The previously highlighted line of code is executed (testing IsNumeric) and the next line of code to be executed is highlighted (Figure 3-96).

⑥ **Press the F8 key six times to see line-by-line execution. Click the End button on the Standard toolbar.**

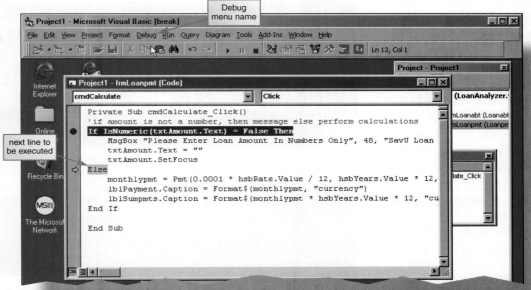

FIGURE 3-96

In the preceding steps, you set a watch expression, a breakpoint, and then stepped through code. In the **line-by-line execution**, the code statements for the input error message box were skipped because the preceding IsNumeric condition was True. A watch expression can be removed by highlighting it in the Watches window and then pressing the DELETE key.

More About

The Immediate Window

You can open the Immediate window during design time by clicking its name on the View menu or pressing CTRL+G. The Immediate window can be dragged and positioned anywhere on your screen unless you have made it a dockable window on the Docking tab in the Options dialog box. You can close the window by clicking its Close button.

Using the Immediate Window

The **Immediate window** allows you to test out code statements without changing any of your procedures. You can cut and paste code to and from the Immediate window. Perform the steps on the next page to use the Immediate window to check the value of a property.

To Use the Immediate Window

1 **Click the Start button on the Standard toolbar. Enter** 18000 **for the loan amount,** 6 **for the number of years, and** 5.5 **as the APR. Click the Calculate button. Click View on the menu bar and then click the Immediate Window command. Click the Immediate window and then type** print txtAmount.Text **as the entry.**

The Immediate window displays as shown in Figure 3-97.

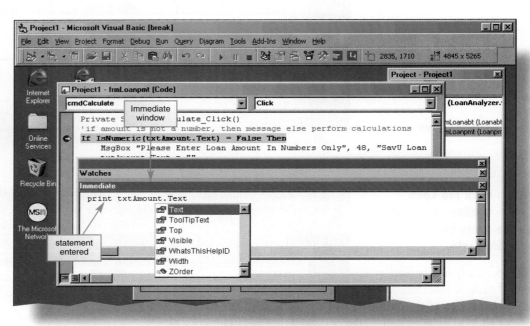

FIGURE 3-97

2 **Press the ENTER key.**

The result of executing the code statement is displayed in the Immediate window (Figure 3-98).

3 **Click the End button on the Standard toolbar.**

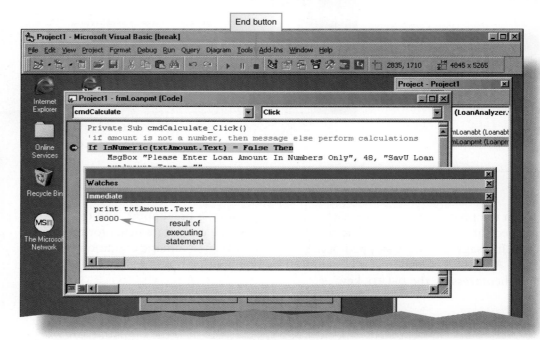

FIGURE 3-98

In the Immediate window, you can type or paste a line of code and then press the ENTER key to run it. You can, however, execute only one line of code at a time.

Making Executable Files

To run an application outside of the Visual Basic programming system, you must **compile**, or convert, the application into an **executable**, or **.exe**, file. Several advanced options are available in the Project1 - Project Properties window on the Compile tab sheet. Perform the following steps to compile the SavU Loan Analyzer using the default compile options and then run the stand-alone application.

 To Make and Run an EXE File

1 **Click the red circle in the Code window margin. Click File on the menu bar and then point to Make LoanAnalyzer.exe.**

The File menu displays (Figure 3-99).

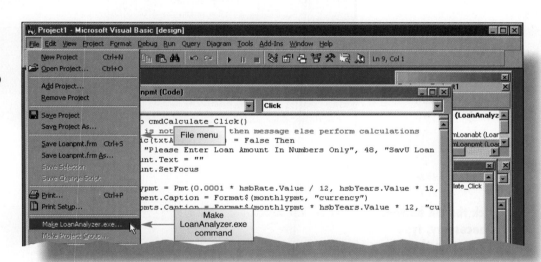

FIGURE 3-99

2 **Click Make LoanAnalyzer.exe and then point to the Options button in the Make Project dialog box.**

The Make Project dialog box displays (Figure 3-100).

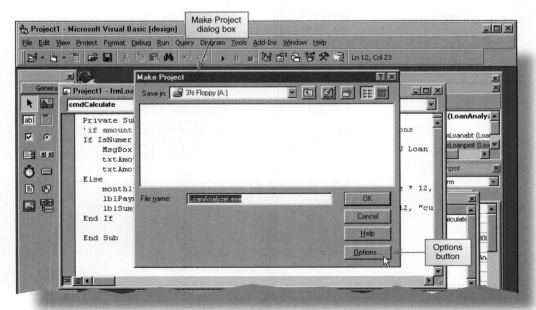

FIGURE 3-100

3 **Click the Options button. If necessary, enter the data and make the selections as shown in the Make tab sheet (Figure 3-101). Point to the OK button.**

The Make tab sheet displays (Figure 3-101).

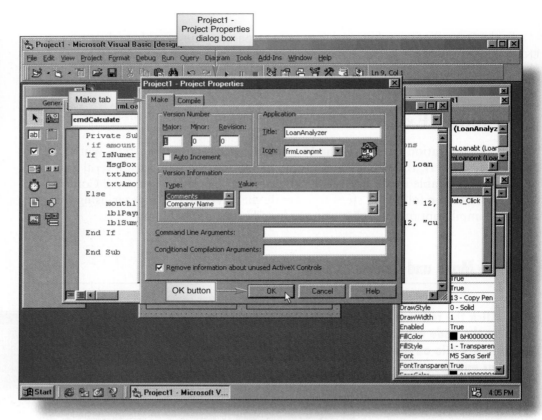

FIGURE 3-101

4 **Click the OK button. If necessary, type** LoanAnalyzer **in the File name text box and change the location for saving the file to 3½ Floppy (A:). Point to the OK button.**

The Project1 - Project Properties dialog box closes and the Make Project dialog box displays (Figure 3-102).

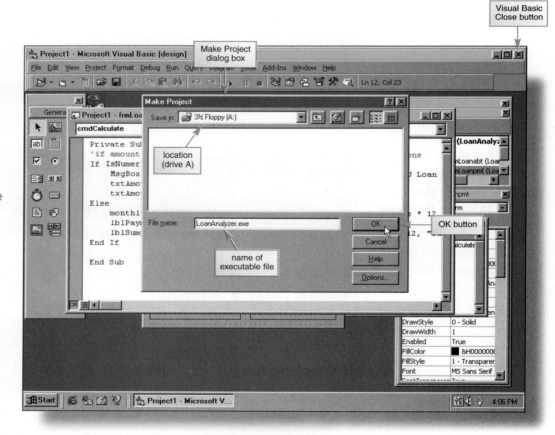

FIGURE 3-102

5 Click the OK button. Close Visual Basic. If prompted to save changes, click the Yes button. Click the Start button on the taskbar and then point to Run on the Start menu.

The Start menu displays (Figure 3-103).

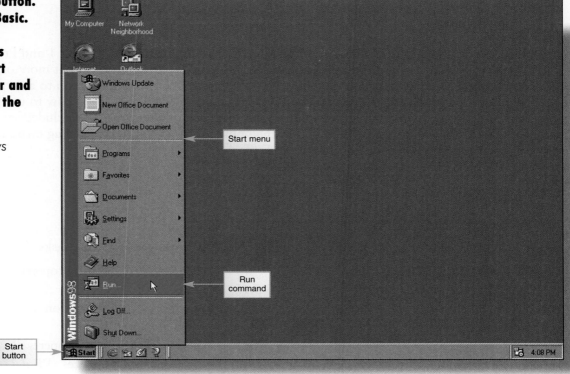

FIGURE 3-103

6 Click Run. Type `a:\LoanAnalyzer.exe` in the Open text box and then click the OK button. Run the application.

The application is opened on the desktop (Figure 3-104).

7 Close the SavU Loan Analyzer application.

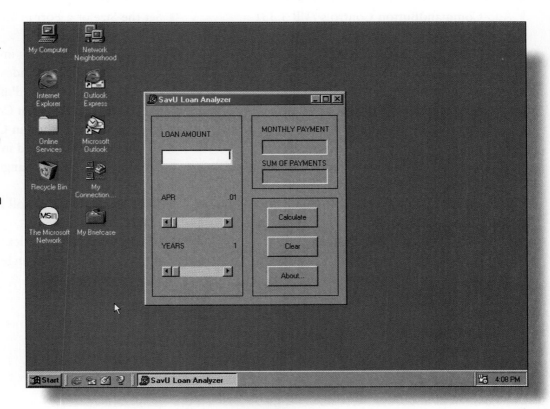

FIGURE 3-104

Other Ways

1. Press ALT+F then press K

Project Summary

Project 3 extended the basics of application building that were presented in Project 1 and Project 2. The application in this project consisted of multiple forms and dialog boxes. You learned about more of the Form control's properties and its WindowState and modality. You also learned how to add an icon to a form.

Several new properties of familiar controls were presented. You also learned how to use Image, Line, and ScrollBar controls. You wrote multiple event procedures for multiple forms that included several new functions and methods. At the end of the project, you learned how to use Visual Basic's Debug menu to isolate and correct errors in code and how to create and run an EXE file.

What You Should Know

Having completed this project, you now should be able to perform the following tasks.

- Add a Graphic to an Image Control *(VB 3.18)*
- Add Label and CommandButton Controls *(VB 3.10)*
- Add a Line Control *(VB 3.12)*
- Add a New Form *(VB 3.23)*
- Add a TextBox Control *(VB 3.31)*
- Add Additional Label Controls *(VB 3.29)*
- Add an Image Control *(VB 3.11)*
- Add Borderless Label Controls *(VB 3.27)*
- Add CommandButton Controls *(VB 3.33)*
- Add ScrollBar Controls *(VB 3.32)*
- Add Shape Controls *(VB 3.24)*
- Make and Run an EXE File *(VB 3.63)*
- Name Controls *(VB 3.37)*
- Save a Project *(VB 3.56)*
- Save a Form File *(VB 3.21)*
- Save the Form *(VB 3.41)*
- Set a Breakpoint and Immediate Watch *(VB 3.57)*
- Set a Form's Icon Property *(VB 3.40)*
- Set a Startup Form *(VB 3.42)*
- Set a Watch Expression and Step Through Code *(VB 3.59)*
- Set the Scroll Bars Properties *(VB 3.39)*
- Set the Alignment Property *(VB 3.35)*
- Set the BorderStyle Property *(VB 3.15)*

- Set the BorderWidth Property of the Line Control *(VB 3.20)*
- Set the Control's Caption and Text Properties *(VB 3.35)*
- Set the ControlBox Property *(VB 3.14)*
- Set the Font Properties *(VB 3.17)*
- Set the Name, Caption, and AutoSize Properties *(VB 3.16)*
- Set the Size of a Form Using the Properties Window *(VB 3.8, VB 3.23)*
- Use Line Continuations in Code *(VB 3.55)*
- Use the Immediate Window *(VB 3.62)*
- Use the IsNumeric and Pmt Functions and If...Then...Else Block in Code *(VB 3.51)*
- Use the Show Method in Code *(VB 3.53)*
- Use the Unload Method in Code *(VB 3.54)*
- Write the ScrollBar Change Event Procedure *(VB 3.45)*
- Write the ScrollBar Scroll Event Procedure *(VB 3.45)*
- Write the cmdClear_Click Event *(VB 3.52)*
- Write the hsbRate_Change and Scroll Event Procedures *(VB 3.46)*

Test Your Knowledge

1 True/False

Instructions: Circle T if the statement is true or F if the statement is false.

T F 1. Dialog boxes are used during run time to give information about the application or prompt you to supply information to the application.

T F 2. Image controls can contain graphical images.

T F 3. The WindowState property cannot be changed at run time.

T F 4. When you create multiple forms in a project, it is important to name them.

T F 5. You must close the first form before adding a new form to a project.

T F 6. When a form's Icon property is set and the form is minimized, a button with the icon displays on the taskbar.

T F 7. Entries within the parentheses in a Pmt function are called values.

T F 8. The MsgBox statement can be used to display message dialog boxes.

T F 9. The Unload method removes a form from the desktop at run time.

T F 10. To help remove errors in code, use the Debug window.

2 Multiple Choice

Instructions: Circle the correct response.

1. The size of a form can be set by changing the _____ and _____ properties values.
   a. Top, Bottom
   b. Left, Right
   c. Height, Width
   d. Bottom, Right

2. The BorderStyle property of a form can have one of _____ different values.
   a. 8
   b. 5
   c. 4
   d. 6

3. Visual Basic creates a file with an extension of _____ when a form with graphical data is saved.
   a. .frx
   b. .ico
   c. .bmp
   d. .exe

4. To change the appearance of a Line control, set the _____ property and the _____ property.
   a. Text, DrawMode
   b. Name, Visible
   c. BorderStyle, BorderWidth
   d. Caption, DrawMode

(continued)

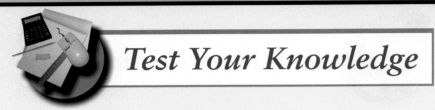

Microsoft **Visual Basic 6**

Test Your Knowledge

Multiple Choice *(continued)*

5. Use the Shape control to group visually the related _____ and _____.
   a. inputs, outputs
   b. OptionButton controls, CheckBox controls
   c. TextBox controls, Label controls
   d. captions, text

6. The _____ property of a scroll bar sets the amount that the value changes when the scroll arrows are clicked.
   a. Min
   b. SmallChange
   c. LargeChange
   d. Max

7. By default, the _____ form is the first project form moved into memory at run time.
   a. Form1
   b. first
   c. last
   d. Startup

8. The code that checks to see if the contents of a TextBox control are numbers or text is _____.
   a. IsText
   b. IsNumber
   c. IsNumeric
   d. IsAmount

9. Use the _____ method to reposition the insertion point in a TextBox control at run time.
   a. MovePoint
   b. SetFocus
   c. MoveFocus
   d. SetCursor

10. When a dialog box displays preventing work with other windows until it is closed, the dialog box is a(n) _____ type.
    a. modeless
    b. event
    c. eventless
    d. modal

3 Understanding Code Statements

Instructions: Carefully read each of the following descriptions of writing code statements to accomplish specific tasks. Record your answers on a separate sheet of paper. Number your answers to correspond to the code descriptions.

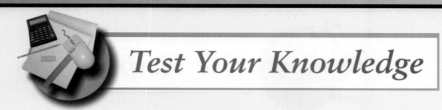

Test Your Knowledge

1. Write a code statement to convert the amount displayed as the caption of lblCharge for a ScrollBar control from an integer number to a decimal number.
2. Write a code statement that will display a message dialog box titled, Important Information. It should display an exclamation point icon and an OK button. The message text should read, A Fatal Error Has Occurred.
3. Write a code statement that will make a TextBox control named txtCursor the active control and place the insertion point in the control.
4. Write a code statement that will cause a form named frmSeeAbout to display on the desktop in a modal state.
5. Write a code statement that will cause a form named, frmGoneAbout, to be removed from the desktop.
6. Write a code statement that will cause a form named, frmSmallAbout, to be minimized on the desktop.

4 Changing Alignment and Font Properties at Run Time

Instructions: Start Visual Basic. Open the project, Text Font Properties, from the Student Data Disk. This application has one CheckBox control group and one Option-Button control group. The CheckBox control group is used to set the Font property of the text in the TextBox control. The OptionButton control group is used to set the Alignment property of the caption for the Label control. Perform the following tasks to complete this application as shown in Figure 3-105.

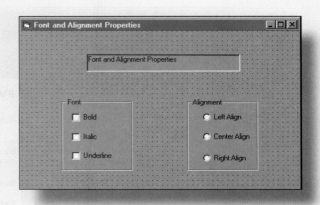

FIGURE 3-105

1. Add two CheckBox controls to the Font CheckBox control group. One should have a caption of Italic and the other should have a caption of Underline. Name the CheckBox controls.
2. Add two OptionButton controls to the OptionButton control group. One should have a caption of Center Align and the other should have a caption of Right Align. Name the OptionButton controls.
3. Open the Code window for the Italic OptionButton control and enter lblFontAlign.FontItalic = chkItalic.Value adding a comment to your code to indicate what the command is accomplishing.
4. Open the Code window for the Underline OptionButton control and enter lblFontAlign.FontUnderline = chkUnderline.Value adding a comment to your code to indicate what the command is accomplishing.
5. Open the Code window for the Center Align CheckBox control and enter lblFontAlign.Alignment = 2 adding a comment to your code to indicate what the command is accomplishing.
6. Open the Code window for the Right Align CheckBox control and enter lblFontAlign.Alignment = 1 adding a comment to your code to indicate what the command is accomplishing.
7. Save the form and project using the file name, Font and Alignment Properties.
8. Run the application and make any necessary corrections and resave using the same project file name.
9. Print the project Form Image, Code, and Form As Text.

Use Help

1 Reviewing Project Activities

Instructions: Perform the following tasks using a computer.

1. Click Help on the menu bar and then click Contents. The MSDN Library Viewer for Visual Studio 6.0 will display with the Contents tab selected. If necessary, select Visual Basic Documentation as the Active Subset in the drop-down list box.

2. In the navigation area under this tab, double-click MSDN Library Visual Studio 6.0 to open the books. Double-click the Visual Basic Documentation book. Double-click the Reference book. Double-click the Language Reference book. Double-click the Functions book. Double-click the letter F book.

3. Click the FV Function topic and read the information in the topic area. Click Double, named arguments, Integer, Variant, and arguments underlined links. Print each topic by right-clicking and selecting Print on the shortcut menu. Use the Back button to return each time to the FV Function page. Click the Example link to display an example of the topic currently being viewed (Figure 3-106). Right-click in the example window and print the example. Return to the FV Function page by clicking the Back button.

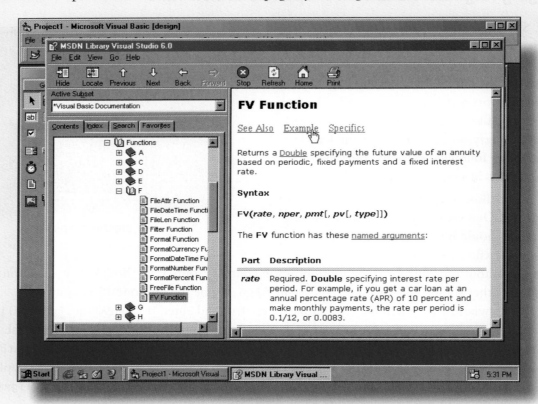

FIGURE 3-106

4. Click the See Also link to display the Topics Found dialog box. Double-click the Pmt Function topic. Read and print the information. Click the Example link to display an example of the topic currently being viewed. Right-click in the example window and print the example. Return to the Pmt Function page by clicking the Back button.

Use Help

5. Click the See Also link to display the Topics Found dialog box. Double-click the PV Function topic. Read and print the information. Click the Example link to display an example of the topic currently being viewed. Right-click in the example window and print the example.

6. Close the MSDN Library and submit all printouts to your instructor.

2 Learning More of the Basics

Instructions: Use the MSDN Library to understand the topics and answer the questions listed below. Answer the questions on your own paper to submit to your instructor.

1. Click Help on the menu bar and then click Contents. The MSDN Library Viewer for Visual Studio 6.0 will display with the Contents tab selected. If necessary, select Visual Basic Documentation as the Active Subset in the drop-down list box.

2. In the navigation area under this tab, double-click MSDN Library Visual Studio 6.0 to open the books. Double-click the Visual Basic Documentation book. Double-click the Using Visual Basic book. Double-click the Programmer's Guide (All Editions) book. Double-click the Part 1: Visual Basic Basics book. Double-click the Programming Fundamentals book. Double-click the Introduction to Variables, Constants, and Data Types book (Figure 3-107). Read the information in the topic area. As you read, answer the following questions.

    a. What are variables?   b. What are constants?   c. What are data types?

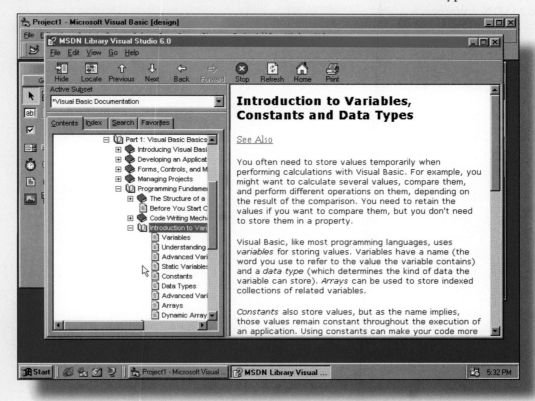

FIGURE 3-107

(continued)

Use Help

Learning More of the Basics (continued)

3. Click Data Types in the navigation area and then answer the following questions.
   a. How many data types are included in Visual Basic?
   b. Give at least one example of each data type.
4. Double-click the Forms, Controls, and Menus book in the navigation area and then click Understanding Focus. Answer the following questions.
   a. What are the focus events, including the one used in this project?
   b. How do each of the focus events work?
   c. Give an example of each one of the focus events.
5. Double-click Part 2: What Can You Do With Visual Basic? in the navigation area. Double-click Creating a User Interface and then double-click Dialog Boxes. One by one, click the topics below Dialog Boxes in the navigation area, reading the information in the topic area. Answer the following questions using the information you read.
   a. What are all of the dialog box types?
   b. What does the owner argument do?
   c. What are the differences between an InputBox and a MsgBox?
   d. How can a custom dialog box be created using a form?
   e. What can be done to customize the form?
   f. How is a custom dialog box displayed?
6. Close the MSDN Library.

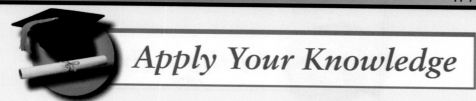

Apply Your Knowledge

1 Writing Code in a Visual Basic Application

Instructions: Start Visual Basic and open the project, Scroll Bars in the Visual Basic folder on the Student Data Disk. This application consists of a form that contains one round Shape control and two ScrollBar controls (Figure 3-108).

1. If necessary, click the View Form button in the Project window.
2. One at a time, change the Name property of each of the two scroll bars. For each of the ScrollBar controls, set the Min property to 480, set the Max property to 3600, set the LargeChange property to 200, set the SmallChange property to 50, and set the Value property to 480.
3. Click the View Code button in the Project window.

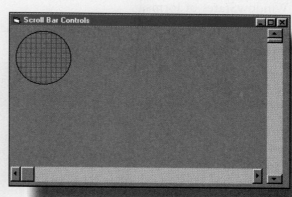

FIGURE 3-108

4. For the horizontal ScrollBar control, add a comment to indicate what the code for this scroll bar is accomplishing. Enter a code statement similar to `Shape1.Width = HScroll1.Value` replacing Shape1 and HScroll1 with the appropriate control names.
5. For the vertical scroll bar (VScrollBar) control, add a comment to indicate what the code for this scroll bar is accomplishing. Enter a code statement similar to `Shape1.Height = VScroll1.Value` replacing Shape1 and VScroll1 with the appropriate control names.
6. Save the form and the project using the file name, Scroll Bar Controls.
7. Click the Start button on the Standard toolbar to run the application. Click the scroll arrows on the horizontal and vertical scroll bars several times. Click the End button and make corrections to the code statements, if necessary. Save the form and project again using the same file name.
8. Print the Form Image, Code, and Form As Text.

In the Lab

1 Creating and Modifying a WindowStates Form

Problem: You are a tutor in the computer laboratory at school. The students are having difficulty understanding what the WindowStates of forms is and exactly how it works. You want a simple application to demonstrate the various WindowStates of forms.

Instructions: Build an application with a user interface that resembles the one shown in Figure 3-109. All of the controls should be named properly.

1. Open a new project in Visual Basic.
2. Add a second form to the project. Size the forms and position them side by side on the desktop.
3. One by one, add three CommandButton controls to the first form and one CommandButton control to the second form by double-clicking the Command-Button button in the Toolbox. Position the CommandButton controls on the forms as they are added.

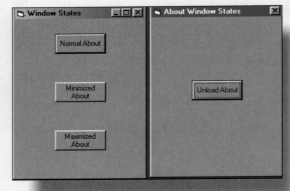

FIGURE 3-109

4. Change the captions on each of the forms. Caption the first form, Window States, and the second form, About Window States. Name the second form, frmAppAbout.
5. The three command buttons on the Window States form should show the About Window States form in a normal, minimized, and maximized state. Change the Caption property of the CommandButton controls to Normal About, Minimized About, and Maximized About. The CommandButton control on the About Window States form should unload the form from the desktop. Change the Caption property of this CommandButton control to Unload About.
6. Set the BorderStyle property for the Window States form to 2 - Sizable and set the BorderStyle property to 1 - Fixed Single for the About Window States form.
7. Make the Window States form the Startup form. Click Project on the menu bar and then click Properties. Click the General tab. Click the Startup Object box arrow, click the name of the Window States form, and click the OK button.
8. Open the Code window for the Normal About command button. Type an appropriate comment to explain the purpose of the code. Type the code statements frmAppAbout.Show and frmAppAbout.WindowState = 0 for the Normal About CommandButton control. Click the Minimized About command button in the Object list box. Type the code statements frmAppAbout.Show and frmAppAbout.WindowState = 1 and then click the Maximized About command button in the Object list box. Type the code statements frmAppAbout.Show and frmAppAbout.WindowState = 2 and then close the Code window.
9. Open the Code window for the Unload About command button on the About Window States form. Type Unload frmAppAbout as the code statement.

In the Lab

10. Save the About Window States form using the file name AbtWinStates.frm. Save the Window States form and the project using the file name, Window States.
11. Run the application to make certain no errors occur. If any errors are encountered, correct them and save the form and project again using the same file name.
12. Print the project Form Image, Code, and Form As Text.

2 Creating a Comparison Application

Problem: You are working in the library and frequently receive telephone calls requesting population information. You decide that a simple application would be very helpful when answering these questions. It should be generic enough to accept and display city, state, or country names. The application will calculate the difference between the population at the beginning of the year and at the end of the year. It also will display a message dialog box stating an increase or decrease in population.

Instructions: Perform the following tasks to build an application similar to the one shown in Figure 3-110.

1. Open a new project in Visual Basic.
2. Change the Caption property of the form to Compare Population.
3. Place TextBox controls to accept and display the city, state, or country as well as the beginning and ending populations.
4. Place Label controls to display the percentage of increase or decrease in population.
5. Place a CommandButton control to calculate the percentage of increase or decrease in population, and to display the message dialog boxes. Place another Command-Button control on the form to clear all the TextBox controls and the Label controls.

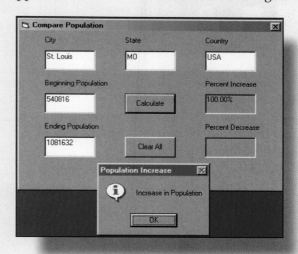

FIGURE 3-110

6. Center the form on the desktop. *Hint:* Use the StartUpPosition property.
7. Open the Code window for the CommandButton control for calculations. Write the necessary code statements to calculate the percent of increase or decrease in population and display the percentage of increase or decrease in the appropriate Label control. Write the code to display either a message dialog box to indicate a population increase or a message dialog box to indicate a population decrease.
8. Save the form and the project using the file name, Compare Population.
9. Run the project and make any necessary changes. Remember to save the form and project again if any changes have been made.
10. Print the project Form Image, Code, and Form As Text.

In the Lab

3 Creating and Using a Future Value Calculator

Problem: You have been investing money on a regular basis and want an application that will calculate the value of the investment. You have decided to develop an application that will allow entry of different amounts, the selection of different even annual interest rates from 1 percent to 25 percent without typing in values, and different numbers of years from 1 to 50 without typing in values. Then, when you click a command button, you want the application to display the future value of the investment based on annual compounding. This will aid you in determining how much your investment could be worth in the future.

Instructions: Perform the following tasks to create the investment calculator as shown in Figure 3-111.

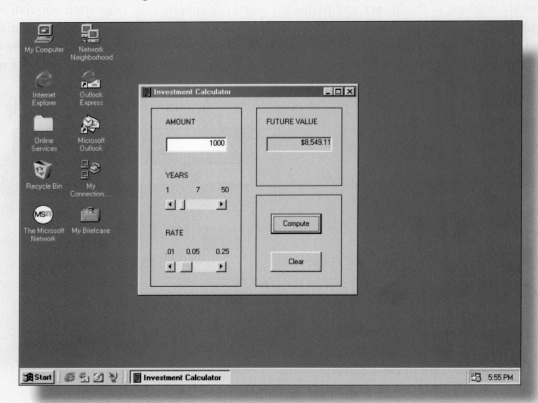

FIGURE 3-111

1. Open a new project in Visual Basic.
2. Size the form appropriately and center it by setting the StartUpPosition property.
3. Add one TextBox control, two ScrollBar controls, ten Label controls, and two CommandButton controls to the form.
4. Set the form's Caption property to Investment Calculator. Set the Icon property to the Calculator icon on the Student Data Disk.

In the Lab

5. Set the Text property of the TextBox control to be blank.

6. Set the Caption property of the two CommandButton controls.

7. Write code statements to clear all control values that should be cleared or set them to minimum values when the form is loaded into memory. The code statements for when the form is cleared are the same as when the form is loaded into memory.

8. Each ScrollBar control should have three corresponding Label controls. Write the code statements for the Label control changes that are triggered by use of the ScrollBar controls. For each scroll bar, set the Caption property of the Label controls to reflect values as follows: the minimum value of the scroll bar, the maximum value of the scroll bar, and the change as the scroll bar is used.

9. Write the code statement for the CommandButton control that performs the computations. The code statements should display an error message if the investment amount entered in the TextBox control is not numeric. They should compute the value of the future investment. The amount should be formatted as currency and displayed as the caption of the separate Label control. Remember that the number of years should be multiplied by four and the annual interest rate should be divided by four.

10. Save the form and the project using the file name, Investment Calculator.

11. Run the application and make any necessary corrections. Remember to save the form and project again if any changes have been made.

12. Make the application executable.

13. Print the project Form Image, Code, and Form As Text.

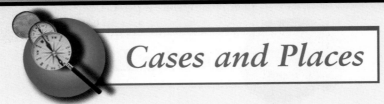

Cases and Places

The difficulty of these case studies varies:
▶ are the least difficult; ▶▶ are more difficult; and ▶▶▶ are the most difficult.

1 ▶ As a student worker employed by various faculty members, you have been given an interesting assignment by a history instructor. Various lands in the United States were purchased from other nations for small sums of money. Your instructor wants to know if the same amount of money were invested in an interest-bearing account, what the investment would be worth today. The application should accept and display the original amount, the interest rate should be selected using a scroll bar, and the period of time should be selected using a scroll bar. An appropriate message should display if the original amount entered is not numeric. The current value of the investment should display on the form. As an example of data that could be entered, use Manhattan Island, which was purchased in 1626 for $24.00.

2 ▶ You recently were hired at Sparkling Gems to build applications for its accounting department. One of your first assignments is to develop an application to calculate employee yearly raises. You have decided that the yearly salary must be entered with a message displaying if the amount is not numeric. Use OptionButton controls to select the raise percentage rates of 10% for sales, 5% for labor, or 15% for management. The number of years from 1 to 40 can be selected using a ScrollBar control. Use a CheckBox control for people who have worked more than 15 years because they are entitled to an additional 2% raise.

3 ▶▶ As a part-time employee of Mannequin, a clothing store, you have been asked to develop a small application for the salespeople. They require an application that allows them to enter the cost price of a clothing item and select the margin (markup) using a scroll bar. The application then should compute both the selling price of the item and the gross profit of the item. The selling price and gross profit should display for the salesperson. The salesperson should be notified if any errors occur when entering the cost price. You have decided to use the knowledge gained in this project to develop an appropriate application to perform these calculations.

4 ▶▶ Wire-Gram has hired you as a consultant to build an application that will calculate the cost of a telegram. The application should include a way to enter the message and compute the cost based on $4.20 for the first 100 characters and $.02 for each letter over 100. The total number of letters and the total cost should display for the person entering the telegram. You want the company to remember your work and decide to include a form with information about yourself and the application. *Hint*: Search the MSDN Library for the MultiLine property of a TextBox control as well as the Len function for string data.

Cases and Places

5   ▶▶   Your friend, who owns Lullaby Land, knows what a knowledgeable programmer you are and has requested your assistance. She is going to provide around-the-clock child-care. She and her coworkers require a quick, easy way to be able to calculate the total amounts owed by her clients. The application would have to provide a way to enter the beginning and ending times. The rate structure is $3.50 per hour from 8:00 a.m. up to and including 5:00 p.m. and $4.25 per hour after 5:00 p.m. up to and including 8:00 a.m. The number of hours from 8:00 a.m. to 5:00 p.m. should be displayed along with a subtotal amount for this time period. The number of hours from 5:00 p.m. to 8:00 a.m. also should be displayed along with a subtotal amount for this time period. The two subtotals should be added and displayed for a final total amount due. Appropriate error messages should be used with icons and one or more command buttons. An About form also should be developed for the application. *Hint*: See the MsgBox function in the Functions section of the Language Reference in the MSDN Library.

6   ▶▶▶   As a programmer for Tootsies shoe stores, you have been asked to develop a program to calculate discounts and taxes on items purchased. The form should be neatly arranged. The salespeople should be able to enter the list price of an item as well as the tax rate. Provide a method to select the discount rate. The gross list price should display along with the tax rate and the discount rate. After the calculations have been performed, the net list price also should display. You will want to provide appropriate error messages where necessary. You also want to provide an About form with information about the application and about you. This should be a compiled application.

7   ▶▶▶   You are working as a manager trainee with a well-known national company. One of the benefits of the job is that you can request payroll investment deductions on a quarterly basis. The amount deducted is determined by you at the beginning of each year. The money is invested for a period of years at an annual percentage rate, both of which can vary. You would like to experiment with different values for the investment amount, the period of time, and the annual interest rate to see how much you can earn. You want the form to be well organized. Error messages also should display if amounts entered are not numeric. You also want to remember what the application is for and when you designed it. *Hint*: See the FV function in the Functions section of the Language Reference in the MSDN Library. This should be a compiled application.